TURKISH
PHRASEBOOK

Tom Brosnahan
Jim Masters
Perihan Masters

Turkish phrasebook
   2nd edition

Published by
   Lonely Planet Publications
   Head Office: PO Box 617, Hawthorn, Vic 3122, Australia
   Branches: 150 Linden Street, Oakland CA 94607, USA
                10a Spring Place, London NW5 3BH, UK
                1 rue du Dahomey, 75011 Paris, France

Printed by
SNP Printing Pte Ltd, Singapore

Cover Illustration
Now is the Time to Dance! by Maria Vallianos

Published
   February 1999

National Library of Australia Cataloguing in Publication Data

   Turkish phrasebook
   2nd ed.
   Includes index.
   ISBN 0 8442 436 1.

© Lonely Planet Publications Pty Ltd, 1999
Cover Illustration © Maria Vallianos

About the Authors

Jim and Perihan Masters are a husband and wife team, living on the Aegean Coast of Turkey just 50 miles south of Izmir. Jim was born in Shanghai, China, of American military parentage. Peri was born on the Black Sea coast of Turkey near Trabzon, of Turkish military parentage.

First at Brown University and then at the University of North Carolina, Jim pursued studies in Mathematics and Computer Science. Upon graduation and during the late 60s and early 70s, he worked as a computer programmer/analyst on both US coasts before taking a position in London as Technical Director for a computer facilities management firm. Enticed by a Financial Times advertisement, he joined a NATO sponsored enterprise in Ankara in 1974 where he met the beautiful and brainy Perihan, a rising young Turkish banking executive. It was uninhibited love at first sight, except that neither spoke the other's language! So they embarked on a mad language learning scramble, which continues to this day, that culminated in their marriage now celebrating it's 25th year.

After spending fifteen working years in the United States, with numerous visitations to Turkey, the two opted to return permanently to Turkey in 1992 to take up residence in Gümüldür, a seaside resort town in the heart of what was once the ancient Ionian Empire. There they live an idyllic life by the sea writing, drawing and painting, teaching English, and providing computing service support to local businesses. They also sponsor the MSNBC award-winning *Learning Practical Turkish* Website (http://www2.egenet.com.tr/mastersj) which has built an enthusiastic international following of devoted Turkophiles and inquisitive language students of all ages.

Tom Brosnahan was born and raised in Pennsylvania, went to college in Boston, then set out on the road. His first two years in Turkey, during which he learned to speak fluent Turkish, were spent as a US Peace Corps Volunteer. He studied Middle east history and the Ottoman Turkish language for eight years but abandoned the writing of his PhD dissertation in favour of travelling and writing phrasebooks and guidebooks.

From the Authors

The authors (Jim and Perihan Masters) wish to thank our dear parents, our beloved children, our cherished sisters, and one remarkable brother for their support, patience, and understanding during all these years. We also extend a special thanks to our esteemed friend Taşkın Çalı whose damned hard work with us on the *LPT* website is valued beyond measure. And, lastly but not leastly, we send their thanks and admiration to the incredible Lonely Planet editors who've put this whole package together without ever having seen our faces! *Yaşasın Internet!, Yaşasın Lonely Planet!* (Long Live Internet!, Long Live Lonely Planet!).

From the Publisher

This book was put together by a group of tough hardened phrasebook professionals. Justin Rudelson edited the book with proofing by Vicki Webb and Peter D'Onghia. Fabrice Rocher designed the cover and laid out his final phrasebook with the help of Brendan Dempsey. Maria Vallianos drew the wonderful illustrations and cover. Martin Hughes produced the clever and supposedly witty crossword clues.

Many thanks to Tom Bosnahan who wrote the first edition of the Lonely Planet Turkish phrasebook, from which this edition developed.

CONTENTS

INTRODUCTION 9

Abbreviations 10   How to Use This Book 11

PRONUNCIATION 15

Vowels 15   Transliteration System 17
Consonants 16

GRAMMAR 19

Word Order 19   Past 27
Articles 20   Future 28
Nouns 20   Imperative 28
Adjectives 24   To Be 28
Pronouns 24   To Have 29
Verbs 25   Possession 30
Infinitives 26   Questions 31
Present 26   Negatives 33

MEETING PEOPLE 35

You Should Know 35   Language Difficulties 43
Greetings & Goodbyes 36   Nationalities 46
Body Language 37   Cultural Differences 47
Polite Phrases 38   Age 48
Forms of Address 39   Occupations 48
First Encounters 40   Feelings 49
Making Conversation 42   Crossword 50

GETTING AROUND 51

Finding Your Way 51   Train 57
Addresses 53   Boat 57
Buying Tickets 53   Taxi 58
Air 55   Car 59
Bus 56   Bicycle 61

ACCOMMODATION 63

Finding Accommodation 63   Paperwork 66
Booking Ahead 63   Requests & Complaints 69
Checking In 64   Checking Out 70

AROUND TOWN 71

Looking For 71
At the Bank 71
At the Post Office 73
Telecommunications 74
Bureaucracy 77
Sightseeing 77

GOING OUT 81

Where to Go 81
Arranging to meet 83
Romance 84
Crossword 86

FAMILY & INTERESTS 87

Family 87
Staying in Touch 88
Common Interests 90
Stars 96
Social Issues 97
Sport 99
Games 102
Crossword 104

SHOPPING 105

Looking For 105
Making A Purchase 105
Bargaining 107
Prices 108
Essential Groceries 109
Souvenirs 110
Clothing 110
Materials 110
Colours 111
Toiletries 111
For the Baby 112
Stationery &
    Publications 112
Music 113
Photography 114
Smoking 115
Sizes & Comparisons 116

FOOD 117

Vegetarian & Special
    Meals 117
Eating Out 118
Meals 119
Menu Decoder 120
Typical Dishes 129
Self-catering 134
At the Market 134
Spices & Condiments 137
Drinks 137
Paying the Bill 139
Cooking Terms 140

IN THE COUNTRY 141

Camping 141
Hiking 141
At the Beach 147
Weather 148
Geographical Terms 149
Sights 150
Animals 150
Flora & Agriculture 151
Crossword 152

HEALTH 153

In an Emergency 153
At the Doctor 155
Ailments 157
Women's Health 159
Special Health Needs 162

Alternative Treatments 163
Parts of the Body 163
At The Chemist 164
At the Dentist 165
Crossword 166

SPECIFIC NEEDS 167

Disabled Travellers 167
Gay Travellers 168
Travelling with the
    Family 168
Looking For A Job 169

On Business 170
On Tour 172
Pilgrimage & Religion 173
Tracing Roots &
    History 174

TIMES, DATES & FESTIVALS 175

Telling the Time 175
Days 176
Months 176
Seasons 177
Dates 177

Present 177
Past 178
Future 178
During the Day 179
Festivals 180

NUMBERS & AMOUNTS 183

Cardinal Numbers 183
Ordinal Numbers 184

Fractions 184

EMERGENCIES 185

Health Emergencies 185

Dealing with Police 186

ENGLISH-TURKISH DICTIONARY 191

TURKISH-ENGLISH DICTIONARY 227

INDEX 261

INTRODUCTION

Turkish is so different from European languages that it can be bewildering at first. But it has advantages. There are no gender distinctions (he, she, it), only one irregular noun (su, 'water'), one irregular verb (olmak, 'to be'), and few articles (a, an, the). It also has a logical, if complex, structure. Context counts for a lot in Turkish, so you can say a few words and phrases to Turks and they will pick up the rest easily.

The Turkish language is a member of the Ural-Altaic language family, which also includes such lesser-known tongues as Kyrgyz, Kazakh, Uyghur, Azerbaijani, Manchu, Chuvash, and Mongolian. Surprisingly, Korean and Japanese are also Ural-Altaic languages.

'Pure' Oğuz Turkish, as spoken by nomads of Central Asia 1500 years ago, was a simple, logical and expressive language. When the Turks encountered Islam in AD 670, they adopted the Arabic alphabet, even though it was ill-suited to record the sounds of Turkish.

As the erstwhile tribesmen gained worldliness and sophistication, their language took on grammatical and vocabulary borrowings from the Persians and the Arabs. At the height of the Ottoman Empire's power, the Turkish spoken by the Ottoman upper classes was overly complex, full of flowery phrases and wordy academic usages.

After the fall of the empire, Kemal Atatürk, the founding-father and first president of modern Turkey, undertook to reform and 'purify' Turkish to encourage literacy. He established the Turkish Language Society, with instructions for it to rid the Turkish language of Arabic and Persian words and grammatical usages, and to replace them with revitalised Turkish ones. With the changes, Turks could say 'you', instead of 'your exalted personage' (Persian), and 'me', instead of 'your humble servant'.

In the interests of literacy, Atatürk ordered that the Arabic alphabet be abandoned in favour of a modified Latin one. On 1 November 1928, Parliament decreed that after two months no materials could be published in the Arabic script – only in the

INTRODUCTION

modern Turkish alphabet. Atatürk himself took blackboard and chalk to village squares and taught the new letters to the people.

In ensuing years, Turkish changed so drastically that today's Turkish school children and university students cannot read Ottoman works of a century ago without special instruction in alphabet, grammar and vocabulary. Indeed, Turkish has changed so much since the 1930s that even Atatürk's speeches (he died in 1938) seem archaic and mysterious today. Most have been 'translated' into öztürkçe, the modern 'pure Turkish'.

The language reforms introduced many new or 'revived' words and phrases into Turkish. Thus you may find that there are two or more ways to say something: the 'old' way and the 'new' way. Both ways are completely acceptable.

Modern Turkish is spoken by the nearly 60 million citizens of the Turkish Republic and also by Turkish Cypriots and small communities of ethnic Turks in Greece. Ethnic Turkish minorities in Bulgaria and Yugoslavia speak dialects of Ottoman Turkish. If you can speak Turkish, you can make yourself understood from Belgrade, Yugoslavia, to Xinjiang, China.

ABBREVIATIONS USED IN THIS BOOK

adj	adjective	m	masculine
art	article	n	noun
col	colloquial	pl	plural
f	feminine	pol	polite
fam	familiar	sg	singular
lit	literally		

HOW TO USE THIS PHRASEBOOK
You *Can* Speak Another Language

It's true – anyone can speak another language. Don't worry if you haven't studied languages before, or that you studied a language at school for years and can't remember any of it. It doesn't even matter if you failed English grammar. After all, that's never affected your ability to speak English! And this is the key to picking up a language in another country. You don't need to sit down and memorise endless grammatical details and you don't need to memorise long lists of vocabulary. You just need to start speaking. Once you start, you'll be amazed how many prompts you'll get to help you build on those first words. You'll hear people speaking, pick up sounds from TV, catch a word or two that you think you know from the local radio, see something on a billboard – all these things help to build your understanding.

Plunge In

There's just one thing you need to start speaking another language – courage. Your biggest hurdle is overcoming the fear of saying aloud what may seem to you to be just a bunch of sounds.

The best way to start overcoming your fear is to memorise a few key words. These are the words you know you'll be saying again and again, like 'hello', 'thank you' and 'how much?'. Here's an important hint though: right from the beginning, learn at least one phrase that will be useful but not essential. Such as 'good morning' or 'good afternoon', 'see you later' or even a conversational piece like 'lovely day, isn't it?' or 'it's cold today' (people everywhere love to talk about the weather). Having this extra phrase (just start with one, if you like, and learn to say it really well) will enable you to move away from the basics, and when you get a reply and a smile, it'll also boost your confidence. You'll find that people you speak to will like it too, as they'll understand that at least you've tried to learn more of the language than just the usual essential words.

Ways to Remember

There are several ways to learn a language. Most people find they learn from a variety of these, although people usually have a preferred way to remember. Some like to see the written word and remember the sound from what they see. Some like to just hear it spoken in context (if this is you, try talking to yourself in Turkish, but do it in the car or somewhere private, to give yourself confidence, and so others don't wonder about your sanity!). Others, especially the more mathematically inclined, like to analyse the grammar of a language, and piece together words according to the rules of grammar. The very visually inclined like to associate the written word and even sounds with some visual stimulus, such as from illustrations, TV and general things they see in the street. As you learn, you'll discover what works best for you – be aware of what made you really remember a particular word, and if it sticks in your mind, keep using that method.

Kicking Off

Chances are you'll want to learn some of the language before you go. The first thing to do is to memorise those essential phrases and words. Check out the basics (page 35) ... and don't forget your extra phrase. Try the sections on making conversation or greeting people for a phrase you'd like to use. Write some of these words down on a separate piece of paper and stick them up around the place. On the fridge, by the bed, on your computer, as a bookmark – somewhere where you'll see them often. Try putting some words in context – the 'How much is it?' note, for instance, could go in your wallet.

Building the Picture

We include a chapter on grammar in our books for two main reasons.

Firstly, some people have an aptitude for grammar and find understanding it a key tool to their learning. If you're such a person, then the grammar chapter will help you build a picture of the language, as it works through all the basics.

The second reason for the grammar chapter is that it gives answers to questions you might raise as you hear or memorise some key phrases. You may find a particular word is always used when there is a question – check out the grammar heading on questions and it should explain why. This way you don't have to read the grammar chapter from start to finish, nor do you need to memorise a grammatical point. It will simply present itself to you in the course of your learning. Key grammatical points are repeated throughout the book.

Any Questions?

Try to learn the main question words (see page 31). As you read through different situations, you'll see these words used in the example sentences, and this will help you remember them. So if you want to hire a bicycle, turn to the Bicycles section in Getting Around (use the Contents or Index pages to find it quickly). You've already tried to memorise the word for 'where' and you'll see the word for 'bicycle'. When you come across the sentence 'Where can I hire a bicycle?', you'll recognise the key words and this will help you remember the whole phrase. If there's no category for your need, try the dictionary (the question words are repeated there too, with examples), and memorise the phrases 'Please write that down' and 'How do you say ...?' (see page 43).

I've Got a Flat Tyre

Doesn't seem like the phrase you're going to need? Well in fact, it could be very useful. As are all the phrases in this book, provided you have the courage to mix and match them. We have given specific examples within each section. But the key words remain the same even when the situation changes. So while you may not be planning on any cycling during your trip, the first part of the phrase 'I've got ...' could refer to anything else, and there are plenty of words in the dictionary that, we hope, will fit your needs. So whether it's 'a ticket', 'a visa' or 'a condom', you'll be able to put the words together to convey your meaning.

INTRODUCTION

Finally

Don't be concerned if you feel you can't memorise words. On the inside front and back covers are the most essential words and phrases you'll need. You could also try tagging a few pages for other key phrases.

PRONUNCIATION

Despite daunting oddities such as the 'soft g', the ğ, and the 'undotted i', the ı, Turkish is phonetic and fairly easy to pronounce. Note that each Turkish letter has a distinct pronunciation – there are no double-consonants like 'th' or 'ch' as in English, and there is only one unpronounced or silent letter, the ğ.

VOWELS

A, a	as the 'a' in 'art' or 'bar'
E, e	as the 'e' in 'fell'
İ, i	as the 'ey' in 'key'
I, ı	as the 'e' in 'glasses' or the 'a' in 'about'
O, o	as the 'o' in 'hot' or the 'aw' in 'awe'
Ö, ö	as the 'e' in 'her'
U, u	as the 'oo' in 'moo'
Ü, ü	as an exaggerated, rounded-lip 'oo' or 'yoo'

Turkish has two extremely different sounds represented by the letters i and ı. Notice that one, i, has a dot while the other, ı, does not. It's easy for the eye to ignore this difference when reading, so stay alert because mispronunciation can cause confusion. For example, ısırır is pronounced '**ih-sih-rihr**', but ikinci is pronounced '**ee- keen-jee**'. Keep your eye out for the dot on the capital I and İ as well: Isparta is pronounced '**ihss-spahr-tah**' not '**eess-spahr-tah**', and İzmir is pronounced '**eez-meer**' not '**ihz-mihr**'.

As for ö and ü, purse your lips when saying them. For ü, shape your lips to say 'oo', but then say 'ee'.

PRONUNCIATION

VOWEL HARMONY

Turkish divides vowels into two groups: those formed 'in the front of the mouth' (e, i, ö, ü) and those formed 'in the back of the mouth' (a, ı, o, u). The principle of vowel harmony follows one's inclination to keep the mouth in the same position while pronouncing a word or sound as when you hum 'la-la-la' or 'du-du-du'. This distinction is very important when forming words with suffixes. Turkish requires that the vowel(s) in the suffix(es) must be of the same type, either front or back, as the vowel(s) in the root word.

For example, when forming the word hepinizi, 'all of you', the root hep, 'all', has a front vowel e. So the suffix -iniz, 'you', and the suffix -i, 'of' all must be front vowels, the dotted i rather than the undotted ı. The e of hep and the i in -inizi have vowel harmony because both are 'front' vowels. With hep you can't use the forms of the suffix made with an undotted ı (-ınızı) because ı is a 'back' vowel. To form arabanızı, 'your car', from araba, 'car', and -ınızı, 'of you', the use of ı is correct because the a vowels in araba are 'back' vowels as is ı.

After a while you'll get a feel for vowel harmony and won't have to think about it. And even if you make mistakes, you will probably still be understood.

CONSONANTS

Most consonants are pronounced as in English. The most unusual exception is c, which is always pronounced like an English 'j'.

C, c	as the 'j' in 'jet' or 'jigsaw'
Ç, ç	as the 'ch' in 'church'
G, g	always hard; as the 'g' in 'get', not as in 'gentle'
Ğ, ğ	silent; lengthens preceding vowel
H, h	weak; as the 'h' in 'half'
J, j	as the 'z' in 'azure'
S, s	unvoiced; as the 's' in 'sun', not as the 's' in 'ease'
Ş, ş	as the 'sh' in 'show'
V, v	as the 'w' in 'weather'

The 'soft g', the ğ, is never pronounced, and it never begins a word. It does lengthen the preceding vowel slightly, but you can ignore it altogether. Whatever you do, don't pronounce it. For example, soğan sounds like English 'so on' not 'sewn'. In eastern Turkic dialects of Central Asia, ğ is pronounced as a guttural 'r' but in Turkey, the western extreme of the language, the sound became silent.

The Turkish h, however, is pronounced, though it is weak. Start saying 'hot', but stop with the 'h'. That's the sound. It is important to note that h does not combine with other consonants. When t and h are together as in mithat, the word is pronounced 'meet-haht', not like the English 'me-thought', and meshut is 'mess-hoot', not 'meh-shoot'.

The Turkish v is soft, somewhere between an English 'v' and 'w' but closer to 'w'. When a Turk says 'very,' it sounds much like 'wery'.

Double Consonants

Double consonants like kk in dikkat or ll in yollar are held for a longer time. For instance, dikkat sounds like '**dik-kaht**' not 'dikat'. You'll have no trouble with double consonants if you remember that the first consonant of the double ends a word and the second begins a new word. Thus, yollar is pronounced '**yol lar**', not 'yolar'.

TRANSLITERATION SYSTEM

The transliteration system provided in this phrasebook is intended to assist you in learning to pronounce Turkish letters and sounds. Since Turkish has several letters with special markings not found in English, our transliteration system will help you become comfortable speaking Turkish as you use it on your journey.

Stress is much less pronounced in Turkish than in English. Turkish spoken with little stress is considered the most correct and standerd variety therefore stress is not indicated throughout this phrasebook.

PRONUNCIATION

Vowels

A, a	ah
E, e	eh
I, ı	ih
İ, i	ee
O, o	oh
Ö, ö	er
U, u	oo
Ü, ü	yu

Consonants

Most Turkish consonants are pronounced in the same way as their English counterparts, with the exception of the following:

C, c	j
Ç, ç	ch
Ğ, ğ	(silent, no letter)
J, j	zh
Ş, ş	sh

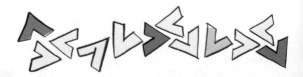

Turkish is a systematic and logical language with no gender distinction, only one irregular noun (su, 'water') and one irregular verb (olmak, 'to be'). It's an agglutinative language, which means that suffixes are added to a short word-root to form an adjective, noun, verb or verbal noun. If several suffixes are added, a single word can become an entire sentence. The method of using 'building blocks' to make words is sensible, but so different from anything English speakers are used to that it can be very confusing at first. Still, if you learn to use several important suffixes, you'll be able to express yourself.

The grammar rules for use of suffixes are logical, but the rules are complicated somewhat by the need for certain 'buffer' letters s, n, or y, added for ease of pronunciation with certain combinations of words and suffixes. You will probably still be understood most of the time, even if you ignore these rules or make mistakes.

WORD ORDER

Pronouns, nouns and adjectives usually come first, followed by the verb. The final suffix on the verb is the subject of the sentence:

I'll go to Istanbul.	İstanbul'a gideceğim.
	(lit: Istanbul-to go-will-I)
I want to buy (some) biscuits.	Biskuvi almak istiyorum.
	(lit: biscuits to-buy wanting-am-I)
We stayed for only one night.	Yalnız bir gece kaldık.
	(lit: only one night stayed-we)

Some complex sentences can be merely a few long words packed with suffixes. How about this doozy of a one-word-sentence:

> You seem to be one of those who is incapable of being naughty.
> Yaramazlastırılamıyabilenlerdenmipsiniz.

Broken apart by suffixes its meaning is unravelled as:

> Yaramaz-lastırıla-mıyabilen-ler-den-mip-siniz.
> (lit: naughty-be-with-unable-them-from-seems-you)

ARTICLES

It is frequently stated that Turkish does not have articles (a, an, the). Often it is context that indicates whether 'the' is intended in a sentence. However, the word bir, which usually means 'one' in Turkish, is used as an article in Turkish to convey the meaning of the English articles a or an.

> My wife is a jealous woman.   Eşim kıskanç bir kadındır.
> (lit: wife-my jealous a woman)

> I now have one black eye.   Şimdi, bir siyah gözüm var.
> (lit: now, ozne black eye-mine have)

The positioning is important. As long as the bir fronts the noun (bir kadındır), it should be translated as 'a' or 'an'. But if bir fronts the adjective (bir siyah), then it should be translated as 'one'.

NOUNS

Nouns in Turkish don't have gender. Nouns are pluralised by adding -ler or -lar depending upon vowel harmony (see page 16). The plural suffix is -ler for root words with front vowels (e, i, ö, ü) and -lar for root words with back vowels (a, ı, o, u).

meal	yemek	meals	yemekler
airplane	uçak	airplanes	uçaklar

Noun Cases

The six Turkish cases with their corresponding suffixes mark the role of a noun in a sentence, whether it is the subject, direct object, or indirect object, etc. The different suffixes added to nouns indicate a noun's relationship to other words in a sentence. Each case suffix has spelling variations which follow vowel harmony. For instance, the suffix indicating 'to' is -e for front vowels and -a for back vowels.

Nominative

The nominative case is the subject of the verb in a sentence. This case does not take on a suffix. It is the noun in its simplest form as in postane (post-office) or araba (car).

Where is the post office?	Postane nerede?
	(lit: post-office where)
How may hours is the journey?	Yolculuk kaç sa'at?
	(lit: journey how-many hour)

Accusative

The accusative case refers to the direct object of the sentence. It is the 'whom' or 'what' to which the verb refers. It's formed with the suffix -ı or -u.

Could I see the room?	Odayı görbilir miyim?
	(lit: room see-can question-me)
How do you like Turkey?	Türkiye'yi nasıl buluyorsunuz?
	(lit: Turkey how liking-you-pl?)

Genitive

The genitive case refers to ownership or possession. It's the 'whose', 'of whom' or 'of what'.

What's this wine called?	Bu şarabın adı nedir?
	(lit: this wine name what-call)
Your passport, please.	Pasaportunuz, lütfen.
	(lit: passport-your, please)

GRAMMAR

Dative

The dative indicates indirect objects and is formed with the suffix
-a or -e.

to   -a, -e

ship	vapur	to the ship	vapura
sea	deniz	to the sea	denize

Does this bus go to Izmir?   Bu otobüs İzmir'e gider mi?
(lit: this bus Izmir-to go
question)

When does the bus to   Ankara'ya giden otobüs ne
Ankara depart?   zaman kalkar?
(lit: Ankara-to going bus what
time depart)

Locative

The locative tense indicates where the action of the sentence takes
place. It's formed with the suffix -de or -da.

Can I camp in the garden?   Bahçede kamp yapabilir
miyim?
(lit: garden-in camp do-able
question-me)

Can you show me on   Haritada gösterebilirmisin?
the map?   (lit: map-on show-able-
question-you)

Ablative

The ablative tense indicates 'from where' or 'from whom' an action takes place. It's formed with the suffix -dan, or -den.

car	araba	from the car	arabadan
hotel	otel	from the hotel	otelden

I think my ancestors came   Benim atalarım buralardan
from this area.   gelmişler.
(lit: my fathers-my places-
from came-they)

I'll have one of those.   Şunlardan bir tane istiyoyum.
                              (lit: those-from one piece
                              want-I)

Noun Suffixes

- with, of, of a quality   -lı, -li, -lu, -lü

Ireland	İrlonda	Irish	İrlondalı
sugar	şeker	sweet	şekerli

- without   -sız, -siz, -suz, -süz

mind	akıl	mindless/stupid	akılsız
fee	ücre	without fee	ücretsiz

- '-ness'   -lık, -lik, -luk, -lük

child	çocuk	childhood	çocukluk
traveller	yolcu	journey	yolculuk

- 'er': profession   -cı, -ci, -cu, -cü

tea	çay	teahouse waiter	çaycı
watch/clock	saat	watchmaker	saatçi

Noun suffixes and other endings alter the meaning of a root word.
The word anahtar, 'key', can take on the following meanings
with the addition of various suffixes:

key	anahtar
keys	anahtarlar
my key	anahtarım
your keys	anahtarlarınız
(the) key's ...	anahtarın
characterised by a key, having a key	anahtarlı
keyless	anahtarsız
'key thing' (key ring, key holder, etc)	anahtarlık
key-person (key cutter, locksmith)	anahtarcı

ADJECTIVES

Turkish adjectives are simple and useful. Often an adjective and a
noun have the same meaning. The adjective genç, for example,
means 'young', but can also be used as a noun, 'a youth'. Adjectives
don't change according to the case of the noun they modify.

Adjectives are formed by adding an -i suffix to the noun. Religion, din, becomes religious, dini. For nouns ending in -at, the
ending -at is dropped and -i is added. Politics (siyaset) becomes
political (siyasi) this way.

Comparison

Comparison is easy in Turkish. Taking 'long', uzun, as an example, the comparative is formed by putting daha in front of it –
daha uzun 'longer'. For 'longest', put en in front of it – en uzun

cheap ucuz	cheaper daha ucuz	cheapest en ucuz
beautiful güzel	more beautiful daha güzel	most beautiful en güzel
much; a lot çok	more daha çok	most en çok

PRONOUNS
Personal Pronouns with Verbs

I	ben
you (sg inf)	sen
he/she/it	o
we	biz
you (pl, sg pol)	siz
they	onlar

The second person plural – you, siz – is also used for the polite singular. You can say sen to a friend or relative, but to be polite you must say siz to a stranger or important person. As a traveller it is best to always use the second person plural form siz, whether talking to one Turk or several.

The suffixes -im, -iz, -sin, -siniz, and -ler are added to verbs to indicate the person acting. Therefore, personal pronouns are not really necessary and infrequently used. Turks use them mostly for emphasis or to make a point more clearly. In other words, gelirim and ben gelirim mean the same thing – 'I come'. Here's an example of where the personal pronoun is useful:

Are they leaving?	Gidiyorlar mı?
	(lit: leaving-they question)
No, we're leaving.	Hayır, biz gidiyoruz
	(lit: no, we leaving-we)

VERBS

Verbs are always placed at the end of a sentence or clause. Turkish verbs also use suffixes to change the meaning of a simple root. This can be as simple as the combination of gel-, the root for 'come', and -ir, the suffix for the simple present tense, making gelir, 'he comes'.

To form Turkish verbs, you add suffixes to the third person singular (he/she/it) which is the simplest form of the verb. The present tense forms of the verb -gel 'to come' are:

I come	gelirim
you come (sg inf)	gelirsin
he/she/it comes	gelir
we come	geliriz
you come (pl, sg pol)	gelirsiniz
they come	gelirler

GRAMMAR

The preceding tense suffixes that apply to the verb gel- can change slightly according to the root of the verb and vowel harmony, but the various forms of the suffix are all fairly similar. For instance, instead of -ir in gelir, 'to come', it might be -ür in götürür, 'to take'. But the tense suffix's main 'clue', the r, is always there.

The personal suffix also changes, according to vowel harmony, so gelir is formed as gelirim, 'I come', and götürür becomes götürürüm, 'I take'. The personal suffix's main 'clue', the 'm' indicating first person, is always there.

INFINITIVES

All Turkish infinitives end with -mak or -mek. The infinitive of 'to come' is the verbal stem gel with the suffix -mek, gelmek. The infinitive 'to read' is the verbal stem oku with -mak, okumak. To form various tenses of verbs, -mek is removed from the verb and corresponding endings are added to the verb stem.

PRESENT
Simple Present

The simple present tense is formed by adding the suffix -ar, -er, -ır, -ir, -ur, -ür to the verb stem and then adding personal endings. The third person singular of a verb does not take a personal ending and is the form to which personal endings are added.

Thus, the personal suffixes -im, -sin, -iz, -siniz, -ler are added to the root gelir (he/she/it comes) to form the simple present:

I come	gelirim	we come	geliriz
you come (sg inf)	gelirsin	you come (pl, sg pol)	gelirsiniz
he/she/it comes	gelir	they come	gelirler

Continuous Present

The continuous present is formed by adding -ıyor, -iyor to the verbal stem and then adding personal endings. This tense corresponds to the -ing suffix of English.

I am coming	geliyorum
you are coming (sg inf)	geliyorsun
he/she/it is coming	geliyor
we are coming	geliyoruz
you are coming (pl, sg pol)	geliyorsunuz
they are coming	geliyorlar

PAST
Simple Past

The simple past, 'I came, I saw, I conquered', is formed by adding -dı, -di, -du, -dü to the verb stem and then by adding the personal suffixes.

I came	geldim	we came	geldik
you came (sg inf)	geldin	you came (pl, sg pol)	geldiniz
he/she/it came	geldi	they came	geldiler

Continuous Past

The continuous past, or imperfect, is formed by a compound of the continuous ending -iyor with the past ending -di. To this are added the personal suffixes. The verb of third person plural (they) places the plural suffix -ler before the past ending -di.

I was coming	geliyordim
you were coming (sg inf)	geliyordin
he/she/it were coming	geliyordi
we were coming	geliyordik
you were coming (pl, sg pol)	geliyordiniz
they were coming	geliyorlerdi

FUTURE

The future tense is formed by adding -acak, -ecek, -acağ-, -eceğ-
to the verb stem and then by adding the personal suffixes.

I will come	geleceğim
you will come (sg inf)	geleceksin
he/she/it will come	gelecek
we will come	geleceğiz
you will come (pl, sg pol)	geleceksiniz
they will come	gelecekler

IMPERATIVE

The imperative of a verb is formed simply by adding -in and its
variant spellings according to vowel harmony (-ın, in, -un, -ün)
to the verb stem.

Come!	gelin	Look!	bakın
Wait!	bekleyin	Stop!	durun

The negative imperative is formed by adding -meyin and variant
spellings to the verb stem.

Don't come! gelmeyin   Don't do it! yapmayın

TO BE
Present

The verb 'to be' in Turkish is most commonly indicated through
the use of personal suffixes added to the noun, adjective or adverb.
These endings follow the personal suffixes used throughout the
language -(y)im, -sin, (no ending), -(y)iz, -isiniz, -ler, and their
spelling variations, following the laws of vowel harmony.

For example, serseri (a ne'er-do-well) plus sin (you) gives
serserisin which means, 'you're a deadbeat!'

I'm tired	(ben) yorgunum
you are tired (sg, inf)	(sen) yorgunsun
he is tired	(o) yorgun

we're tired	(biz) yorgunuz
you are tired (pl, sg pol)	(siz) yorgunsunuz
they are tired	(onlar) yorgunlar

Past

The past tense of 'to be' is formed by adding to adjectives and nouns an ending similar to that used for the regular past tense -dim, -din, -di, -dik, -diniz, -diler and their spelling variations, following the laws of vowel harmony.

I am tired	(ben) yorgundum
you are tired (sg inf)	(sen) yorgundun
he is tired	(o) yorgundu
we are tired	(biz) yorgunduk
you are tired (pl, sg pol)	(siz) yorgundunuz
they are tired	(onlar) yorgundular

Two particular verbs indicate 'to be' in Turkish. They are olmak which also means 'to exist', 'to occur' as in olan oldu 'it is too late now', and bulunmak 'to be present' as in the phrase:

| I am very glad to be here. | Burada bulunmaktan çok memnunum. |
| | (lit: this-place to-be-present-from very delighted-me) |

TO HAVE
Present

The most common way of expressing 'to have' in the present tense is by adding possessive suffixes to the noun and placing the word var at the end of the sentence. To indicate 'not having', yok is placed at the end of the sentence.

I have time.	Menim vaktim var.
	(lit: my time-my have)
You do not have a home.	Siz eviniz yok.
	(lit: you home-your not-have)

Past

To express 'to have' in the past, the same endings are added to the noun, but to var is added the part ending -dı (vardı) and to yok is added -tu (yoktu).

I did not have time.	Menim vaktim yoktu.
	(lit: my time-my not-had)
You had a house.	Siz eviniz vardı.
	(lit: you home-your had)

POSSESSION
Possessive Pronouns

There are several ways to show possession. While not strictly correct, the easiest way is simply to use the possessive pronoun:

my/mine	benim
your/yours	senin
his/her/its	onun
our/ours	bizim
your/yours	sizin
their/theirs	onların

Here are some examples:

pen	kalem
your pen	sizin kalem
ticket	bilet
his ticket	onun bilet

Possessive Suffix

You can also add a suffix to a noun to show possession. This is fully correct:

my	(i)m
your (sg inf)	(i)n
his/her/its	(s)i
our	(i)miz
your (pl, sg pol)	(i)niz
their	leri

Possessive suffixes, like others, are subject to vowel harmony, so it might be, for example, -im for one word, -um for another.

ticket	bilet	my ticket	biletim
suitcase	bavul	my suitcase	bavulum

Using either the possessive pronoun or the possessive suffix will allow you to make yourself understood. However, to emphasise ownership (as in 'not my pen, your pen'), use both the pronoun and the suffix together:

your	sizin	pen	kalem	your pen	sizin kaleminiz
his	onun	suitcase	bavul	his suitcase	onun bavulu

QUESTIONS

To form a question, add the suffix -mi, -mı, -mu, -mü, depending on vowel harmony, to the very end of the verb. Though the suffix -mi is part of the same word, a space is customarily left in front of it.

The bus is coming.	Otobüs geliyor. (lit: bus coming)
Is the bus coming?	Otobüs geliyor mu? (lit: bus coming question)

GRAMMAR

KEY VERBS

agree	rah-zih olh-mahk	*razı olmak*
ask	sohr-mahk	*sormak*
begin	bahsh-lah-mahk	*başlamak*
bring	gheh-teer-mehk	*getirmek*
buy	ahl-mahk	*almak*
come	gehl-mehk	*gelmek*
depart (leave)	geet-mehk	*gitmek*
do	yahp-mahk	*yapmak*
drink	eech-mehk	*içmek*
eat	yeh-mehk	*yemek*
enter	geer-mehk	*girmek*
find	bool-mahk	*bulmak*
forget	oon-oot-mahk	*unutmak*
give	vehr-mehk	*vermek*
go	geet-mehk	*gitmek*
know (someone)	tah-nih-mahk	*tanımak*
know (something)	beel-mehk	*bilmek*
leave	bihr-ahk-mahk	*bırakmak*
like	sehv-mehk	*sevmek*
live	yahsh-ah-mahk	*yaşamak*
look	bahk-mahk	*bakmak*
lose	kahy-beht-mahk	*kaybetmek*
love	sehv-mehk	*sevmek*
make	yahp-mahk	*yapmak*
meet	tah-nihsh-mahk	*tanışmak*
prefer	tehr-jeeh eht-mehk	*tercih etmek*
read	oh-koo-mahk	*okumak*
return	geh-ree dern-mehk	*geri dönmek*
say	sery-leh-mehk	*söylemek*

	KEY VERBS	
see	gerr-mehk	*görmek*
sell	saht-mahk	*satmak*
sleep	oo-yoo-mahkfs	*uyumak*
speak	koh-noosh-mahk	*konuşmak*
stay	kahl-mahk	*kalmak*
take	ahl-mahk	*almak*
understand	ahn-lah-mahk	*anlamak*
wait	behk-leh-mehk	*beklemek*
want	ees-teh-mehk	*istemek*
work	chah-lihsh-mahk	*çalışmak*
write	yahz-mahk	*yazmak*

NEGATIVES

To form the negative, place the suffix -me(z)- or -ma(z)- after the verb root and before any other suffixes and there may be a *y* added as a buffer:

to come	gelmek
not to come	gelmemek

I came	geldim
I didn't come	gelmezdim
I'll go	gideceğim
I won't go	gitmeyeceğim

To make a negative in sentences with an unstated verb 'to be', use the word değil, 'not', where the verb would be.

They are not Turks.	Türklar değiller.
	(lit: Turks not-they)
It's not expensive.	Pahalı değil.
	(lit: expensive not)

GRAMMAR

TO BE ABLE

'To be able' is expressed using the verbal suffix -(y)ebil or -(y)abil.
To form the verb meaning 'I can come', merge -ebil into gelirim,
'I come'. To ask the question 'Can I come?', place the suffix -mi
after -ebil and before the personal ending.

I come	gelirim
I can come.	gelebilirim.
Can I come?	gelebilir miyim?

TO NEED

To need is expressed by placing ihtiyacı- with a personal ending
followed by var, as in 'I have a need'.

I need a better computer.	Daha iyi bilgisayara ihtiyacım var.
	(lit: more good computer need-I have)

MEETING PEOPLE

Ottoman etiquette was complex, graceful and flowery, with all sorts of polite words and phrases. Today Turks are much more informal, but vestiges of Ottoman politeness remain. If you visit a Turk's home, you'll be shown to the best seat in the room, welcomed formally, offered sweets, cigarettes and tea or coffee, and expected to exchange pleasantries for a few minutes. On an intercity bus ride, the *yardımcı*, 'bus driver's assistant', will come through the bus with a bottle of lemon cologne and shake some into your hands so that you can refresh your face and neck. They still offer sweets before takeoff on Turkish Airlines flights, not just to help your ears adjust to altitude, but as a welcoming symbol of Turkish hospitality as well.

YOU SHOULD KNOW

Hi/Hello!	mehr-hah-bah!	*Merhaba!*
Good night.	ee-yee geh-jeh-lehr	*İyi geceler.*
Goodbye.	ahl-lah-ah	*Allaha ısmarladık.*
(person leaving)	ihs-mahr-lah-dihk	

Yes.	eh-veht	*Evet.*
No.	hah-yihr	*Hayır.*
Please.	lyut-fehn	*Lütfen.*

Thank you. (pol)
   teh-shehk-kyur eh-deh-reem   *Teşekkür ederim.*
Thanks. (inf)
   teh-shehk-kyur-lehr   *Teşekkürler.*
Thanks. (inf)
   sah ohl/ohl-loon   *Sağ ol/olun.*
You're welcome.
   beer shehy deh-eel   *Bir şey değil.*
Pardon me.
   af-feh-dehr-see-neez   *Affedersiniz.*

GREETINGS & GOODBYES

Use a greeting whenever you approach someone. The all-purpose informal greeting, *merhaba*, 'hello', is good in any situation, with anyone, at any time of day. Muslims in the more traditional towns may say *salaam aleikum*, 'peace be with you', but they usually only say it to other Muslims. The correct response is *aleikum salaam*, 'and with you, peace'.

To get someone's attention, whether a man, woman or group of people, say *efendim*. With a child you can use *çocuk*, 'child'. Ticket-takers on buses or ferryboats may use *evet*, 'yes' to get your attention so they can check your tickets. If you bump someone inadvertently, say *affedersiniz*, 'pardon me'. You can also get away with simply saying *pardon*, pahr-dohn

Turks will welcome you into a shop or a restaurant, offer you a seat, a cigarette or anything at all using the word *buyurun(uz)*, which means 'be my guest' or 'help yourself'. The closest equivalent in another language is the German politeness-word 'bitte'. You'll hear *buyurun* a lot, and sometimes the plural/extra-polite *buyurunuz*. You can use it yourself if you offer an elderly person your seat on the bus or offer food, etc to someone.

Turks may assume that you're German and greet you with 'guten tag' – any Turks who were formerly 'guest-workers' in Germany do speak German, but many know little more than this greeting.

Sir!; Miss!; Madam!; Ladies and gentlemen!
eh-fehn-deem! *Efendim!*

Good morning/day.
gyu-nay-dihn *Günaydın.*

Good evening.
ee-yee ahk-shahm-lahr *İyi akşamlar.*

How are you?
nah-sihl-sih-nihz? *Nasılsınız?*

Very well, thank you.
chohk ee-yee-yeem, *Çok iyiyim, teşekkür*
tesh-eh-kyur eh-deh-reem *ederim.*

And how are you?
seez nah-sihl-sih-nihz? *Siz nasılsınız?*

Come on in!/Help yourself!		
booy-roon(ooz)!		*Buyurun(uz)!*
Bon voyage/		
Goodbye. (person staying)		
gyu-leh gyu-leh		*güle güle.*
Let's go!		
gee-deh-leem!		*Gidelim!*

You've gone to a lot of trouble.		
chohk zahh-meht		*Çok zahmet ettiniz.*
eht-tee-neez		
There's none/No.	yohk	*Yok.*
I/we have it/there is	vahr	*Var.*
Of course.	tah-bee-ee	*Tabii.*

BODY LANGUAGE

Turks indicate 'yes' by nodding the head once, forward and down. They may also say *var*, 'we have it' – more literally 'it exists', the same way. To indicate 'no' in Turkey, nod your head up and back, lifting your eyebrows at the same time – simply raising your eyebrows also signifies 'no'. Remember, when Turks seem to be giving you a mean look, they are often only saying 'no'. They may also make the sound 'tsk', which also means 'no'.

Wagging your head from side to side doesn't mean 'no' in Turkish, it means 'I don't understand'. So if a Turk asks you, 'Are you looking for the bus to Ankara?' and you shake your head, he or she will assume you don't understand English and will probably ask you the same question again, this time in German.

MEETING PEOPLE

There are other body-language signs that can cause confusion, especially when you're out shopping. For instance, if you want to indicate length – 'I want a fish this big' – don't hold your hands apart at the desired length, rather hold out your arm and place a flat hand on it, measuring from your fingertips to the hand. Thus, if you want a pretty big fish, you must 'chop' your arm with your other hand at about the elbow.

Height is indicated by holding a flat hand the desired distance above the floor or some other flat surface such as a counter or table top.

Turks will invite you to follow them by waving one of their hands downward and toward themselves in a scooping motion. Some Turks, particularly women, will hold their hand in the same way, but flutter their fingers instead of scooping. Both signs mean 'follow me'. Wiggling an upright finger would never occur to a Turk, except perhaps as a vaguely obscene gesture.

POLITE PHRASES

Besides the normal everyday pleasantries such as 'hello' and 'thank you', on certain occasions Turks will automatically hold forth with a special phrase appropriate to the occasion. When you sit down to a meal, it's *Afiyet olsun!*, 'May it contribute to your health!'. If you have suffered illness or injury, or if you have a sudden and very troubling problem, the appropriate phrase is *Geçmiş olsun!*, 'May it be in your past!' The giveaway in these phrases is the last word … *olsun*, 'Let it be (that)…'. If you hear it, and the context seems right, just say *sağ ol*, 'thanks', in response.

May it contribute to your health!
(said to someone sitting down to a meal)
   ah-fee-eht ohl-soon!   *Afiyet olsun!*

May your life be spared!
(said to someone who has just experienced
a death in the family)
   bah-shih-nihz sah ohl-soon!   *Başınız sağ olsun!*

May your soul be safe from harm!
(said to someone who has just accidentally
broken something)
   jah-nih-nihz sah ohl-soon!   *Canınız sağ olsun!*

May it be in your past!
(said to someone who is ill, injured
or otherwise distressed)
   gech-meesh ohl-soon!   *Geçmiş olsun!*

May it last for hours!
(said to someone who just emerged from a bath
or shower, a shave or a hair cut. It's a corruption of
Sıhhatler olsun!, 'May it keep you healthy!')
   saaht-lahr ohl-soon!   *Saatler olsun!*

Health to your hand!
(said to a cook who has prepared a delicious meal)
   el-lee-nee-zeh sah-lihk!   *Elinize sağlık!*

In your honour!/To your health!
(toast when drinking)
   sheh-reh-fee-nee-zeh!   *Şerefinize!*

FORMS OF ADDRESS

In Ottoman times, the hierarchy of forms of address had many
levels. However, the only Ottoman forms of address you're likely
to run into are *Bey*, 'Mr' and *Hanım*, 'Ms', preceded by a person's first name, as in *Mehmet Bey* or *Ayşe Hanım*. Women have
never been separated into 'Miss' and 'Mrs' in Turkish – there was
and is only 'Ms', even under the Ottomans. The Ottoman form
of address is the one commonly used in most situations today, so
you will usually address people as *Ahmet Bey* or *Perihan Hanım*.
Just to use a person's name with no title is very informal, and is
impolite if you don't know the person well.

The romantic old word *Efendi* is not used much anymore; in
fact it is now used only to indicate someone of very low social
position. The dustman may be *Hasan Efendi*, but the higher-

status driver of the rubbish truck is *Ahmet Bey*. You shouldn't use *Efendi* at all. Note that *Efendim* is the polite, completely acceptable non-specific form of address for men and women, singly or in a group – just be sure to add that final *m*!

Under Atatürk's republic, the Turkish Language Society introduced the 'pure Turkish' forms of address *Bay*, 'Mr' and *Bayan*, 'Ms' followed by the family name: eg *Bay Kocatürk*, 'Mr Kocatürk' or *Bayan Kocatürk*, 'Ms Kocatürk'. These are used in more formal situations – in addressing envelopes, in television interviews and game shows, by government officials, on official forms, etc. You may find yourself being addressed this way occasionally.

It's also common to use a job title followed by *Bey* or *Hanım* instead of the person's given name. This is useful because in many situations you'll know the person's job or title but not their name.

Mr Official (police or civil)
    Meh-moor Behy   *Memur Bey*
Ms Director
    myu-dyur hah-nihm   *Müdür Hanım*
Mr Driver (taxi or bus)
    shoh-ferr behy   *şoför Bey*
Mr/Ms Doctor
    dohk-tohr behy/hahn-ihm *Doktor Bey/Hanım*
Mr Waiter
    gahr-sohn behy   *Garson Bey*
Mr Conductor (Ticket-Taker)
    bee-leht-chee behy   *Biletçi Bey*

FIRST ENCOUNTERS

Even though tourists are now a common sight in Turkey, many Turks will still be curious about you, where you come from and how you are enjoying their country. In hotel lobbies, on bus and train trips, in cafés and teahouses, you may be greeted, offered cigarettes and tea, and engaged in conversation.

What's your name?
　ees-mee-neez neh?　　　　　*İsminiz ne?*

My name's Julia.
　ees-meem Julia　　　　　　*İsmim Julia.*

Is this your first visit to Turkey?
　tyur-kee-yeh-yeh
　eelk deh-fah mih
　geh-lee-yohr-soo-nooz?　　*Türkiye'ye ilk defa mı
　　　　　　　　　　　　　geliyorsunuz?*

How do you like Turkey?
　tyur-kee-yeh-yee nah-sihl
　boo-loo-yohr-soo-nooz?　　*Türkiye'yi nasıl
　　　　　　　　　　　　　buluyorsu-nuz?*

Thanks. I don't smoke.
　teh-she-kyur eh-deh-reem.
　see-gah-rah eech-mee-
　yoh-room　　　　　　　　*Teşekkür ederim. Sigara
　　　　　　　　　　　　　içmiyorum.*

MAKING CONVERSATION

Do you live here?
　boo-rah-dah mih
　oh-too-roo-yohr-soon?　　*Burada mı oturuyorsun?*

Where are you going?
　neh-reh-deh
　gee-dee-yohr-soon?　　　*Nerede gidiyorsun?*

What are you doing?
　neh yah-pih-yohr-soon?　　*Ne yapıyorsun?*

What do you think about ...?
　... neh dyu-shyu-nyu-yohr
　soon?　　　　　　　　　*... ne düşünüyorsun?*

Can I take a photo (of you)?
　rehs-mee-nee che-keh-bee-
　leer-mee-yeem?　　　　　*Resmini çekebilirmiyim?*

What's this called?
　boo-noon ees-mee neh-deer?　*Bunun ismi nedir?*

LANGUAGE DIFFICULTIES

Do you speak English?
  een-gee-leez koh-noo-
  shoo-yohr-moo-soo-nooz?

*İngilizce
konuşuyormusunuz?*

Yes, I speak it.
  eh-veht
  koh-noo-shoo-yohr-room

Evet, konuşuyorum.

No, I don't speak it.
  hah-yihr, koh-noosh-
  moo-yohr-room

Hayır, konuşmuyorum.

I speak a little.
  bee-rahz koh-noosh-
  oo-yohr-room

Biraz konuşuyorum.

Do you understand?
  ahn-lih-yohr-moo-soo-
  nooz?

Anlıyormusunuz?

Yes, I understand.
  eh-veht, ahn-lih-
  yohr-room

Evet, anlıyorum.

No, I don't understand.
  hah-yihr,
  ahn-lah-mih-yohr-room

Hayır, anlamıyorum.

Could you repeat that?
  tehk-rahr
  eh-dehr-mee-see-neez?

Tekrar edermisiniz?

Please write it down.
  lyut-fehn yah-zih-nihz
  lyut-fehn yah-zihn

Lütfen yazınız. (pl, pol)
Lütfen yazın. (sg inf)

How do you say ...?
  ... nah-sihl sery-lyu-yohr-
  soon?

... nasıl söylüyorsun?

What does ... mean?
  ... neh deh-mehk?

... ne demek?

Beautiful, isn't it!
> chohk gyu-zehl deh-eel mee!   *Çok güzel, değil mi!*

It's very nice here.
> boo-rah-sih chohk gyu-zehl   *Burası çok güzel.*

We love it here.
> boo-rah-sih-nih   *Burasını seviyoruz.*
> seh-vee-yohr-rooz

What a cute baby!
> neh sheh-reen beh-behk!   *Ne şerin bebek!*

Are you waiting too?
> sehn deh mee   *Sen de mi bekliyorsun?*
> beh-klee-yohr-soon?

That's strange!
> oh too-hahf   *O tuhaf.*

That's funny. (amusing)
> oh koh-meek   *O komik.*

Are you here on holiday?
> boo-rah-dah tah-teel   *Burada tatil için mi*
> ee-cheen mee boo-loon-   *bulunuyorsunuz?*
> noo-yohr-soon-ooz?

I'm here ...	boo-rah-dah ...	*Burada ...*
for a holiday	tah-teel ee-cheen	*tatil için*
on business	eesh ee-cheen	*iş için*
to study	oh-koo-mahk ee-cheen	*okumak için*

How long are you here for?
> boo-rah-dah neh kah-dahr   *Burada ne kadar*
> kah-lah-jahk-sih-nihz?   *kalacaksınız?*

I'm/We're here for (five) days.
> boo-rah-dah (behsh) gyun   *Burada (beş) gün*
> ee-cheen kah-lah-jah-ihm/   *kalacağım/kalacağız.*
> kah-lah-jah-ihz

Do you like it here?
  boo-rah-dahn
  hohsh-lahn-dih-nihz mih?   *Buradan hoşlandınız mı?*

We like it here very much.
  beez boo-rah-dahn chohk   *Biz buradan çok*
  hohsh-lahn-dihk   *hoşlandık.*

USEFUL PHRASES

Sure	eh-meen	*Emin.*
Just a minute.	beer dah-kee-kah	*Bir dakika*
It's OK.	tah-mahm/ peh-kee	*Tamam/Peki.*
It's important.	er-nehm-lee	*Önemli.*
It's not important.	er-nehm-lee deh-eel	*Önemli değil*
It's possible.	myum-kyun	*Mümkün.*
It's not possible.	myum-kyun deh-eel	*Mümkün değil.*
Look!	bah-kihn! bahk!	*Bakın! (pol)* *Bak! (inf)*

Listen/Listen to this!
  deen-leh-yeen/deen-leh   *Dinleyin! (pol)/Dinle! (inf)*
I'm ready.
  hah-zihr-ihm   *Hazırım.*
Are you ready?
  hah-zihr-mih-sihn?   *Hazırmısın?*
Good luck!
  ih-yee shahns-lahr!   *İyi şanslar!*
Just a second!
  beer sah-nee-yeh!   *Bir saniye!*

MEETING PEOPLE

NATIONALITIES

Unfortunately we can't list all countries here, however you'll find that many country names in Turkish are similar to English. Remember though that even if a word looks like the English equivalent, it will have a Turkish pronunciation.

Where are you from?
   neh-reh-lee-see-neez?   *Nerelisiniz?*

I'm American.
   ah-meh-ree-kah-lih-yihm   *Amerikalıyım*

I'm Australian.
   ah-voo-strahl-yah-lih-yihm   *Avustralyalıyım.*

I'm British.
   een-geel-teh-reh-lee-yeem   *İngitereliyim.*

I'm Canadian.
   kah-nah-dah-lih-yihm   *Kanadalıyım.*

I'm English.
   een-gee-lee-zeem   *İngilizim.*

The following are countries and the words for their corresponding nationalities, not languages. 'French language', for example, is *Fransızca*, while a 'French person' is *Fransız*.

MEETING PEOPLE

France	frahn-sa	*Fransa*
French	frahn-sihz	*Fransız*
Germany	ahl-mahn-yah	*Almanya*
German	ahl-mahn	*Alman*
Israel	ee-srah-yeel	*İsrail*
Israeli	ee-srah-yeel-lee	*İsrailli*
Italy	ee-tahl-yah	*İtalya*
Italian	ee-tahl-yah-lih/	*İtalyalı/*
	ee-tahl-yahn	*İtalyan*
Japan	zha-pohn/	*Japon/*
	zha-pohn-yah	*Japonya*
Japanese	zha-pohn-yah-lih	*Japonyalı*
Spain	ee-spahn-yah	*İspanya*
Spanish	ee-spahn-yohl	*İspanyol*
Sweden	ee-swehch	*İsveç*
Swedish	ee-swehch-lee	*İsveçli*
Switzerland	ee-sveech-reh	*İsviçre*
Swiss	ee-sweech-reh-lee	*İsviçreli*

CULTURAL DIFFERENCES

How do you do this in your country?

seh-neen yul-kehn-deh   *Senin ülkende bunu nasıl*
boo-noo nah-sihl   *yapıyorsun?*
yah-pih-yohr-soon?

Is this a local or national custom/tradition?

boo mah-hal-lee mee meel-lee   *Bu mahalli mi milli mi*
mee ah-deht/geh-leh-nehk?   *adet/gelenek?*

I don't want to offend you.

seh-nee gyu-jehn-deer-mehk   *Seni gücendirmek*
ee-steh-mehm   *istemem.*

I'm sorry, it's not the custom in my country.

yuz-gyu-nyum, beh-neem   *Üzgünüm, benim ülkemde*
yul-kem-deh ah-deht deh-eel   *adet değil.*

MEETING PEOPLE

I'm not accustomed to this.
  boo-nah ah-lih-shihk   *Buna alışık değilim.*
  deh-eel-eem
I don't mind watching, but
I'd prefer not to participate.
  sehy-reht-meh-meen   *Seyretmemin sakıncası*
  sah-kihn-jah-sih yohk,   *yok, fakat katılmamayı*
  fah-kaht kah-tihl-mah-   *tercih ederim.*
  mah-yih tehr-jeeh eh-deh-reem

AGE

How old are you?
  kahch   *Kaç yaşındasınız?*
  yah-shihn-dah-sih-nihz?
I'm 25.
  yeer-mee-besh   *Yirmibeş yaşındayım.*
  yah-shihn-dah-yihm

OCCUPATIONS

What do you do?
  neh eesh yah-pahr-sih-nihz?   *Ne iş yaparsınız?*
I'm a businessman/
businesswoman.
  eesh ah-dah-mihm/   *İşadamım/İşkadınım.*
  eesh-kah-dih-nihm
I'm a doctor.
  dohk-tohr-room   *Doktorum.*
I'm an engineer.
  myu-hehn-dee-seem   *Mühendisim.*
I'm a musician.
  myu-zee-syeh-neem/   *Müzisyenim/Müzikçiyim.*
  myu-zeek-chee-yeem
I'm a student.
  er-rehn-jee-yeem   *Öğrenciyim.*

I'm a teacher.
   er-reht-mehn-eem   *Öğretmenim.*

I'm a journalist.
   gah-zeh-teh-jee-ycem   *Gazeteciyim.*

I'm a (factory) worker.
   eesh-chee-yeem   *İşçiyim.*

I'm a nurse.
   hem-shee-reh-yeem   *Hemşireyim.*

FEELINGS

To express most feelings, add the suffix *-im*, *-ım*, *-um*, or *-üm*, depending on vowel harmony, to an adjective. To say 'we're ...', add the suffix *-ız*, *-iz*, *-uz*, or *-üz*.

I'm tired.	yohr-goon-oom	*Yorgunum.*
We're tired.	yohr-goon-ooz	*Yorgunuz.*
I'm hungry.	ah-chihm	*Açım.*
We're thirsty.	soo-sooz-ooz	*Susuzuz.*
I'm happy.	moot-loo-yoom	*Mutluyum.*
I'm angry.	kihz-gihn-ihm	*Kızgınım.*
We're sorry.	yuz-gyun-yuz	*Üzgünüz.*

Some feelings are expressed by idioms:

I'm sleepy. (my sleep has come)
   ooy-koom gehl-dee   *Uykum geldi.*

MEETING PEOPLE

CROSSWORD

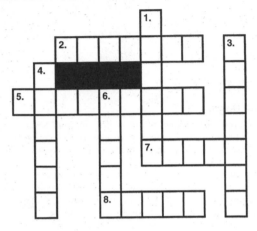

Across

2. '... John' leads to a broken heart
5. wallpaper in teenagers' bedrooms
7. money, not coins (1st word)
8. expression of consent

Down

1. baby-faced travellers may need this to get alcohol
3. Abraham Lincoln shouldn't have gone there
4. not good, resembling excrement
6. bat one's eyelids, dally amorously (2nd word)

Answers on page 259

FINDING YOUR WAY

Where's a/the ...?	... neh-reh-deh?	... *nerede?*
railway station	gahr/ees-tah-syohn	*gar/istasyon*
bus station	oh-toh-gahr	*otogar*
airport	hah-vaah-lah-nih	*havaalanı*
dock/pier	ees-keh-leh	*iskele*
ticket office	bee-leht sah-tihsh oh-fee-see	*bilet satış ofisi*
checkroom	eh-mah-neht-chee	*emanetçi*

When does it leave?
  neh zah-mahn kahl-kahr? *Ne zaman kalkar?*
When does it arrive?
  neh zah-mahn geh-leer? *Ne zaman gelir?*
Is there an earlier/later one?
  dah-hah ehr-kehn/gech vahr mih? *Daha erken/geç var mı?*
How many hours is the journey?
  yohl-joo-look kahch sah-aht? *Yolculuk kaç saat?*

Directions

Is it nearby; far away?
  yah-kihn/oo-zahk mih? *Yakın/Uzak mı?*
It's nearby; far away.
  yah-kihn/oo-zahk *Yakın/Uzak.*
You can go on foot.
  yyu-ryu-yeh-rehk gee-deh-bee-leer-see-neez *Yürüyerek gidebilirsiniz.*
Go straight ahead.
  doh-roo gee-deen *Doğru gidin.*

to the left/right	soh-lah/sah-ah	*sola/sağa*
here	boo-rah-dah	*burada*
there	shoo-rah-dah	*şurada*
over there	oh-rah-dah	*orada*

GETTING AROUND

Cross the road at the next corner.
    geh-leh-jehk ker-sheh-dehn   *Gelecek köşeden*
    yoh-loo kahr-shih-yah gehch   *yolu karşıya geç.*
Cross the road at the traffic signal.
    trah-feek ih-shih-ihn-dahn   *Trafik ışığından yolu*
    yoh-loo kahr-shih-yah gehch   *karşıya geç.*
Cross the road at the roundabout.
    ger-behk-tehn yoh-loo   *Göbekten yolu karşıya geç.*
    kahr-shih-yah gehch
Go straight.
    doh-roo gee-deen/   *Doğru gidin. (pol);*
    geet doh-roo geet   *Doğru git. (inf)*
It's two streets down.
    ee-kee soh-kahk   *İki sokak aşağıda.*
    ah-shah-ih-dah

Cross the road at ...	yoh-loo kahr-shih-yah gehch ...	*yolu karşıya geç ...*
avenue/street	jahd-deh	*cadde*
square; town centre	mehy-dahn	*meydan*
street/road	soh-kahk	*sokak*

after	dehn sohn-rah	*den sonra*
behind	ahr-kah-sihn-dah/	*arkasında/*
	ahr-kah-sih-nah	*arkasına*
between	ah-rah-sihn-dah	*arasında*
far	dehn oo-zahk	*den uzak*
in front of	er-nyun-deh	*önünde*
near	yah-kihn/yah-kihn-dah	*yakın/yakında*
next to ...	... een yah-nihn-dah	*... in yanında*
opposite	kahr-shih	*karşı*

north	koo-zehy	*kuzey*
south	gyu-nehy	*güney*
east	doh-oo	*doğu*
west	bah-tih	*batı*

ADDRESSES

Addresses in Turkish cities are often given in the form of directions:

> Cumhuriyet Caddesi Sepetçi Sokak No. 23/5,
> Gülistan Ap. 3. Kat, Taksim.

In the Taksim neighbourhood, take Republic Ave (main thoroughfare), to Basketmaker's St (side street) and look for building number 23 (the Rose Garden Apartments), then go to apartment 5 on the 3rd floor.

If you stand in the street looking puzzled for a few seconds, some helpful person is sure to approach you and ask if you need help finding an address.

Written addresses, however, look like:

> Perihan Inozu
> Cinnah Cad. 12946/A
> Çankaya – Ankara

This means – to a woman named Perihan Inozu at an apartment building numbered 12946 in Flat A on Cinnah Avenue in the Çankaya district of the city of Ankara.

BUYING TICKETS

I want a ticket to ...	... beer bee-leht ees-tee-yohr-room	... *bir bilet istiyorum*
How many liras is a ticket to ...?	... beer bee-leht kahch lee-rah?	... *bir bilet kaç lira?*
Istanbul	ih-stahn-boo-lah	*İstanbul'a*
Edirne	eh-deer-neh-yeh	*Edirne'ye*
map	hah-ree-tah	*harita*
timetable	tah-ree-feh	*tarife*

GETTING AROUND

ticket	bee-leht	*bilet*
reserved seat (numbered place)	noo-mah-rah-lih yehr	*numaralı yer*
1st class	beer-een-jee mehv-kee/ sih-nihf	*birinci mevki/ sınıf*
2nd class	ee-keen-jee mehv-kee/ sih-nihf	*ikinci mevki/ sınıf*
single; one way	gee-deesh	*gidiş*
return; round trip	gee-deesh-der-nyush	*gidiş-dönüş*
student (ticket)	er-rehn-jee/tah-leh-beh (bee-leh-tee)	*öğrenci/talebe (bileti)*
for today	boo-gyun ee-cheen	*bugün için*
for tomorrow	yah-rihn ee-cheen	*yarın için*
for Friday	joo-mah gyu-nyu ee-cheen	*cuma günü için*
daily	hehr-gyun	*hergün*

TRAFFIC SNARLS

Eşol eşek, 'son of a donkey', is the very first offensive remark that pops from a Turkish car-driver's mouth if he (or she) perceives he's been wronged on the road. Since he/she always perceives such wrongdoing, it may be heard on every road at every hour of the day and night, as Turks constantly compete with each other to win the 'Road Rudeness Award'. It is stunning how a people who are so friendly, kind, and courteous 'on dry land' can become the complete opposite when they get behind the wheel of a car. Turkey actually posts large roadside signs imploring drivers to 'Control the Traffic Monster Inside You!'

AIR

Turkish airlines have a useful schedule of flights, and competition is increasingly provided by smaller airlines.

Will you please check this luggage?
  boo bah-gahzh kahy-deh-dehr   *Bu bagaj kaydeder*
  mee-see-neez?   *misiniz?*

arrival	geh-leesh/vah-rihsh	*geliş/varış*
departure	gee-deesh/kahl-kihsh	*gidiş/kalkış*
airplane	oo-chahk	*uçak*
airport	hah-vaah-lah-nih	*havaalanı*
boarding pass	bee-neesh kahr-tih	*biniş kartı*
flight	oo-choosh	*uçuş*
gate (door)	kah-pih	*kapı*
gate number	noo-mah-rah-lih	*numaralı*
	chih-kihsh	*çıkış*
	kah-pih-sih	*kapısı*
one/two	beer/ee-kee	*bir/iki*
security check	gyu-vehn-leek	*güvenlik*
	kohn-troh-lyu	*kontrolü*

At Customs

customs	gyum-ryuk	*gümrük*

I have nothing to declare.
  beh-yahn eh-deh-jehk beer   *Beyan edecek bir şeyim yok.*
  sheh-yeem yohk

I have something to declare.
  beh-yahn eh-deh-jehk beer   *Beyan edecek bir şeyim var.*
  sheh-yeem vahr

Do I have to declare this?
  boo-noo beh-yahn   *Bunu beyan etmelimiyim?*
  eht-meh-lee-mee-yeem?

I didn't know I had to declare it.
    boo-noo beh-yahn eht-mehm
    geh-rehk-tee-ee nee
    beel-mee-yohr-doom

Bunu beyan etmem gerektiğini bilmiyordum.

This is all my luggage.
    bah-gahzh-lahr-ih-mihn
    hehp-see boo

Bagajlarımın hepsi bu.

BUS

You'll undoubtedly do some of your Turkish travelling by bus. The intercity-bus network operated by private companies is possibly the busiest in the world. Big, comfortable, modern buses shuttle between cities frequently, even if the cities are at opposite ends of the country. Minibuses (*dolmuş*) serve the shorter routes. Though most cities have modern bus stations, some still have only collections of bus ticket offices, often near the market. Turkish bus stations, whether modern or not, are often very busy, and seemingly chaotic.

At any city bus station, agents will approach you and ask where you want to go, then lead you to the ticket counter of a bus company operating buses to that destination. The agents don't expect tips, and they are not con men. But their company's bus may or may not be the next departure for your destination. It's good to check around on your own and ask about departure times before buying your ticket.

Does this bus/train go to Izmir?
    boo oh-toh-byus/trehn   *Bu otobüs/tren İzmir'e*
    eez-meer-eh gee-dehr mee?   *gider mi?*
When does the bus to Ankara depart?
    ahn-kah-rah-yah gee-dehn   *Ankara'ya giden otobüs ne*
    oh-toh-byus neh zah-mahn   *zaman kalkar?*
    kahl-kahr?

bus	oh-toh-byus	*otobüs*
bus terminal	oh-toh-gahr	*otogar*
minibus	dohl-moosh	*dolmuş*
direct (bus)	dee-rehk(t)	*direk(t)*
indirect (route)	ahk-tahr-mah-lih	*aktarmalı*

TRAIN

Turks are passionate travellers. Some of the trains operated by the
Turkish State Railways are very fast and comfortable, and like the
buses, train fares are surprisingly cheap.

train	trehn	*tren*
railway	deh-meer-yoh-loo	*demiryolu*
railway station	gahr/ees-tahs-yohn	*gar/istasyon*
sleeping car	yah-tahk-lih vah-gohn	*yataklı vagon*
dining car	yeh-mehk-lee vah-gohn	*yemekli vagon*
couchette	koo-sheht	*kuşet*
no-smoking car	see-gah-rah ee-cheel-mee-yehn vah-gohn	*sigara içilmeyen vagon*

BOAT

berth	yah-tahk	*yatak*
cabin	kah-mah-rah	*kamara*
class	mehv-kee/sih-nihf	*mevki/sınıf*
dock	ees-keh-leh	*iskele*
ferryboat	feh-ree-boht	*feribot*
port tax	lee-mahn vehr-gee-see	*liman vergisi*
ship	geh-mee	*gemi*

GETTING AROUND

TAXI

Is this taxi available?
boo tahk-see
myu-sah-eet mee?

Bu taksi müsait mi?

Please take me to (Sultanahmet).
lyut-fehn beh-nee
(sool-tahn-ah-meht)-eh
ger-tyu-ryu-nyuz

*Lütfen beni (Sultanahmet)'e
götürünüz.*

How much does it cost to go to (Sultanahmet)?
(sool-tahn-ah-meht)-eh
geet-mehk neh kah-dahr
too-tahr?

*(Sultanahmet)'e gitmek ne
kadar tutar?*

How much is the fare?
yuj-reh-tee-neez
neh kah-dahr?

Ücretiniz ne kadar?

Do we pay extra for luggage?
bah-gahzh ee-cheen eks-trah
erdeh-yeh-jehk-mee-yeez?

*Bagaj için ekstra
ödeyecekmiyiz?*

THEY MAY SAY ...

tah-mahm/peh-kee *Tamam/Peki.*	OK/That's fine.
tah-mahm *Tamam.*	Sure/OK.
gee-deh-lihm *Gidelim.*	Let's go.
behk-leh-yihn/behk-leh *Bekleyin (pol)/Bekle (inf)*	Wait.
beer dah-kee-kah *Bir dakika.*	Just a minute.
hah-zihr mih-sih-nihz? *Hazır mısınız?*	Are you ready?
hah-zihr-ihm *Hazırım.*	I'm ready.

Instructions

Let's go!
gee-deh-leem! *Gidelim!*

I'm in a hurry.
ah-jeh-lehm vahr *Acelem var.*

Slow down!
yah-vahsh gee-deen! *Yavaş gidin!*

Stop (here)!
(boo-rah-dah) doo-roon! *(Burada) durun!*

Wait here!
boo-rah-dah bek-leh-yeen! *Burada bekleyin!*

Careful! deek-kaht! *Dikkat!*
Slow! yah-vahsh! *Yavaş!*

CAR

air (for tyres)	hah-vah (lahs-teek)	*hava (lastik)*
auto electric repairman	oh-toh ee-lehk-treek-chee	*oto elektrikçi*
brake(s)	frehn(lehr)	*fren(ler)*
climbing lane	tihr-mahn-mah sheh-ree-dee	*tırmanma şeridi*
headlamp	fahr	*far*
highways	kah-rah-yoh-lah-rih	*karayolları*
long vehicle	oo-zoon ah-rahch	*uzun araç*
lubrication	yah-lah-mah	*yağlama*
motor oil	moh-tohr yah-ih	*motor yağı*
motorway/ expressway	oh-toh-yohl	*otoyol*
normal/regular	nohr-mahl	*normal*
petrol/gasoline	behn-zeen	*benzin*
road construction	yohl yah-pih-mih	*yol yapımı*
road repairs	yohl oh-nah-rih-mih	*yol onarımı*
super/extra	syu-pehr	*süper*
tyre repairman	oh-toh lahs-teek-chee	*oto lastikçi*
(car) washing	yih-kah-mah	*yıkama*
wide vehicle	geh-neesh ah-rahch	*geniş araç*

Car Problems

We need a mechanic.
tah-meer-jee-yeh
ee-tee-yah-jih-mihz vahr
Tamirciye ihtiyacımız var.

What make is your car?
ah-rah-bah-nihz neh
mahr-kah?
Arabanız ne marka?

The car broke down at ...
ah-rah-bah ...-deh
boh-zool-doo
Araba ...'de bozuldu.

The battery is flat.
ah-kyu-syu beet-tee
Aküsü bitti.

The radiator is leaking.
rahd-yah-ter dahm-lih-yohr
Radyatör damlıyor.

I have a flat tyre.
   lahs-tee-yeem paht-lah-dih   *Lastiğim patladı.*

It's overheating.
   chohk ih-sih-nih-yohr   *Çok ısınıyor.*

It's not working.
   chah-lihsh-mih-yohr   *Çalışmıyor.*

I've lost my car keys.
   ah-rah-bah-mihn   *Arabamın anahtarını*
   ah-nahh-tah-rih-nih   *kaybettim.*
   kahy-beht-teem

I've run out of petrol.
   behn-zee-neem beet-tee   *Benzinim bitti.*

BICYCLE

Can you go by bicycle?
   bee-see-kleht-leh   *Bisikletle gidilebilir mi?*
   gee-dee-leh-bee-leer mee?

Where can I hire a bicycle?
   neh-reh-dehn bee-see-kleht   *Nereden bisiklet*
   kee-rah-lah-yah-bee-lee-reem?   *kiralayabilirim?*

Where can I find secondhand
bikes for sale?
   neh-reh-den ee-keen-jee ehl   *Nereden ikinci el satılık*
   sah-tih-lihk bee-see-kleht   *bisiklet bulabilirim?*
   boo-lah-bee-lee-reem?

My tyre blew.
   lahs-tee-yeem paht-lah-dih   *Lastiğim patladı.*

How much is it for ...?	... neh kah-dahr?	*... ne kadar?*
an hour	beer sah-ah-tee	*bir saati*
the morning	sah-bahh-lah-rih	*sabahları*
the afternoon	er-gleh-dehn sohn-rah-lah-rih	*öğleden sonraları*
the day	byu-tyun gyun	*bütün gün*

bike	bee-see-kleht	*bisiklet*
brake(s)	frehn(lehr)	*fren(ler)*
to cycle	bee-see-kleht been-mehk	*bisiklet binmek*
gear stick	vee-tehs	*vites*
handlebars	gee-dohn(lahr)	*gidon(lar)*
helmet	kahsk	*kask*
inner tube	eech lahs-teek	*iç lastik*
light(s)	ih-shihk(lahr)/ fahr(lahr)	*ışık(lar)/far(lar)*
mountain bike	dah bee-see-kleh-tee	*dağ bisikleti*
padlock	ahs-mah kee-leet	*asma kilit*
pump	pohm-pah	*pompa*
puncture	paht-lahk/dehl-meh	*patlak/delme*
racing bike	yah-rihsh-mah bee-see-kleh-tee	*yarışma bisikleti*
saddle	seh-leh	*sele*
tandem	tahn-dehm/ ee-kee-lee bee-see-kleht	*tandem/ ikili bisiklet*
wheel	teh-kehr-lehk	*tekerlek*

ACCOMMODATION

Turkey has all classes of accommodation, from student dormitories and little family-run pensions to international-class luxury hotels. Some Turks will assume that, as a foreigner, you'll want to stay at a four-star place. But when you ask them for directions to a good, cheap hotel they'll readily oblige and recommend a place where they would stay.

FINDING ACCOMMODATION

Where's a hotel?
beer oh-tehl neh-reh-deh?   *Bir otel nerede?*

Where's a clean, cheap hotel?
oo-jooz teh-meez beer   *Ucuz, temiz bir otel*
oh-tehl neh-reh-deh?   *nerede?*

I want a room for only
(20,000) liras.
yahl-nihz (yeer-mee been)   *Yalnız (yirmi bin) lira için*
lee-rah ee-cheen beer oh-dah   *bir oda istiyorum.*
ees-tee-yoh-room

BOOKING AHEAD

I'd like to book a room, please.   *Bir oda ayırtmak*
beer oh-dah ah-yihrt-mahk   *istiyorum.*
ees-tee-yohr-room

Do you have any rooms available?
oh-dah-nihz vahr mih?   *Odanız var mı?*

For (three) nights.
(yuch) geh-jeh ee-cheen   *(Üç) gece için.*

How much per night?
beer geh-jeh-leek neh   *Bir gecelik ne kadar?*
kah-dahr

I'll be staying ...	... kah-lah-jah-ihm	... *kalacağı.*
We'll be staying ...	... kah-lah-jah-ihz	... *kalacağız.*
one night	beer geh-jeh	*bir gece*
two nights	ee-kee geh-jeh	*iki gece*
three nights	yuch geh-jeh	*üç gece*
a few nights	beer kahch geh-jeh	*bir kaç gece*
(at least) a week	(ehn ah-zihn-dahn)	*(en azından)*
	beer hahf-tah	*bir hafta*

I'm not sure how long I'm staying.
heh-nyuz   *Henüz bilmiyorum.*
beel-mee-yoh-room
We will be arriving at
...'deh geh-leh-jeh-eez   ... *'de geleceğiz.*
My name is ...
ah-dihm ...   *Adım ...*

CHECKING IN
Even in the smallest hotels and pensions there will probably be someone who speaks a few words of English.

I want a ...	beer ... ees-tee-yoh-room	*Bir ... istiyorum.*
We want a ...	beer ... ees-tee-yoh-rooz	*Bir ... istiyoruz.*
bed	yah-tahk	*yatak*
room	oh-dah	*oda*
single room	kee-shee-leek oh-dah	*kişilik oda*
double room	ee-kee kee-shee-leek oh-dah	*iki kişilik oda*
triple room	yuch kee-shee-leek oh-dah	*üç kişilik oda*

room with one bed	tehk yah-tahk-lih oh-dah	*tek yataklı oda*
room with two beds	ee-kee yah-tahk-lih oh-dah	*iki yataklı oda*
room with twin beds	cheeft yah-tahk-lih oh-dah	*çift yataklı oda*
double bed	geh-neesh yah-tahk	*geniş yatak*
room with bath	bahn-yoh-loo oh-dah	*banyolu oda*
room without bath	bahn-yoh-sooz oh-dah	*banyosuz oda*
room with shower	doosh-loo oh-dah	*duşlu oda*
room with washbasin	lah-vah-boh-loo oh-dah	*lavabolu oda*
quiet room	sah-keen beer oh-dah	*sakin bir oda*

ACCOMMODATION

How many liras?
kahch lee-rah?   *Kaç lira?*
That's too expensive.
chohk pah-hah-lih   *Çok pahalı*
Is there a cheaper (room)?
dah-hah oo-jooz-oo vahr mih?   *Daha ucuzu var mı?*
Could I see the room?
oh-dah-yih ger-reh-bee-leer-mee-yeem?   *Odayı görebilir miyim?*
Is there a better (room)?
dah-hah ee-yee-see vahr mih?   *Daha iyisi var mı?*

included	dah-heel	*dahil*
excluded	hah-reech	*hariç*

Is the tax included?
vehr-gee dah-heel mee?   *Vergi dahil mi?*
Where's the toilet?
too-vah-leht neh-reh-deh?   *Tuvalet nerede?*

ACCOMMODATION

PAPERWORK

name	ee-seem/ahd	isim/ad
father's name	bah-bah-nihn ah-dih	babanın adı
address	ah-dres	adres
date of birth	doh-oom gyu-nyu	doğum günü
place of birth	doh-oom yeh-ree	doğum yeri
age	yahsh	yaş
sex	jeen-see-yeht/jeens	cinsiyet/cins
nationality	ooy-rook-look/	uyrukluk/
	meel-lee-yeht	milliyet
religion	deen	din
profession/work	mehs-lehk	meslek
reason for travel	sehy-yah-hah-tihn	seyahatın
	seh-beh-bee	sebebi
marital status	meh-deh-nee hahl	medeni hal
single	beh-kahr	bekar
married	ehv-lee	evli
divorced	bohsh-ahn-mihsh	boşanmış
widow/widower	dool kah-deen/	dul kadin/
	ehr-kehk	erkek
identification	keem-leek	kimlik
passport number	pah-sah-pohrt	pasaport
	noo-mah-rah-sih	numarası
visa	vee-zeh	vize
driving licence	eh-lee-yeht	ehliyet
customs	gyum-ryuk	gümrük
passport control	pah-sah-pohrt	pasaport
	kohn-trohl	kontrol
security	ehm-nee-yeht	emniyet
purpose of visit	zee-yah-reh-teen	ziyaretin
	seh-beh-bee	sebebi
holiday	tah-teel	tatil
business	eesh	iş
visiting relatives	ah-krah-bah-yih	akrabayı
	zee-yah-reht-eht-meh	ziyaret etme

Is a hot shower included?
sih-jahk doosh dah-heel mee?   *Sıcak duş dahil mi?*

How much is a hot shower?
sih-jahk doosh kahch   *Sıcak duş kaç lira?*
ee-rah?

Where's the manager?
pah-trohn neh-reh-deh?   *Patron nerede?*

Is there someone who
knows English?
een-gee-leez-jeh bee-lehn   *Ingilizce bilen bir kimse*
beer keem-seh neh-reh-deh?   *nerede?*

It's fine, I'll take it.
ee-yee, too-too-yoh-room   *İyi, tutuyorum.*

Is breakfast included?
kahh-vahl-tih dah-heel mee?   *Kahvaltı dahil mi?*

Are meals included?
yeh-mehk-lehr dah-heel mee?   *Yemekler dahil mi?*

I don't want to take meals.
yeh-mehk-lehr   *Yemekler istemiyorum.*
ees-teh-mee-yoh-room

Taking meals is required.
yeh-mehk-lehr ahl-mahk   *Yemekler almak*
mej-boor(door)   *mecbur(dur).*

Do I have to rent sheets (hire
the bedlinen)?
chahr-shahf keer-   *Çarşaf kir alamalımıyım?*
ah-lah-mah-lih-mih-yihm?

I'll pay with a credit card.
kreh-dee kahr-tih ee-leh   *Kredi kartı ileödeyeceğim.*
er-deh-yeh-jehy-ihm

Do you want a deposit?
deh-poh-seet   *Deposit istermisiniz?*
ihs-tehr-mih-sih-nihz?

ACCOMMODATION

I'm going to stay for ...
    ... kah-lah-jah-ihm   *... kalacağım*

I'm going to stay for one day.
    beer gyun kah-lah-jah-ihm   *Bir gün kalacağım.*

I'm going to stay for two days.
    ee-kee gyun kah-lah-jah-ihm   *İki gün kalacağım.*

I'm going to stay for one week.
    beer hahf-tah kah-lah-jah-ihm   *Bir hafta kalacağım.*

I'm not sure how long I'll stay.
    neh kah-dahr kah-lah-jah-ihm   *Ne kadar kalacağımdan*
    -dahn eh-meen deh-ee-leem   *emin değilim.*

THEY MAY SAY ...

yuz-gyu-nyum. doh-loo-yooz
  Üzgünüm. Doluyuz.   I'm sorry. We're full.
neh kah-dahr
kah-lah-jahk-sih-nihz?
  Ne kadar kalacaksınız?   How long will you stay?
kahch gheh-jeh?
  Kaç gece?   How many nights?
kihm-lee-ee-neez vahr mih?
  Kimliğiniz var mı?   Do you have
                      identification?
yu-yeh-leek kahr-tih-nihz vahr mih?
  Üyelik kartınız var mı?   Do you have a
                      membership card?
doh-oom gyu-nyu-nyuz?
  doğum gününüz?   (Your) date of birth?
ees-mee-neez?
  İsminiz?   Name?
ihm-zah
  ımza   signature

REQUESTS & COMPLAINTS

Don't you have anything cheaper?
heech dah-hah oo-jooz
yohk moo

Hiç daha ucuz yok mu?

Can I/we sleep on the roof?
chah-tih-dah yah-tah-
beer-leer mee-yeem/
mee-yeez?

Çatıda yatabilir miyim/ miyiz?

Can I/we camp in the garden?
bahh-cheh-deh kahmp
yah-pah-bee-leer
mee-yeem/mee-yeez?

Bahçede kamp yapabilir miyim/ miyiz?

I/we have a tent.
chah-dihr-ihm/
chah-dihr-ihz vahr

Çadırım/Çadırız var.

It's too small.
chohk kyu-chyuk

Çok küçük.

It's very noisy.
chohk gyu-ryul-tyu-lyu

Çok gürültülü.

It's very expensive.
chohk pah-hah-lih

Çok pahalı.

It won't do.
ohl-moo-yohr

Olmuyor.

ACCOMMODATION

DID YOU KNOW ... Turkish is a member of the Turkic language family. The Turkic people were centred in Mongolia and spread throughout Central Asia. Turkic languages can now be heard from Turkey to Xinjiang Province in western China.

ACCOMMODATION

CHECKING OUT

Could I have the bill?
heh-sah-bihm lyut-fehn   *Hesabım lütfen.*

I'm/W e're checking out ...
... gee-dee-yoh-room/   ... *gidiyorum/gidiyoruz.*
gee-dee-yoh-rooz

now	sheem-dee	*şimdi*
midday	oh-leh-yeh doh-roo	*oğleye doğru*
this evening	boo ahk-shahm	*bu akşam*
tomorrow	yah-rihn	*yarın*

Can I leave my stuff with you until ...?
bah-gazh-ih-mih ...   *Bagajımı ... kadar sizinle*
kah-dahr see-zeen-leh   *bırakabilir miyim?*
bih-rah-kah-bee-leer
mee-yeem?

3 o'clock	sah-aht yuch-eh	*saat üçe*
this afternoon	oh-leh-dehn	*oğleden sonraya*
	sohn-rah-yah	
this evening	ahk-shah-mah	*akşama*

LOOKING FOR ...

Where is ...?	... nch-reh-deh	... *nerede?*

the Hacibaba Restaurant
    hah-jih-bah-bah   *Hacıbaba Lokantası*
    loh-kahn-tah-sih

the (main) post office
    (mehr-kehz) pohs-tah-neh   *(merkez) postane*

a police officer
    poh-lees meh-moo-roo   *polis memuru*

the (Australian) Embassy
    (ah-voos-trahl-yah) byu-yyuk   *(Avustralya) büyük elçiliği*
    ehl-chee-lee-ee

the Turkish bath
    hah-mahm   *hamam*

AT THE BANK

Not all bank branch offices have exchange facilities. If a branch does not, a bank officer will point you toward a branch that does. Sometimes the exchange desk is one flight up from the main floor. Always take your passport when changing money, and hold onto your exchange slips so that you can change unused liras back into your own currency.

Note that most post offices will change foreign currency notes (but not travellers cheques) into Turkish liras.

Do you accept these travellers cheques?
boo seh-yah-haht
chehk-leh-ree kah-bool
eh-dehr mee-see-neez?
Bu seyahat çekleri kabul eder misiniz?

Do you accept Eurocheques?
yu-roh-chek kah-bool
eh-dehr mee-see-neez?
Euroçek kabul eder misiniz?

Would you change this?
boo-noo boh-zahr
mih-sih-nihz?
Bunu bozar mısınız?

cash	eh-fehk-teef	*efektif*
cashier	kah-sah/vehz-neh	*kasa/vezne*
cheque	chek	*çek*
coin(s)	mah-deh-nee pah-rah	*madeni para*
commission (fee)	koh-mees-yohn	*komisyon*
exchange rate	koor	*kur*
(currency) exchange	kahm-bee-yoh	*kambiyo*
foreign currency	der-veez	*döviz*
money	pah-rah	*para*
paper money	kah-iht pah-rah	*kağıt para*
purchase	ah-lihsh	*alış*
sale	veh-reesh	*veriş*
small change	boh-zook pah-rah	*bozuk para*
tax	vehr-gee	*vergi*

THINGS THEY SELL ...

crafts	zah-nah-aht/ eh sah-nah-tih	*zanaat/ el sanatı*
earing(s)	kyu-peh(lehr)	*küpe(ler)*
painting(s)	tah-bloh(lahr)	*tablo(lar)*
poster(s)	poh-stehr(lehr)	*poster(ler)*
scarf (scarves)	eh-sharp(lahr)	*eşarp(lar)*
T-shirt	tee-sherrt	*Ti şört*

AT THE POST OFFICE

I would like an air-mail stamp for a
postcard to (Australia).

(ah-voo-strahl-yah)-yah *(Avustralya)'ya uçakla*
oo-chahk-lah kahrt-pol ıs-tahl *kartpostal için bir pul*
ee-cheen beer pool ree-jah *rica ederim.*
eh-deh-reem

How many liras to send this to (Canada)?

(kah-nah-dah)-yah kahch *(Kanada)'ya kaç lira?*
lee-rah?

Is there a letter for me in poste restante?

pohst-res-tahn-dah bah-nah *Postrestanda bana*
mek-toop vahr mih? *mektup var mı?*

aerogramme	hah-vah mek-too-boo/ eh-roh-grahm	*hava mektubu/ aerogram*
air mail	oo-chahk-lah/ oo-chahk-ee-leh	*uçakla/uçak ile*
customs	gyum-ryuk	*gümrük*
express mail/ special delivery	ehks-press	*ekspres*
facsimile	eh-lek-troh-neek mehk-toop/fahks	*elektronik mektup/fax*
letter	mehk-toop	*mektup*
money order	hah-vah-leh	*havale*
parcel	koh-lee/pah-keht	*koli/paket*
post office	pohs-tah-neh/ pohs-tah-hah-neh	*postane/ postahane*
post-telephone -telegraph	peh-teh-teh	*PTT*
postage stamp	pool	*pul*
postcard	kahrt-pohs-tahl	*kartpostal*
poste restante/ general delivery	pohst-rehs-tahnt	*post restant*
registered mail	kah-yiht-lih	*kayıtlı*

AROUND TOWN

TELECOMMUNICATIONS

Could I please use the telephone?
　teh-leh-foh-noo kool-lah-　　　*Telefonu kullanabilirmiyim?*
　nah-bee-leer-mee-yeem?

I want to call ...
　... teh-leh-fohn et-mehk　　　*... telefon etmek istiyorum.*
　ees-tee-yohr-room

The number is ...
　... noo-mah-rah-sih　　　　　*... numarası.*

How much does a three-minute call cost?
　yuch dah-kee-kah　　　　　　*Üç dakika konuşmak ne*
　koh-noosh-mahk　　　　　　　*kadar?*
　neh kah-dahr?

I want to call (Australia).
　(ah-voo-strahl-yah)-yah　　　*(Avustralya)'ya telefon*
　teh-leh-fohn et-mehk　　　　 *etmek istiyorum.*
　ees-tee-yohr-room

I want to make a reverse-charges/collect call.
　er-deh-meh-lee teh-leh-fohn　*Ödemeli telefon etmek*
　eht-mehk ees-tee-yohr-room　*istiyorum.*

What is the area code for ...?
　... ah-lahn noo-mah-rah-sih　*... alan numarası nedir?*
　neh-deer?

It's engaged/busy.　　　mehsh-gool　　　　*Meşgul.*
I've been cut off.　　　 kes-eel-dee　　　　*Kesildi.*

Is there a local Internet café?
　jee-vahr-dah een-tehr-neht　*Civarda Internet café*
　kah-feh var mih?　　　　　　*var mı?*

I want to connect to the Internet.
　een-tehr-neh-teh　　　　　　*Internete bağlanmak*
　bah-lahn-mahk　　　　　　　 *istiyorum.*
　ees-tee-yohr-room

I want to look at my email.
　eh-mah-ee-lee-meh　　　　　 *E-mailime bakmak*
　bahk-mahk　　　　　　　　　 *istiyorum.*
　ees-tee-yohr-room

operator	oh-peh-rah-terr/	operatör/santral
	sahn-trahl	
phone book	teh-leh-fohn	telefon rehberi
	rehh-beh-ree	
phone box	teh-leh-fohn	telefon külübesi
	kyu-lyu-beh-see	
phonecard	teh-leh-fohn	telefon kartı
	kahr-tih	
telephone	teh-leh-fohn	telefon
telephone debit card	teh-leh-kahrt	telekart
telephone token	zheh-tohn	jeton
urgent	ah-jeel	acil

ON THE STREETS

artist	sah-naht-chih	sanatçı
beggar	dee-lehn-jee	dilenci
busker/street	soh-kahk	sokak
performer	myoo-zees-yeh-nee	müzisyeni
clown	pahl-yah-choh	palyaço
fortune teller	fahl-jih	falcı
magician	see-heer-bahz	sihirbaz
actor;	oh-yoon-joo	oyuncu
performing artist		
portait painter	pohr-treh	portre ressamı
	rehs-sah-mih	
peddler;	sehy-yahr	seyyar satıcı
itinerant seller	sah-tih-jih	
flower seller		
chee-chehk sah-tih-jih-sih		çiçek satıcısı
lottery ticket seller		
loh-toh bee-leht sah-tih-jih-sih		loto bilet satıcısı

AROUND TOWN

Making a Call

Hello, is (Mehmet) there?
  mehr-hah-bah (mehh-meht)   *Merhaba (Mehmet)*
  oh-rah-dah mih?   *orada mı?*

Hello. (answering a call)
  eh-fehn-deem/booy-roon   *Efendim/Buyrun.*

May I speak to (Mehmet)?
  (mehh-met)-lah   *(Mehmet)'la*
  ger-ryu-sheh-   *görüşebilirmiyim?*
  bee-leer-mee-yeem?

Who's calling?
  keem ah-rih-yohr?   *Kim arıyor?*

It's ...
  behn ...   *Ben ...*

Yes, he/she is here.
  eh-veht. boo-rah-dah   *Evet. Burada.*

One moment, (please).
  beer dah-kee-kah, lyut-fehn   *Bir dakika, lütfen.*

I'm sorry, he's not here.
  yuz-gyun-yum,   *Üzgünüm, burada değil.*
  boo-rah-dah deh-eel

What time will she be back?
  neh zah-mahn geh-ree   *Ne zaman geri dönecek?*
  der-neh-jehk?

Can I leave a message?
  meh-sahzh bih-rah-kah-   *Mesaj bırakabilirmiyim?*
  bee-leer-mee-yeem?

Please tell her I called.
  lyut-fehn, oh-nah   *Lütfen, ona aradığımı*
  ah-rah-dih-ih-mih   *söyleyiniz.*
  sery-leh-yee-neez

I'll call back later.
  dah-hah sohn-rah   *Daha sonra arayacağım.*
  ah-rah-yah-jah-ihm

BUREAUCRACY

Turkish official bureaucracy has a well-deserved reputation for slowness and abundant frowns. A bureaucrat's favourite word is *Olmaz!* (Impossible!). Still, as a foreigner you will probably be given special consideration and perhaps even a smile. Bribes are rarely asked of foreigners, and you should not suggest one. Be patient with the creeping wheels of bureaucracy, and above all do not lose your temper.

Wait!	behk-leh-yeen!	*Bekleyin!*
director	myu-dyur	*müdür*
document	behl-geh	*belge*
form	fohr-mah	*forma*
official (person)	meh-moor	*memur*
tomorrow	yahr-ihn	*yarın*

SIGHTSEEING

Where is the tourism office?
  too-reezm byu-roh-soo
  neh-reh-deh?   *Turizm bürosu nerede?*

Do you have a local map?
  sheh-heer plah-nih?   *şehir planı?*

I'd like to see ...
  ... oo gerr-mehk
  ees-tee-yohr-room   *...'u görmek istiyorum.*

What time does it open?
  neh zah-mahn
  ah-chihl-lah-jahk?   *Ne zaman açılacak?*

What time does it close?
  neh zah-mahn
  kah-pah-nah-jahk?   *Ne zaman kapanacak?*

What's that building?
  oh bee-nah neh-deer?   *O bina nedir?*

What's this monument?
  oh ah-bee-deh neh-deer?   *O abide nedir?*

AROUND TOWN

Can we come inside?
  ee-cheh-ree-yeh   *İçeri'ye gelebilirmiyiz?*
  geh-leh-bee-leer-mee-yeez?
When can we visit?
  neh zah-mahn zee-yah-reht   *Ne zaman ziyaret*
  eh-deh-bee-lee-reez?   *edebiliriz?*

May we take photographs?
  foh-toh-graf   *Fotoğraf çekebilirmiyiz?*
  che-keh-bee-leer-mee-yeez?
I'll send you the photograph.
  sah-nah foh-toh   *Sana foto göndereceğim.*
  gern-deh-reh-jeh-eem
Could you take a photograph of me?
  rehs-mee-mee   *Resmimi çekebilirmisin?*
  che-keh-bee-leer-
  mee-see-neez?

castle	kah-leh	*kale*
church/cathedral	kee-lee-seh	*kilise*
cinema	see-neh-mah	*sinema*

SIGNS

SICAK/SOĞAK	HOT/COLD
GİRİŞ	ENTRANCE
ÇIKIŞ	EXIT
GİRİLMEZ	NO ENTRY
SİGARA İÇİLMEZ	NO SMOKING
AÇIK/KAPALI	OPEN/CLOSED
YASAK(TIR)	PROHIBITED
TUVALET(LER)/WC	TOILETS

concert	kohn-sehr	*konser*
crowded	kah-lah-bah-lihk	*kalabalık*
museum	myu-zeh	*müze*
park	pahrk	*park*
statue	hehy-kehl	*heykel*
university	yu-nee-vehr-see-teh	*üniversite*

What's that?
  oh neh-deer?   *O nedir?*

What's happening?
  neh oh-loo-yohr?   *Ne oluyor?*

What happened?
  neh ohl-doo?   *Ne oldu?*

What's that woman/man doing?
  oh kihz/ehr-kehk neh   *O kız/erkek ne yapıyor?*
  yah-pih-yohr?

How much do you want?
  neh kah-dahr   *Ne kadar istiyorsun?*
  ee-stee-yohr-soon?

How much?
    neh kah-dahr?   *Ne kadar?*
Can I take one?
    beer tah-neh ah-lah-bih-leer   *Bir tane alabilir miyim?*
    mee-yihm?

festival	bahy-rahm	*bayram*
news kiosk	gah-zeh-teh	*gazete*
	koo-lyu-beh-see	*kulübesi*
a recycling bin/box	yeh-nee-dehn	*yeniden*
	eesh-leh-meh	*işleme*
	soh-koo-lahn	*sokulan kutu*
	koo-too	
street/road	soh-kahk	*sokak*
street demonstation	soh-kahk	*sokak*
	ger-steh-ree-see	*gösterisi*
suburb	dihsh mah-hahl-leh	*dış mahalle*
tobacco kiosk	tyu-tyun	*tütün*
	koo-lyu-beh-see	*kulübesi*

WHERE TO GO

Where can we dance?
  neh-reh-deh dahns
  eh-deh-bee-leer-eez?

Nerede dans edebiliriz?

Do you want to go to
a Karaoke bar?
  kah-rah-oh-keh
  bah-rah geet-mehk
  ih-stehr-mee-see-neez?

*Karaoke bara gitmek
istermisiniz (pol)?*

How much does it cost to get in?
  ee-cheh-ree geer-eesh
  neh kah-dahr?

İçeri giriş ne kadar?

Is there a charge to enter
the dance salon?
  dahns sah-loh-noo-nah
  geer-eesh yooj-reht-lee mee?

*Dans salonuna
giriş ücretli mi?*

No. It's free of charge.
  hah-yihr. yuj-reht-seez

Hayır. Ücretsiz.

Yes. It's (one) million lira.
  eh-veht. (beer) meel-yohn
  lee-rah

Evet. (Bir) milyon lira.

THEY MAY SAY ...

dih-shah-rih chih-kihp gyu-zehl vah-keet
geh-chee-reh-leem!

Let's go out and have a good time!

It's beautiful here.
    boo-rah-sih chohk gyu-zehl   *Burası çok güzel.*

I'm having a very nice time.
    Chohk gyu-zehl vah-keet   *Çok güzel vakit*
    geh-chee-ree-yoh-room   *geçiriyorum.*

Shall we go someplace else?
    bahsh-kah beer yeh-reh   *Başka bir yere gidelim mi?*
    gee-deh-leem mee?

I don't like the music here.
    boo-rah-dah-kee   *Buradaki müzikten*
    myu-zeek-tehn hohsh-   *hoşlanmıyorum.*
    lahn-mih-yoh-room

I really like Reggae music.
    rehg-gehy myu-zeek-tehn   *Reggae müzikten*
    gehr-chehk-tehn   *gerçekten hoşlanıyorum.*
    hohsh-lah-nih-yoh-room

SHOWING AFFECTION

You can also demonstrate affection for someone or something by attaching the diminutive -*ciğim* or -*cığım*, or -*cuğum* or -*cüğüm*, as a suffix to the given name of the dear one or thing you are addressing.

You just need to remember to add the suffix according to the rule of vowel harmony. When you add *ciğim* (or *cığım*, etc) it gives the meaning of 'my dear little ...' as in **anneciğim**, 'my dear little mom'/ 'mommy'; **babacığım**, 'my dear little dad'/'daddy'; **evciğim**, 'my dear little home' or **Phillipacığım**, 'my dear little Phillipa'/'Pippa'.

ARRANGING TO MEET

At what time shall we meet?
sah-aht kahch-tah
boo-loo-shah-lihm?

Saat kaçta buluşalım?

Where shall we meet?
neh-reh-deh boo-loo-shah-
bee-leer-reez?

Nerede buluşabiliriz?

Let's meet at eight o'clock.
sah-aht seh-keez-deh
boo-loo-shah-lihm

Saat sekizde buluşalım.

OK. See you then.
tah-mahm. oh sah-aht-teh
ger-ryu-shyu-ryuz

*Tamam. O saatte
görüşürüz.*

Agreed.
kah-bool

Kabul.

BAD TURKISH

Damn!	lah-neht ohl-soon!	*Lanet olsun!*
Fuck off!	seek-teer giht!	*Siktir git!*
Shit!	bohm-bohk!	*Bombok!*
Goddamnit!	ahl-lah kahh-reht-seen!	*Allah kahretsin!*
Gosh!	hahy-reht beer shehy!	*Hayret bir şey!*
Oh my God!	ah-mahn ahl-lah-hihm!	*Aman allahım!*
SOB	oh-rohs-poo choh-joo-oo	*orospu çocuğu*
bastard	peech	*piç*
nob/dickhead	seek	*sik*
idiot	ahp-tahl	*aptal*
a screw-up	sehr-sehm	*sersem*
imbecile	sah-lahk	*salak*

GOING OUT

ROMANCE

For when you're cuddling by the fireplace.

girlfriend/boyfriend
  ahr-kah-dahsh   *arkadaş*
a sincere friend, possibly a girlfriend, a boyfriend
  dohst   *dost*
a flirt, a girlfriend, a boyfriend
  flert   *flört*

to flirt	flert eht-mehk	*flört etmek*

(You're) my life	hah-yah-tihm	*hayatım*
I love you.	seh-nee	*Seni seviyorum.*
	seh-wee-ee-yohr-oom	

THEY MAY SAY ...

kah-bool eh-dee-yoh-room!	I agree!
keh-seen-leek-leh!	Definitely!
chok doh-roo!	Very true!
gah-yeht tah-bee-ee!	Certainly!/Of course!
ohl-mahz!	No way!
kah-bool eht-mee-yoh-room!	I don't agree!
doh-roo deh-eel!	That's not true!
oh. er-leh mee?	Oh, is that so ...!
eh-veht, ah-mah ...	Yes, but ...
ryu-yahn-dah ger-ryur-syun!	In your dreams!
yeh-tehr ahr-tihk!	That's enough, now!
hehr nehy-seh ...	Whatever ...

My darling.	sehv-gee-leem	*Sevgilim.*
My dear.	'Jahn-ihm	*Canım.*
My sweet.	aht-lihm	*Tatlım.*

You are everything to me.
   sehn behn-eem   *Sen benim herşeyimsin.*
   hehr-shehy-eem-seen

My everything is yours.
   hehr shehy-eem,   *Her şeyim, senindir.*
   sehn-een deer

I feel myself becoming complete with you.
   sehn-een-leh kehn-deem-ee   *Seninle kendimi*
   byu-tyun-lehsh-mish   *bütünleşmiş*
   hees-sehd-ee-yohr-oom   *hissediyorum.*

Every day that we pass together, you take a
more important place in my heart and feelings.
   beer-leek-teh hehr gehch-ehn   *Birlikte her geçen gün,*
   gyun, kahl-beem-deh veh   *kalbimde ve hislerimde*
   hees-lehr-eem-deh dah-hah   *daha önemli bir yer*
   er-nehm-lee beer yehr   *alıyorsun.*
   ahl-ih-yohr-soon

CROSSWORD

Across
1. Otis Redding sat on one in the bay
5. this place
6. archer, sign of the zodiac
7. something you bought
8. enchanting person

Down
2. full of people
3. the waterfront can be taxing (1st word)
4. seafaring vessel, often transports cars
5. first word when you answer the phone

GOING OUT

Answers on page 259

FAMILY & INTERESTS

FAMILY

Are you married?
ev-lee-mee-see-neez? *Evli misiniz?*

I'm married/I'm not married.
ehv-lee-yeem/ehv-lee
deh-eel-eem *Evliyim/Evli değilim.*

Do you have children?
choh-jook vahr mih? *Çocuk var mı?*

No, none.
hah-yihr, yohk *Hayır, yok.*

Yes, a daughter and a son.
eh-veht, beer kihz
veh beer oh-ool *Evet, bir kız ve bir oğul.*

Is your (husband) here?
(koh-jah-nihz) boo-rah-dah
mih? *(Kocanız) burada mı?*

Do you have a (girlfriend)?
(kihz ahr-kah-dah-sh)-ih-nihz
vahr mih? *(Kız arkaş)-ınız var mı?*

brother	ehr-kehk kar-dehsh	*erkek kardeş*
sister	kihz kar-dehsh	*kız kardeş*
children	choh-jook-lahr	*çocuklar*
girlfriend	kihz ahr-kah-dahsh	*kız arkaş*
boyfriend	ehr-kehk ahr-kah-dahsh	*erkek arkaş*
family	ah-yee-leh/ah-krah-bah	*aile/akraba*
father	bah-bah	*baba*

87

FAMILY & INTERESTS

husband	koh-jah	*koca*
wife	kah-rih	*karı*
mother	ahn-neh	*anne*
older brother	ah-ah-behy	*ağabey*
older sister	ah-blah	*abla*
son	oh-ool	*oğul*
daughter	kihz	*kız*

STAYING IN TOUCH

Once you get back home, you may want to drop a line to people you met. Here are a few lines to help you.

Dear/Esteemed ...
   sehw-gee-lee/sah-yihn ...   *Sevgili (inf)/Sayın (pol) ...*
I'm sorry it's taken me so long to write.
   yuz-gyu-nyum yahz-mahk-tah   *Üzgünüm yazmakta*
   geh-jeek-teem   *geciktim.*

It was great to meet you.
seh-neen-leh tah-nihsh-mahm
hah-ree-kahy-dih

*Seninle tanışmam
harikaydı.*

Thank you so much for your
hospitality.
koh-nook-seh-wehr-lee-een
ee-cheen chohk
teh-shehk-kyur eh-deh-reem

*Konukseverliğin için
çok teşekkür ederim.*

I had a fantastic time in ...
... 'deh hah-ree-kah wah-keet
geh-cheer-deem

*... 'de harika vakit
geçirdim.*

My favourite place was ...
... ehn sehw-dee-eem yehr-dee

... en sevdiğim yerdi.

I hope to visit ... again.
teh-krahr ... eh gehl-meh-yee
yu-meet eh-dee-yohr-room

*Tekrar...'e gelmeyi ümit
ediyorum.*

Say 'hi' to (Mehmet) and
(Perihan) for me.
(mehh-meht) weh
(peh-ree-hahn) behn-dehn
seh-lahm sery-leh-yee-neez

*(Mehmet) ve (Perihan)
benden selâm söyleyiniz.*

I miss you. (sg inf)
seh-nee erz-leh-deem

Seni özledim.

I miss you. (pl, sg pol)
see-zee erz-leh-deem

Sizi özledim.

I'd love to see you again.
seh-nee tehk-rahr
ger-mehk-ten mehm-noon
oh-loor-room

*Seni tekrar görmekten
memnun olurum.*

Write soon!
yah-kihn-dah yahz-zih-nihz!

Yakında yazınız!

With love and regards.
sehw-gee-lehr weh
sahy-gih-lah-rihm-lah

Sevgiler ve saygılarımla.

FAMILY & INTERESTS

COMMON INTERESTS

What do you do in your spare time?

bohsh zah-mahn-lah-rihn-dah   *Boş zamanlarında ne*
neh yap-pahr-sihn?   *yaparsın?*

I like ...

... dehn hohsh-lahn-dihm   *... 'den hoşlandım.*

I don't like ...

... dehn hohsh-lahn-mah-dihm   *... 'den hoşlanmadım.*

Do you like ...?   ...'dehn hohsh-   *... 'den hoşlandınız mı?*
lahn-dih-nihz mih?

film	see-neh-mah	*sinema*
music	myu-zeek	*müzik*
going out	gehz-meh	*gezme*
playing games	oh-yoon ohy-nah-mah	*oyun oynama*
playing soccer	foot-bohl ohy-nah-mah	*futbol oynama*
reading books	kee-tahp-lahr oh-koo-mah	*kitaplar okuma*
shopping	ah-lihsh weh-reesh	*alış veriş*
travelling	seh-yah-haht et-meh	*seyahat etme*
watching TV	teh-leh-weez-yohn sehy-reht-meh	*televizyon seyretme*
art	sah-naht	*sanat*
dancing	dahns eht-meh	*dans etme*
cooking	pee-sheer-meh	*pişirme*
photography	foh-toh-grahf-chih-lihk	*fotoğrafçılık*
the theatre	tee-yah-troh	*tiyatro*
writing	yah-zih yahz-mah	*yazı yazma*

Music

Do you like to listen to music?

myoo-zeek   *Müzik dinlemekten*
deen-leh-mehk-tehn   *hoşlanır mısın?*
hohsh-lah-nihr mih-sihn?

FAMILY & INTERESTS

Do you like to dance?
    dahns eht-mehk-tehn   *Dans etmekten hoşlanır mısın?*
    hohsh-lah-nihr mih-sihn?

Do you play a musical instrument?
    myoo-zeek ah-leh-tee   *Müzik aleti çalar mısın?*
    chah-lahr mih-sihn?

Do you sing?
    shahr-kih sery-lehr   *Şarkı söyler misin?*
    mih-sihn?

Which kind of music do you like?
    hahn-gee myu-zeek-tehn   *Hangi müzikten hoşlanırsın?*
    hohsh-lah-nihr-sihn?

Which group do you like?
    hahn-gee goo-roop-tahn   *Hangi guruptan hoşlanırsın?*
    hohsh-lah-nihr-sihn?

Have you heard (Perihan)'s latest cassete?
    (peh-ree-hahn)'ihn sohn   *(Perihan)'ın son kasetini*
    kah-seh-tee-nee   *dinledin mi?*
    deen-leh-deen mee?

YOU MAY HEAR ...

dehrt deh-eel.	It's no trouble/No problem.
Dert değil.	
hahy-roh-lah ...	Are you OK?
Hayrola ...	There's nothing wrong
	is there?
	All's well I hope.
sahch-mah-lah-mah!	Don't speak nonsense!
Saçmalama!	
tohz ohl-mahk!	Bugger off, get lost
Toz olmak!	(lit: Become dust!)

MY TONGUE IS NOT ARRIVING

'Well said!'
   ah-zih-nah saah-lihk!   *Ağzına sağlık!*
   lit: health to your mouth

This place is immaculate.
   bahl derrk deh yah-lah   *Bal dök de yala*
   lit: pour honey and lick

What's wrong with me/Why am I left out?
   beh-nihm bah-shihm   *Benim başım kel mi?*
   kehl mee?
   lit: does my head have a bald spot?

It's utterly worthless.
   behsh pah-rah eht-mehz   *Beş para etmez*
   lit: it doesn't make five-fortieths of a kuruş
   – a defunct currency unit

He can't do anything right.
   deh-nee-zeh geer-seh   *Denize girse kurutur.*
   koo-roo-toor
   lit: he get's dry if he enters the sea

I can't bring myself to say it.
   dee-leem vahr-mih-yohr   *Dilim varmıyor.*
   lit: my tongue is not arriving

She can talk the legs off a donkey.
   shee-eer gee-bee   *Şiir gibi konuşuyor.*
   koh-noo-shoo-yohr
   lit: she speaks like a poet

To put one's foot in it. To mess up.
   yah-rah-ih-nah yahn   *Yarağına yan*
   bahs-mahk   *basmak*
   lit: to step sideways on your penis

Which station plays Turkish
pop music?

hahn-gee ih-stahs-yohn   *Hangi istasyon türk*
tyurk pohp myu-zeek   *pop müzik çalıyor?*
chah-lih-yohr?

The concert next week will be (fantastic).

geh-leh-jehk hahf-tah   *Gelecek hafta konser*
kohn-sehr (hah-ree-kah)   *(harika) olacak.*
oh-lah-jahk

It's a (lousy) film.

oh fee-lihm (ker-tyu)   *O film (kötü).*

The weather was beautiful yesterday.

dyun-kyu hah-wah   *Dünkü hava güzeldi.*
gyu-zehl-dee

Yesterday's trip was super!   *Dünkü seyahat süperdi!*

doon-koo seh-yah-haht
syu-pehr-dee!

Tomorrow's party will really
be (superb).

yah-rihn-kee pahr-tee   *Yarınki parti gerçekten*
gehr-chehk-tehn   *(şahane) olacak.*
(shah-hah-neh) oh-lah-jahk

Cool!	Seh-reen!	*Serin!*
It's amazing!	hahy-reht beer shehy!	*Hayret bir şey!*
It's great!	fehw-kah-lah-deh!	*Fevkalade!*
That's brilliant!	ah-kihl-lih beer shehy!	*Akıllı bir şey!*
Splendid.	mooh-teh-shehm	*Muhteşem.*
Crazy.	deh-lee	*Deli.*
Heavy.	ah-ihr	*Ağır.*
Crappy.	bohk-tahn	*Boktan.*
Dreadful.	behr-baht	*Berbat.*
Full of shit.	bohm-bohk	*Bombok.*

Cinema & Theatre

documentary
behl-geh-sehl   *belgesel*

drama
drah-mah   *drahma*

film noir
see-yah sih-neh-mah   *siyah sinema*

horror film(s)
kohr-koo fee-leem(leh-ree)   *korku filim(leri)*

period drama(s)
chah drahm(lah-rih)   *çağ dram(ları)*

realism
gehr-chehk-chee-leek   *gerçekçilik*

science fiction film(s)
bee-lihm-koor-goo   *bilimkurgu filim(leri)*
fee-leem(leh-ree)

short film(s)
kih-sih fee-leem(leh-ree)   *kısa filim(leri)*

thriller film(s)
geh-ree-leem   *gerilim filim(leri)*
fee-leem(leh-ree)

war film(s)
sah-wahsh fee-leem(leh-ree)   *savaş filim(leri)*

Opinions

Did you like the film?
feel-mee beh-ehn-deen mee?   *Filmi beğendin mi?*

Did you like the performance?
shoh-voo beh-ehn-deen mee?   *Şovu beğendin mi?*

Did you like the play?
oh-yoo-noo beh-ehn-deen mee?   *Oyunu beğendin mi?*

I liked it a lot.
chohk hohsh-lahn-dihm   *Çok hoşlandım.*

I didn't like it very much.
chohk fahz-lah   *Çok fazla hoşlanmadım.*
hohsh-lahn-mah-dihm

**FAMILY &
INTERESTS**

I thought it was ...
  ... dyu-shyun-dyum   ... *düşündüm.*
I thought it was excellent.
  myu-kehm-mehl   *Mükemmel*
  ohl-doo-oo-noo   *olduğunu düşündüm.*
  dyu-shyun-dyum
I thought the ... was quite ordinary.
  sih-rah-dahn ohl-doo-oo-noo   *Sıradan olduğunu*
  dyu-shyun-dyum   *düşündüm.*
I had one or two problems with
the language.
  lee-sahn ee-leh beer ee-kee   *Lisan ile bir iki*
  proh-bleh-mihm ohl-doo   *problemim oldu.*

DID YOU KNOW ... Turkish linguists have identified
no less than 20 Turkish
dialects spoken worldwide.
However, if you stick to
standard vocabulary and
speak clearly, you can be
understood in any of the
regions where the dialects
are spoken. And those
regions cover a very large
span of territory from en-
claves in Lithuania, Belarus,
Hungary, Yugoslavia,
Ukraine, Macedonia,
Bulgaria, and Greece to
Turkey itself.

FAMILY & INTERESTS

STARS
Astrology

When is your birthday?
doh-oom gyun-yun
neh zah-mahn?

Doğum günün ne zaman?

What's your astrological sign?
hahn-gee boorch-tahn-sihn?

Hangi burçtansın?

I don't believe in astrology.
boorch-lah-rah
ee-nahn-mih-yoh-room

Burçlara inanmıyorum.

I'm a/an ...	behn ...	Ben ...
Capricorn	oh-lahk	Oğlak
Aquarius	koh-wah	Kova
Pisces	bah-lihk	Balık
Aries	kohch	Koç
Taurus	boh-ah	Boğa
Gemini	ee-keez-lehr	İkizler
Cancer	yehn-gech	Yengeç
Leo	ahs-lahn	Aslan
Virgo	bah-shahk	Başak
Libra	teh-rah-zee	Terazi
Scorpio	ah-krehp	Akrep
Sagittarius	yahy	Yay

Ah, that explains it!
shihm-dee ah-chihk-lih-ah
kah-voosh-too!

Şimdi açıklığa kavuştu!

(Leo's) are very ...	(ahs-lahn)-lahr chohk ...	(Aslan)lar çok ...
aggressive	sahl-dihr-gahn	*saldırgan*
caring	bah-kihm ger-steh-rehn	*bakım gösteren*
charming	cheh-kee-jee	*çekici*
crafty	hee-leh-kar	*hilekâr*
creative	yah-rah-tih-jih	*yaratıcı*
emotional	dooy-goo-loo	*duygulu*
indecisive	kah-rahr-sihz	*kararsız*
intense	gehr-geen	*gergin*
interesting	ehn-teh-reh-sahn	*enteresan*
jealous	kihs-kahnch	*kıskanç*
loyal	sah-dihk	*sadık*
likeable/attractive	sehm-pah-teek	*sempatik*

SOCIAL ISSUES

What do people feel about (taxes)?
een-sahn-lahr (vehr-gee-lehr) hahk-kihn-dah neh hihs-seh-dee-yohr-lahr?	*İnsanlar (vergiler) hakkında ne hissediyorlar?*

What do you think about (taxes)?
(vehr-gee-lehr) hahk-kihn-dah neh dyu-shyu-nyu-yohr-soo-nooz?	*(Vergiler) hakkında ne düşünüyorsunuz (pol)?*

I'm in favour of/not in favour of ...
... yah-nah-yihm/ kahr-shih-yihm	*... yanayım/karşıyım.*

I'm in favour/not in favour of abortion.
choh-jook ahl-dihr-mah-yah yah-nah-yihm/ kahr-shih-yihm	*Çocuk aldırmaya yanayım/karşıyım.*

I'm in favour/not in favour of animal rights.

hahy-wahn hah-klah-rih-nah yah-nah-yihm/ kahr-shih-yihm	*Hayvan haklarına yanayım/karşıyım.*

I'm in favour/not in favour of equal opportunity.

fihr-saht eh-shiht-lee-ee-neh yah-nah-yihm/ kahr-shih-yihm	*Fırsat eşitliğine yanayım/ karşıyım.*

I'm in favour/not in favour of euthanasia.

yu-teh-nehy-sah-yah yah-nah-yihm/ kahr-shih-yihm	*Üteneysaya yanayım/ karşıyım.*

I'm in favour/not in favour of immigration.

gerch eht-meh-yeh yah-nah-yihm/ kahr-shih-yihm	*Göç etmeye yanayım/ karşıyım.*

I'm in favour/not in favour of party politics.

pahr-tee see-yah-seh-tee-neh yah-nah-yihm/ kahr-shih-yihm	*Parti siyasetine yanayım/karşıyım.*

I'm in favour/not in favour of taxes.

vehr-gee-leh-reh yah-nah-yihm/ kahr-shih-yihm	*Vergilere yanayım/ karşıyım.*

I'm in favour/not in favour of unions.

sehn-dee-kah-lah-rah yah-nah-yihm/kahr-shih-yihm	*Sendikalara yanayım/ karşıyım.*

What's the latest policy concerned with immigration?

gerch-mehn-lehr-leh eel-gee-lee sohn poh-lih-tee-kah neh-deer?	*Görçmenlerle ilgili son politika nedir?*

Is there an unemployment problem here?

boo-rah-dah eesh-seez-leek proh-bleh-mee vahr mih?	*Burada işsizlik problemi var mı?*

FAMILY &
INTERESTS

SPORT

Do you like sport?
  spohr-dahn
  hohsh-lah-nihr-mih-sih-nihz?   *Spordan
    hoşlanırmısınız?*

I like playing sport.
  spohr yahp-mahk-tahn
  hohsh-lah-nihr-rihm   *Spor yapmaktan
    hoşlanırım.*

I prefer to watch rather than play sport.
  ohy-nah-mahk-tahn-sah
  sehy-reht-meh-yee tehr-jeeh
  eh-deh-reem   *Oynamaktansa
    seyretmeyi
    tercih ederim.*

Do you play ...?
  ... ohy-nahr-mih-sih-nihz?   *... oynarmısınız?*

Would you like to play ...?
  ... ohy-nah-mahk
  ees-tehr-mee-see-neez?   *... oynamak
    istermisiniz?*

Useful Words

baseball	behys-bohl	*beysbol*
basketball	bah-skeht-bohl	*basketbol*
boxing	bohks	*boks*
cricket	kree-keht	*kriket*
diving	dahl-gihch	*dalgıç*
football	foot-bohl	*futbol*

THEY MAY SAY ...

er-nehm-lee	It's important.
er-nehm-lee deh-eel	It's not important.
myum-kyun (deh-eel)	It's (not) possible.
beer shehy deh-eel	You're welcome/ It's nothing.
fahr-keht-mehz	It doesn't matter/ It's not important.

hockey	hoh-kehy	*hokey*
kayaking	kah-yahk	*kayak*
martial arts	ahs-keh-ree erz-gyu	*askere özgü*
	spohr-lar (zhoo-doh, kah-rah-teh)	*sporlar (judo, karate)*
rugby	roog-bee	*rugbi*
soccer	foot-bohl	*futbol*
surfing	serf	*sörf*
swimming	yyuz-meh	*yüzme*
tennis	teh-nees	*tenis*
gymnastics	zheem-nahs-teek	*jimnastik*
skiing	skee	*ski*

FAMILY & INTERESTS

THEY MAY SAY ...

hahy-dee! hahy-dee! gohl!	Come on! Let's Go! Goal!
peh-nahl-tih vehr-meh-see lah-zihm!	They have to give a penalty!
hah-kehm hahk-sihz-lihk yah-pih-yohr!	The ref is wrong!
fah-ool!	Foul!
ohf-sahyt!	Offside!
ehn byu-yyuk (gah-lah-tah-sah-rahy).	The (Galatasaray) team is great!
shahns-lih-sihn!	You're lucky!
shahn-sihn yohk!	Hard luck!
shahn-sihm yah-vehr gih-dee-yohr!	I'm on a roll!
hee-leh yahp-tihn!	Cheat!
boo-gyun ker-yu gyu-nyum-deh-yihm!	I'm jinxed today!

Soccer

seat	kohl-took	*koltuk*
ticket for the match	mahch bee-leh-tee	*maç bileti*
ticket booth	gee-seh	*gişe*

Do you like football?
   foot-bohl
   seh-wee-yohr-moo-soon?   *Futbol seviyormusun?*

Which team do you support?
   hahn-gee tah-kihm-ih
   too-too-yohr-soon?   *Hangi takımı tutuyorsun?*

I support (Trabzonspor).
   (trahb-zohn-spohr)'loo-yoom   *(Trabzonspor)'luyum.*

What an ordinary team!
   sih-rah-dahn beer tah-kihm!   *Sıradan bir takım!*

(Beşiktaş) is much better than
the other team.
   (beh-shihk-tahsh) er-teh-kee   *(Beşiktaş) öteki takımdan*
   tah-kihm-dahn chohk   *çok daha iyi.*
   dah-hah ee-yee

Soccer Teams

Every Turkish football fan, regardless of where he/she lives, fervently favours one of the three top Istanbul soccer teams listed below. Trabzonspor, a Black Sea coastal favourite and perennial soccer powerhouse, is also very popular.

   You might hear chants like these at a game:

Galatasaray Cim Bom Bom	gah-lah-tah-sah-rahy
	jeem bohm bohm
Fenerbahçe Sarı Kanarya	feh-nehr-bah-cheh
	sah-rih kah-nahr-yah
Beşiktaş Kara Kartal	beh-shihk-tahsh
	kah-rah kahr-tahl
Trabzonspor Bordo Mavi	trahb-zohn-spohr
	bohr-doh mah-vee

GAMES

How do you play (Backgammon)?
(tahv-lah-yih) nah-sihl
ohy-noo-yohr-soo-nooz?

*(Tavlayı) nasıl
oynuyorsunuz?*

What are the rules?
koo-rahl-lahr-ih neh-deer?

Kuralları nedir?

Whose turn is it?
kih-mihn sih-rah-sih?

Kimin sırası?

It's my turn.
behn-ihm sih-rahm

Benim sıram.

I'm winning/losing.
kah-zah-nih-yoh-room/
kahy-beh-dee-yoh-room

*Kazanıyorum/
Kaybediyorum.*

Cards

Do you want to play cards?
kahrt ohy-nah-mahk ees-tehr
mee-seen?

Kart oynamak ister misin?

Do you want to play bridge?
breech ohy-nah-mahk
ihs-tehr mee-seen?

Briç oynamak ister misin?

Do you want to play poker?
poh-kehr ohy-nah-mahk
ees-tehr mee-seen?

*Poker oynamak ister
misin?*

I don't know how to play.
oh-yoon beel-mee-yoh-room

Oyun bilmiyorum.

I'll teach you.
er-reh-tee-reem

Öğretirim.

Your turn.
seh-neen sih-rahn

Senin sıran.

I pass.
pahs

Pas.

I bet (two) million lira.
(ee-kee) yyuz meel-yohn
koh-yoo-yoh-room

*(İki) yüz milyon
koyuyorum.*

I'm in.
vahr-ihm   *Varım.*

I raise (one) million lira.
(beer) meel-yohn   *(Bir) milyon*
yyuk-sehl-tee-yoh-room.   *yükseltiyorum.*

ace	ahs	*as*
king	pah-pahz	*papaz*
queen (cards)	kihz	*kız*
queen (chess)	veh-zeer	*vezir*
jack	vah-leh/oh-lahn	*vale/oğlan*
clubs	see-nehk	*sinek*
diamonds	kah-roh	*karo*
hearts	kahlp	*kalp*
spades	mah-chah	*maça*

CROSSWORD

Across

2. a kiosk selling the Turkish Daily News (1st word)
5. you could turn green with this (not the drinking water)
6. it's no big deal
8. ET could have done with one of these
9. room for two platonic friends (1st word)

Down

1. difficult, no walk in the ...
3. no prizes for reinventing this
4. balancing scales, astrologically
7. not a clock with four legs

Answers on page 259

SHOPPING

Many Turkish crafts and trades are named simply by the object dealt with followed by the *-cı, -ci, -cu, -cü* suffix. Thus 'book' is *kitap* and 'bookseller' is *kitapçı* (lit: book-person), whereas shoe is *ayakkabı* and cobbler is *ayakkabıcı* (lit: shoe-person).

LOOKING FOR ...

Where is (a) ...?	... neh-reh-deh?	... nerede?
shopping district	chahr-shih	*çarşı*
covered bazaar	kah-pah-lih chahr-shih	*kapalı çarşı*
barber	beer behr-behr	*bir berber*
bookshop	beer kee-tahp-chih	*bir kitapçı*
chemist/pharmacy	beer ej-zah-neh	*bir eczane*
tailor	beer tehr-zee	*bir terzi*
watch-repair shop	beer sah-aht-chee	*bir saatçi*
market	chahr-shih	*çarşı*
shop	dyuk-kahn	*dükkan*

MAKING A PURCHASE

I want to buy ...	... sah-tihn ahl-mahk ees-tee-yoh-room	... *satın almak istiyorum.*
Do you have ...?	vahr mih?	... *var mı?*
Which?	hahn-gee?	*Hangi?*
this much	boo kah-dahr	*bu kadar*
this one	boo-noo	*bunu*

Where can I buy (bus tickets)?
  (oh-toh-byus bee-leht-leh-   *(Otobüs biletleri) nereden*
  ree) neh-reh-den sah-tihn   *satın alabilirim?*
  ah-lah-bee-lee-reem?

film	fee-leem	*filim*
price	fee-yaht	*fiyat*
tax	vehr-gee	*vergi*

SHOPPING

I'm just looking around.
shery-leh beer bah-kih-yoh-room
Şöyle bir bakıyorum.

How much is this?
boo neh kah-dahr?
Bu ne kadar.

Can you write down?
yah-zah-bee-leer mee-see-neez?
Yazabilir misiniz?

I'd like to buy (a book).
beer (kee-tap) ahl-mahk
ee-stee-yoh-room
Bir (kitap) almak istiyorum.

I'll take/buy it.
ah-lih-yoh-room.
Alıyorum.

Can I look at it?
oh-nah bah-kah-bee-leer
mee-yeem?
Ona bakabilir miyim?

I don't like it.
beh-ehn-meh-deem
Beğenmedim.

Do you have others?
bahsh-kah-lah-rih vahr mih?
Başkaları var mı?

I'd like to return this please.
boo-noo geh-ree vehr-mehk
ee-stee-yoh-room, lyut-fehn
Bunu geri vermek istiyorum, lütfen.

Can I use a credit card?
kreh-dee kahr-tih
kool-lah-nah-bee-leer
mee-yeem?
Kredi kartı kullınabilir miyim?

Will you give me a receipt, please?
lyut-fehn, beer feesh
veh-reer mee-see-neez?
Lütfen, bir fiş verir misiniz?

Is there a guarantee?
gahr-ahn-tee-see vahr mih?
Garantisi var mı?

Can you send it overseas?
oh-noo dih-shahr-ih-yah
gern-deh-reh-bee-leer
mee-see-neez?
Onu dışarıya gönderebilir misiniz?

BARGAINING

In food markets, prices are regulated and bargaining is usually futile, but for most other items bargaining is necessary. Some shops mark prices and stick to them, but others mark them only in order to 'give you a special discount', so bargaining is in order. Remember, there is never an obligation to buy unless the shopkeeper accepts your price. Don't feel guilty about walking away if you can't agree upon a price.

How many liras/ dollars/pounds ...?	... kahch lee-rah/ doh-lahr/stehr-leen?	... kaç lira/ dolar/sterlin?
is this one	boo-noo	bunu
is that one	shoo-noo	şunu
is two kg	ee-kee kee-loh	iki kilo
is three metres	yuch meh-treh	üç metre
for all of them	hehp-see	hepsi

(It's) very expensive.	chohk pah-hah-lih	Çok pahalı.
(It's) very cheap.	chohk oo-jooz	Çok ucuz.
Do you have something cheaper?	dah-hah oo-jooz beer shehy vahr mih?	Daha ucuz bir şey var mı?

SHOPPING

THEY MAY SAY ...

yahr-dihm eh-deh-bee-leer mee-yeem?	May I help you?
bahsh-kah beer shehy ee-stehr mee-see-neez?	Will there be anything else?
heh-dee-yeh-leek pah-keht ee-stee-yohr moo-soo-nooz?	Do you want it wrapped?
kahl-mah-dih/ kahl-mah-mihsh	We don't have any left in stock.

SHOPPING

PRICES

I'll give you ...	... veh-reh-jeh-yeem	... *vereceğim.*
$20	yeer-mee doh-lahr	*yirmi dolar*
40,000 TL	kihrk been lee-rah	*kırk bin lira*
£10	ohn stehr-leen	*on sterlin*

ESSENTIAL GROCERIES

laundry detergent	deh-tehr-zhahn	*deterjan*
matches	kee-breet	*kibrit*
aspirin	ahs-pee-ree-nah	*aspirina*
bottled spring water	shee-sheh-deh	*şişede*
	mem-bah soo-yoo	*memba suyu*
batteries	peel-lehr	*piller*
bread	ehk-mehk	*ekmek*
butter	teh-reh-ya-ih	*tereyağı*
cheese	pehy-neer	*peynir*
egg(s)	yoo-moor-tah(lahr)	*yumurta(lar)*
flour	oon	*un*
gas cylinder	tyup	*tüp*
ham	zhahm-bohn	*jambon*
honey	bahl	*bal*
milk	syut	*süt*
pepper	bee-behr	*biber*
salt	tooz	*tuz*
shampoo	shahm-poo-ahn	*şampuan*
soap	sah-boon	*sabun*
sugar	sheh-kehr	*şeker*
toilet paper	too-vah-leht	*tuvalet*
	kah-ih-dih	*kağıdı*
toothpaste	deesh mah-joo-noo	*diş macunu*
yoghurt	yoh-oort	*yoğurt*

SHOPPING

I WONDER ...

ah-jah-bah ...   *Acaba* ...   I wonder ...

This 'phrase' is added to questions in Turkish to
increase politeness. For example:

poh-stah-neh neh-reh-deh, ah-jah-bah?
Postane nerede, acaba?
    Where is the post office, I wonder?

SOUVENIRS

(hand)bag	chan-tah	*çanta*
carpet	hah-lih	*halı*
clothing	ehl-bee-seh/gee-see	*elbise/giysi*
cloth	koo-mahsh	*kumaş*
jewellery	myu-jehv-heh-raht	*mücevherat*
porcelain	chee-nee	*çini*
leather clothing	deh-ree gee-yeem	*deri giyim*
old copper (items)	ehs-kee bah-kihr	*eski bakır*

CLOTHING

It's very big/small.
    chohk byu-yyuk/kyu-chyuk   *Çok büyük/küçük.*
Put (try) it on.
    gee-yeen   *Giyin.*
It's too short/long.
    chohk kih-sah/oo-zoon   *Çok kısa/uzun.*
It doesn't fit/match.
    ooy-mahz   *Uymaz.*
Do you have a larger/smaller size?
    dah-hah byu-yyuk/   *Daha büyük/küçük var mı?*
    kyu-chyuk vahr mih?
I don't like the colour.
    rehn-gee   *Rengi beğenmiyorum.*
    beh-ehn-mee-yoh-room
I don't like (it/them).
    beh-ehn-mee-yohr-room   *Beğenmiyorum.*

MATERIALS

brass	toonch	*tunç*
copper	bah-kihr	*bakır*
gold	ahl-tihn	*altın*
leather	deh-ree	*deri*
silver	gyu-myush	*gümüş*
suede	syu-eht	*süet*

COLOURS

colour	rehnk	*renk*
another colour	bahsh-kah rehnk	*başka renk*
black	see-yahh	*siyah*
blue	mah-vee	*mavi*
brown	kah-veh-rehn-gee	*kahverengi*
green	yeh-sheel	*yeşil*
pink	pehm-beh	*pembe*
red	kihr-mih-zih	*kırmızı*
white	beh-yahz	*beyaz*
yellow	sahr-rih	*sarı*
dark(er)	(dah-hah) koh-yoo	*(daha) koyu*
light(er)	(dah-hah) ah-chihk	*(daha) açık*

TOILETRIES

comb	tah-rahk	*tarak*
condom	preh-zehr-vah-teef	*prezervatif*
facial tissue; paper handkerchief	kah-iht mehn-dee-lee	*kağıt mendili*
flea powder	pee-reh-leh-reh kahr-shih poo-drah	*pirelere karşı pudra*
hand cream	ehl kreh-mee	*el kremi*
lotion	lohs-yoh-noo	*losyonu*
medicine	ee-lahch	*ilaç*
mirror	ahy-nah	*ayna*
mosquito repellent	see-vree-see-neh-eh kahr-shih ee-lahch	*sivrisineğe karşı ilaç*
sanitary pad	hee-zheh-neek kah-dihn bah-ih	*hijenik kadın bağı*
shampoo	sham-poo-ahn	*şampuan*
shaving cream	trahsh kreh-mee	*traş kremi*
soap	sah-boon	*sabun*
sticking plaster; adhesive bandage	tihb-bee fih-lahs-tehr	*tıbbi filaster*
tampon	tahm-pohn	*tampon*

SHOPPING

FOR THE BABY

tinned baby food	kohn-sehr-veh	*konserve*
	beh-behk	*bebek yemeği*
	yeh-meh-ee	
baby powder	beh-behk	*bebek pudrası*
	poo-drah-sih	
bib	mah-mah	*mama önlüğü*
	ern-lyu-yur	
disposable nappy/	tehk	*tek*
diaper	kool-lah-nihm-lihk	*kullanımlık*
	cho-jook beh-zee	*çocuk bezi*
dummy/pacifier	ehm-zeek	*emzik*
feeding bottle	bee-beh-rohn	*biberon*
nappy/diaper	choh-jook beh-zee	*çocuk bezi*
nappy/diaper	ee-see-leek kreh-mee	*isilik kremi*
rash cream		
powdered milk	syut-toh-zoo	*süttozu*

STATIONERY & PUBLICATIONS

Is there an English-language bookshop here?
een-gee-leez-jeh kee-tahp   *İngilizce kitap satılan*
sah-tih-lahn kee-tahp-chih   *kitapçı var mı?*
vahr mih?

Is there an English-language section?
een-gee-leez-jeh ber-lyu-myu   *İngilizce bölümü var mı?*
vahr mih?

Is there a city entertainment guide?
sheh-heer eh-lehn-jeh   *Şehir eğlence*
rehh-beh-ree vahr mih?   *rehberi var mı?*

Do you sell ...?	... sah-tih-yohr-moo-soon?	... *satıyormusun?*
book	kee-tahp	*kitap*
dictionary	lyu-gaht/serz-lyuk	*lügat/sözlük*
envelopes	zahrf	*zarf*
paper	kah-iht	*kağıt*

today's newspaper	boo-gyun-kyu gah-zeh-teh	*bugünkü gazete*
English-language newspaper	een-gee-leez-jeh beer gah-zeh-teh	*igilizce bir gazete*
magazine	mej-moo-ah	*mecmua*
notebook	dehf-tehr	*defter*
paper	kah-iht	*kağıt*
pen (ballpoint)	tyu-kehn-mehz	*tükenmez*
pencil	koor-shoon-kah-lehm	*kurşunkalem*
postcard	kahrt-pohs-tahl	*kartpostal*

MUSIC

I'm looking for a ... CD.
... CD ah-rih-yohr-room   *... CD arıyorum.*

Do you have any ...?
... vahr mih?   *... var mı?*

What is his/her best recording?
ehn ee-yee ahl-byu-myu hahn-gee-see?   *En iyi albümü hangisi?*

I heard a band/singer called ...
... goo-roo-boo/shahr-kih-jih-yih dooy-doom   *... Gurubu/şarkıcıyı duydum.*

Can I listen to this CD here?
see-dee-yee boo-rah-dah deen-leh-yeh-bee-leer-mee-yeem?   *CD'yi burada dinleyebilirmiyim?*

I need a blank tape.
bohsh kah-seh-deh eeh-tee-yah-jihm vahr   *Boş kasede ihtiyacım var.*

PHOTOGRAPHY

How much would it cost to print this film?
boo feel-mee bah-sahrt-mahk · *Bu filmi basartmak için*
ee-cheen kahch lee-rah? *kaç lira?*

When will it be ready?
neh zah-mahn hah-zihr *Ne zaman hazır olur?*
oh-loor?

I'd like a film for this camera.
boo kah-meh-rah ee-cheen *Bu kamera için filim*
fee-leem ees-tee-yohr-room *istiyorum*

My camera doesn't work.
kah-meh-rahm *Kameram çalışmıyor.*
chah-lish-mih-yohr

It shoots too slow/fast.
yah-vahsh/chah-book *Yavaş/çabuk çekiyor.*
cheh-kee-yohr

It needs new batteries.
yeh-nee peel-lehr lah-zihm *Yeni piller lazım.*

SHOPPING

SAY CHEESE		
battery	peel	pil
film	fee-leem	filim
flash bulb	fee-lahsh	filaş
photo	foh-toh	foto
slide/	slahyt/	slayt/
diapositive	dee-ah-poh-zee-teef	diapozitif
36-exposure (film)	oh-tooz ahl-tih pohz	otuz altı poz

SMOKING

A packet of cigarettes, please.
beer pah-keht see-gah-rah, *Bir paket sigara, lütfen.*
lyut-fehn
Are these cigarettes strong or mild?
boo see-gah-rah sehrt mee, *Bu sigara sert mi,*
hah-feef mee? *hafif mi?*
Do you have a light?
ah-teh-shee-neez vahr mih? *Ateşiniz var mı?*
Please don't smoke.
lyut-fehn, see-gah-rah *Lütfen, sigara içmeyiniz.*
eech-meh-yee-neez
Do you mind if I smoke?
see-gah-rah eech-meh-meen *Sigara içmemin mahsuru*
mah-soo-roo vahr mih? *var mı?*
I'm trying to give up.
bih-rahk-mah-yah *Bırakmaya çalışıyorum.*
chah-lih-shih-yohr-room

cigarettes	see-gah-rah (lahr)	*sigara(lar)*
cigarette papers	see-gah-rah kah-ihd-lah-rih	*sigara kağıdları*
filtered	feel-treh-lee see-gah-rah	*filtreli sigara*
lighter	chahk-mahk	*çakmak*
match(es)	kee-breet(lehr)	*kibrit(ler)*
menthol	mehn-tohl-lyu	*mentollü*
pipe	pee-poh	*pipo*
tobacco	tyu-tyun	*tütün*

SIZES & COMPARISONS

small	kyu-chyuk/oo-fahk	*küçük/ufak*
big	byu-yyuk	*büyük*
heavy	ah-ihr	*ağır*
huge	koh-jah-mahn	*kocaman*
light	hah-feef	*hafif*
more	dah-hah	*daha*
little (amount)	ahz/beer-rahz	*az/biraz*
too much/many	fahz-lah	*fazla*
many	chohk	*çok*
enough	yeh-tehr-lee/kah-fee	*yeterli/kafi*
also	dah-hee/beer deh	*dahi/bir de*
a little bit	kyu-chyuk meek-tahr/	*küçük miktar/*
	ahz-jihk	*azcık*

SHOPPING

Turkish cuisine is based on lamb and mutton, but beef and chicken are also readily available. Though Muslims don't touch pork, you may occasionally find pork products offered at the fancier big-city and resort restaurants. Seafood is a Turkish specialty, and the Muslim prohibition against eating shellfish is ignored by many modern Turks. Wonderful fresh vegetables and fruits are a big part of the Turkish diet. In fact, the Turks have more than 40 ways of preparing eggplant – at least one of these is as a sweet dessert! Turkish bread is a delicious sourdough loaf baked fresh morning and afternoon. You can buy it by the loaf, half loaf, or even quarter loaf.

In a traditional workers' restaurant such as a *kebapçı*, *köfteci* or *pideci*, no alcoholic beverages are ever served, and the simple *lokanta* will observe this rule as well. But in slightly classier restaurants serving a variety of dishes, beer, wine, *rakı*, and other drinks are available.

If you don't eat meat, you can select from the many soups, vegetable dishes, meze plates, and salads available. But you should be aware that many Turkish soups and vegetable dishes are made using small quantities of meat as a flavouring.

| Bon Apetit | ah-fee-yeht ohl-soon | *Afiyet olsun.* |

VEGETARIAN & SPECIAL MEALS

I can't eat ...	... yee-yeh-mee-yoh-room	... *yiyemiyorum.*
any meat	heech-eht	*hiç et*
eggs	yoo-moor-tah	*yumurta*
spicy peppers	ah-jih bee-behr	*acı biber*

I don't even eat meat juices.
eht soo-yoo bee-leh   *Et suyu bile yiyemiyorum.*
yee-yeh-mee-yoh-room

I eat chicken/fish.

   tah-vook/bah-lihk   *Tavuk/balık yiyorum.*
   yee-yoh-room

I eat only fruit and vegetables.

   yahl-nihz mehy-veh veh   *Yalnız meyve ve sebze yiyorum.*
   seb-zeh yee-yoh-room

EATING OUT

Is there a kebap restaurant around here?

   boo-rah-lahr-dah beer   *Buralarda bir kebapçı var mı?*
   keh-bahp-chih vahr mih?

At your service!

   boo-yoo-roon-ooz!   *Buyurunuz!*

Come, look!

   geh-leen, bah-kihn!   *Gelin, bakın!*

Is/are there any ...?	... vahr mih?	... var mı?
shish kebap	sheesh keh-bahp	şiş kebap
appetizers	meh-zeh	meze
fresh fish	tah-zeh bah-lihk	taze balık
wine	shah-rahp	şarap
meatless dishes	eht-seez	etsiz yemekler
	yeh-mehk-lehr	

Please bring ...	lyut-fehn ...	*Lütfen ... getirin.*
	geh-tee-reen	
water	soo	su
salad	sah-lah-tah	salata
salt and pepper	tooz veh bee-behr	tuz ve biber

MEALS

meal/dish of food	yeh-mehk	*yemek*
to eat	yeh-mehk	*yemek*
to eat a meal	yeh-mehk yeh-mehk	*yemek yemek*
breakfast	kahh-vahl-tih	*kahvaltı*
lunch	er-leh yeh-meh-ee	*öğle yemeği*
supper	ahk-shahm yeh-meh-ee	*akşam yemeği*

Utensils

drinking glass	bahr-dahk	*bardak*
fork	chah-tahl	*çatal*
knife	bih-chahk	*bıçak*
napkin	peh-cheh-teh	*peçete*
plate	tah-bahk	*tabak*
spoon	kah-shihk	*kaşık*
cup	feen-jahn	*fincan*

PLACES TO EAT

ayileye mahsustur	ah-yee-leh-yeh mahh-soos-toor	a dining room reserved for couples and single women
büfe	byu-feh	a snack shop
fırın	fih-rihn	a bakery (oven)
kebapçı	keh-bahp-chih	a kebap (roast meat) shop
köfteci	kerf-teh-jee	a köfte (meatball) shop
lokanta	loh-kahn-tah	a simple restaurant with ready food
pastane	pahs-tah-neh	a pastry shop
pideci	pee-deh-jee	a Turkish-style pizza place
restoran	rehs-toh-rahn	fancier than a lokanta, usually serving alcohol

FOOD

MENU DECODER

acı biber	ah-jih bee-behr	spicy peppers
adana kebap	ah-dah-nah keh-bahp	spicy-hot grilled köfte
aile salonu	ah-ee-leh sah-loh-noo	family/ladies' dining room
akşam yemeği	ahk-shahm yeh-meh-ee	supper
alabalık	ah-lah-bah-lihk	trout
armut	ahr-moot	pear
ayileye mahsustur	ah-yee-leh-yeh mahh-soos-toor	couples and single women dining room
ayran	ahy-rahn	tart yoghurt drink
baklava	bahk-lah-vah	flaky pastry with honey and nuts
bal	bahl	honey
balık	bah-lihk	fish
bamya	bahm-yah	okra
barbunya	bahr-boon-yah	red mullet
barbunye	bahr-boon-yeh	red beans
beyaz peynir	behy-yahz pehy-neer	white sheep's milk cheese
beyaz bira	behy-yahz bee-rah	light beer
beyin	behy-yeen	brain (sheep's)
bezelye	beh-zehl-yeh	peas
bıldırcın	bihl-dihr-jihn	quail
biber	bee-behr	pepper
bira	bih-rah	beer
bonfile	bohn-fee-leh	small filet beefsteak
böbrek	ber-brehk	kidneys
börek	ber-rehk	flaky pastry filled with white cheese or meat
büfe	byu-feh	snack shop

FOOD

MENU DECODER

bursa kebap	boor-sah keh-bahp	döner with tomato sauce and browned butter
büyük bardak	byu-yyuk bahr-dahk	big glass
büyük şişe	byu-yyuk shee-sheh	large bottle
buz	booz	ice
cacık	jah-jihk	beaten yoghurt with grated cucumber and garlic
çay	chahy	tea
ciğer	jee-ehr	liver
çikolata	chee-koh-lah-tah	chocolate
çilek	chee-lehk	strawberries
çoban salatası	choh-bahn sah-lah-tah-sih	chopped mixed tomato, cucumber, hot pepper
çorba	chohr-bah	soup
dana rosto	dah-nah rohs-toh	roast veal
dana	dah-nah	veal
dil	deel	tongue
dil balığı	deel bah-lih-ih	sole
domates çorbası	doh-mah-tes chohr-bah-sih	tomato soup
domuz eti	doh-mooz eh-tee	pork (forbidden to Muslims)
dondurma	dohn-door-mah	ice cream
döner kebap	der-nehr keh-bahp	spit-roasted lamb slices
düğün çorbası	dyu-yun chor-bah-sih	egg-and-lemon soup
ekmek	ehk-mehk	bread
ekmek kadayıf	ehk-mehk kah-dah-yihf	crumpet in syrup

FOOD

MENU DECODER

elma	ehl-mah	apple
elma çay	ehl-mah chahy	apple tea
eski kaşar	ehs-kee kah-shahr	cheese aged (yellow)
peynir	pehy-neer	
et	eht	meat
et suyu	eht soo-yoo	mutton broth
(yumurtalı)	(yoo-moor-tah-lih)	(with egg)
etli pide/	eht-lee pee-deh/	flat bread topped
etli ekmek	eht-lee ehk-mehk	with ground lamb
		and spices
etsiz	eht-seez	without meat
etsiz yemekler	eht-seez yeh-mehk-lehr	meatless dishes
ezo gelin	eh-zoh geh-leen	lentil and rice soup
çorbası	chor-bah-sih	
fasulye	fah-sool-yeh	beans
fırın	fih-rihn	bakery (oven)
fırın sütlaç	fih-rihn syut-lach	baked rice pudding (cold)
garson	gahr-sohn	waiter
greyfurut	grehy-foo-root	grapefruit
güveç	gyu-vech	meat and vegetable stew in a crock
hamsi	hahm-see	anchovy (fresh)
haşlama	hahsh-lah-mah	broth with mutton
havuç	hah-vooch	carrot
hindi	heen-dee	turkey
ıspınak	ihs-spih-nahk	spinach
ıstakoz	ihs-tah-kohz	lobster
içki	eech-kee	alcoholic beverages
incir	een-jeer	fig

FOOD

MENU DECODER

işkembe	eesh-kehm-beh	tripe soup
çorbası	chor-bah-sih	
jambon	zhahm-bohn	ham (forbidden to Muslims)
kabak dolması	kah-bahk dohl-mah-sih	stuffed squash/marrow
kabak	kah-bahk	marrow/squash
kahvahltı	kahh-vahl-tih	breakfast
kahve	kahh-veh	coffee
kalkan	kahl-kahn	turbot
karışık ızgara	kah-rih-shuk ihz-gah-rah	mixed grill (lamb)
karışık salata	kah-rih-shihk	see çoban salatası
kara/	kah-rah/	black pepper
siyah biber	see-yahh bee-behr	
karagöz	kah-rah-gerz	black bream
karides	kah-ree-des	shrimp
karnabahar	kahr-nah-bah-hahr	cauliflower
karpuz	kahr-pooz	watermelon
kaşar peynir	kah-shahr pehy-neer	mild yellow cow cheese
kavun	kah-voon	yellow melon
kayısı	kah-yih-sih	apricot
kebapçı	keh-bahp-chih	kebap shop
keçi eti	keh-chee- eh-tee	goat
kefal	keh-fahl	grey mullet
kılıç balığı	kih-lihch bah-lih-ih	swordfish
kırmızı/	kihr-mih-zih/	red/white wine
beyaz şarap	beh-yahz shah-rahp	
kırmızıbiber	kihr-mih-zih bee-behr	red pepper

FOOD

MENU DECODER

kıymalı	kihy-mah-lih	with ground lamb
kiraz	kee-rahz	cherry
koç yumurtası	kohch yoo-moor-tah-sih	testicles (ram's eggs)
komposto	kohm-pohs-toh	stewed fruit
koyun eti	koh-yoon eh-tee	mutton
köfte	kerf-teh	grilled lamb meatballs with onion and spices
köfteci	kerf-teh-jee	(meatball) shop
krem karamel	krehm kah-rah-mehl	baked caramel custard
(süt) kuzu	(syut) koo-zoo	lamb (milk-fed)
küçük bardak	kyu-chyuk bahr-dahk	small glass
küçük sandviç	kyu-chyuk sahnd-weech	small sandwich
küçük şişe	kyu-chyuk shee-sheh	small bottle
kuru fasulye	koo-roo fah-sool-yeh	white beans
lahana dolması	lah-hah-nah dohl-mah-sih	stuffed cabbage
lahana	lah-hah-nah	cabbage
levrek	lehv-rehk	sea bass
limon	lee-mohn	lemon
limonlu	lee-mohn-loo	with lemon juice
lokanta	loh-kahn-tah	restaurant with ready food
lüfer	lyu-fehr	bluefish
makarna	mah-kahr-nah	macaroni/noodles
mandalin	mahn-dah-leen	tangerine/mandarin
margarin	mahr-gahr-reen	margarine

MENU DECODER

marul	mah-rool	Romaine lettuce
memba suyu	mehm-bah soo-yoo	spring water (still)
mercan	mehr-jahn	red coralfish
mercimek çorbası	mehr-jee-mehk chor-bah-sih	lentil soup
meşrubat	meh-shroo-baht	soft drinks
meyva suyu	mehy-vah soo-yoo	fruit juice
meyve	mehy-veh	fruit
meze	meh-zeh	appetizers/ tapas
midye	meed-yeh	mussels
musakka	moo-sah-kah	aubergine and lamb pie
muz	mooz	banana
nohut	noh-hoot	chickpeas/ garbanzos
normal	nohr-mahl	normal-sized
sandviç	sahnd-weech	sandwich
orman kebap	ohr-mahn keh-bahp	roast lamb with onions
öğle yemeği	er-leh yeh-meh-ee	lunch
ördövr	err-dervr	hors d'oeuvre
paça	pah-chah	trotter soup
palamut	pah-lah-moot	tunny/bonito
pasta	pahs-tah	pastry (not noodles)
pastane	pahs-tah-neh	pastry shop
patates	pah-tah-tes	potato
patlıcan salatası	paht-lih-jahn sah-lah-tah-sih	aubergine/ eggplant purée
peynir	pehy-neer	cheese
peynirli	pehy-neer-lee	with cheese

FOOD

MENU DECODER

pide	pee-deh	pizza/flat bread
pideci	pee-deh-jee	Turkish-style pizza place
pilaki/piyaz	pee-lah-kee/ pee-yahz	cold white beans and onions vinaigrette
piliç	pee-leech	roasting chicken
piliç kızartma	pee-leech kih-zart-mah	roast chicken
pirzola	peer-zoh-lah	cutlet (usually lamb)
pisi	pee-see	plaice
portakkal	pohr-tahk-kahl	orange
rakı	rah-kih	arrak, anise brandy
reçel	reh-chehl	fruit jam
restoran	rehs-toh-rahn	fancy restaurant serving alcohol
rom	rohm	rum
saç kavurma	sahch kah-voor-mah	lamb bits fried on an inverted wok
salam	sah-lahm	salami
salata	sah-lah-tah	salad
salatalık	sah-lah-tah-lihk	cucumber
sardalya	sahr-dahl-yah	sardine (fresh)
sarmısak	sahr-mih-sahk	garlic
sebze	seb-zeh	vegetables
sebze çorbası	sehb-zeh chor-bah-sih	vegetable soup
sığır	sih-ih	beef cattle
sığır eti	sih-ihr eh-tee	beef
sirke	seer-keh	vinegar
sirkeli	seer-keh-lee	with vinegar
siyah bira	see-yahh bee-rah	dark beer
soda;maden sodası	soh-dah; mah-dehn soh-dah-sih	mineral soda (fizzy)

MENU DECODER

soğan	soh-ahn	onion
söğüş	ser-yush	sliced tomatoes and cucumbers
su	soo	water
süt	syut	milk
sütlaç	syut-lach	rice pudding
şarap	shah-rahp	wine
şeftali	shef-tah-lee	peach
şehriye çorbası	shehh-ree-yeh chor-bah-sih	vermicelli soup
şeker	sheh-kehr	sugar/candy/sweets
şiş kebap	sheesh keh-bahp	roast skewered lamb chunks
tandır kebap	tahn-dihr keh-bahp	lamb roasted in a crock underground
tarama	tah-rah-mah	roe/red caviar
tarama salatası	tah-rah-mah sah-lah-tah-sih	red caviar in mayonnaise

MENU DECODER

tas kebap	tahs keh-bahp	lamb stew
tavuk	tah-vook	boiling chicken
tavuk çorbası	tah-vook chor-bah-sih	chicken soup
taze balık	taa-zeh bah-lihk	fresh fish
taze fasulye	tah-zeh fah-sool-yah	green (French) beans
tereyağı	teh-reh-yah-ih	butter
testi	tehs-tee	jug
tomates	doh-mah-tes	tomato
trança	trahn-chah	Aegean tuna
turşu	toor-shoo	pickled vegetables
tuz	tooz	salt
türk kahvesi	tyyuk kahh-vehsee	Turkish coffee
un	oon	flour
uskumru	oos-koom-roo	mackerel
üzüm	yu-zyum	grapes
viski	wees-kee	whiskey
vişne	veesh-neh	morello (sour) cherry
yağ	yah	oil
yaprak dolması	yah-prahk dohl-mah-sih	stuffed grape leaves
yayla çorbası	yahy-lah chor-bah-sih	yoghurt and barley soup
yeşil biber	yeh-sheel bee-behr	green pepper (sweet)
yeşil salata	yeh-sheel	green salad
yoğurt	yoh-oort	yoghurt
yumurta	yoo-moor-tah	egg
zencefil	zehn-jeh-feel	ginger
zeytin	zehy-teen	olive
zeytinyağı	zehy-teen-yah-ih	olive oil

FOOD

TYPICAL DISHES

Soups

çorba	chohr-bah	soup
haşlama	hahsh-lah-mah	broth with mutton
tavuk çorbası	tah-vook chor-bah-sih	chicken soup
düğün çorbası	dyu-yun chor-bah-sih	egg and lemon (wedding) soup
ezo gelin çorbası	eh-zoh geh-leen chor-bah-sih	lentil and rice soup
mercimek çorbası	mehr-jee-mehk chor-bah-sih	lentil soup
et suyu (yumurtalı)	eht soo-yoo (yoo-moor-tah-lih)	mutton broth (with egg)
domates çorbası	doh-mah-tes chohr-bah-sih	tomato soup
işkembe çorbası	eesh-kehm-beh chor-bah-sih	tripe soup
paça	pah-chah	trotter soup
sebze çorbası	sehb-zeh chor-bah-sih	vegetable soup
şehriye çorbası	shehh-ree-yeh chor-bah-sih	vermicelli soup
yayla çorbası	yay-lah chor-bah-sih	yoghurt and barley soup

Seafood

A menu is no use in ordering fish (*balık*). You must ask the waiter what's fresh, and then ask the price (*Kaç lira?*). The fish will be weighed and the price computed at the day's per-kg market rate. Sometimes you can haggle. Buy fish that are in season (*mevsimli*), as fish out of season are very expensive. (For names of fish and seafood, see page 135.)

FOOD

Kebaps (Roasted Meats)

Most of us think of *kebap* as shish kebab, but in fact *kebap* can refer to anything roasted. Nevertheless, it's usually meat – generally lamb or mutton. Preparation, spices and extras (onions, peppers, pide) make for the differences among *kebaps*. The meat may be in chunks, or loaded onto a spit and roasted in front of a vertical grill, then sliced off. Or it may be ground and mixed with spices, then formed into meatballs and charcoal-grilled. Some *kebaps* may be ordered *yoğurtlu*, with a side-serving of yoghurt.

adana kebap	ah-dah-nah keh-bahp	spicy-hot grilled köfte
bonfile	bohn-fee-leh	small filet beefsteak
bursa kebap	boor-sah keh-bahp	döner with tomato sauce and browned butter
ciğer	jee-ehr	liver
dana rosto	dah-nah rohs-toh	roast veal
döner kebap	der-nehr keh-bahp	spit-roasted lamb slices
domuz eti	doh-mooz eh-tee	pork (forbidden to Muslims)
etli pide/etli ekmek	eht-lee pee-deh/ eht-lee ehk-mehk	flat bread topped with ground lamb and spices
güveç	gyu-vech	meat and vegetable stew in a crock
karışık ızgara	kah-rih-shuk ihz-gah-rah	mixed grill (lamb)
köfte	kerf-teh	grilled lamb meatballs with onion and spices
(süt) kuzu	(syut) koo-zoo	(milk-fed) lamb
musakka	moo-sah-kah	aubergine and lamb pie
orman kebap	ohr-mahn keh-bahp	roast lamb with onions
piliç	pee-leech	roasting chicken

piliç kızartma	pee-leech kih-zahrt-mah	roast chicken
pirzola	peer-zoh-lah	cutlet (usually lamb)
saç kavurma	sahch kah-voor-mah	lamb bits fried on an inverted wok
sığır	sih-ih	beef
şinitzel	shee-neet-zehl	wienerschnitzel
şiş kebap	sheesh keh-bahp	roast skewered lamb chunks
tandır kebap	tahn-dihr keh-bahp	lamb roasted in a crock underground
tas kebap	tahs keh-bahp	lamb stew
tavuk	tah-vook	boiling chicken

Salads

Most salads (except *söğüş*) come with olive oil. You may be asked if you prefer it *sirkeli*, with vinegar or *limonlu*, with lemon juice. If you don't like hot peppers, say *bibersiz*, though this often doesn't work.

Many visitors are surprised that Turkish chefs do not make Greek-style salads of sliced tomatoes and cucumbers with olives, olive oil, and white cheese. The Turks are catching on, but if your order for a Greek salad meets with incomprehension, order *çoban salatası* or *söğüş*, with olives and white cheese, and make your own.

çoban salatası	choh-bahn	chopped mixed tomato, cucumber, hot pepper
karışık salata	kah-rih-shihk sah-lah-tah	same as *çoban salatası*
marul	mah-rool	Romaine lettuce
patlıcan salatası	paht-lih-jahn	roast aubergine/ eggplant

FOOD

Vegetables

söğüş	ser-yush	sliced tomatoes & cucumbers
turşu	toor-shoo	pickled vegetables
yeşil salata	yeh-sheel sah-lah-tah	green salad

Often a vegetable (*sebze*) is prepared with meat or stock as a flavouring, along with tomato sauce, olive oil, and a spice.

Stuffed Vegetables

... dolma(sı)	... dohl-mah(sih)	stuffed ... (vegetable)
kabak dolması	kah-bahk dohl-mah-sih	squash/marrow
lahana dolması	lah-hah-nah dohl-mah-sih	cabbage
yaprak dolması	yah-prahk dohl-mah-sih	grape leaves

Sweets/Desserts

Many Turkish baked desserts come swimming in sugar syrup. They're delicious, but very sweet.

baklava	bah-lah-vah	flaky pastry with honey and nuts
dondurma	dohn-door-mah	ice cream
ekmek kadayıf	ehk-mehk kah-dah-yihf	crumpet in syrup
fırın sütlaç	fih-rihn syut-lach	baked rice pudding (cold)
komposto	kohm-pohs-toh	stewed fruit
krem karamel	krehm kah-rah-mehl	baked caramel custard
pasta	pahs-tah	pastry (not noodles)
sütlaç	syut-lach	rice pudding

FOOD

Meze

Meze (meh-zeh) is Turkey's answer to the Spanish tapas bar serving drinks and small, delicious snacks of great variety. Turkish appetisers can include almost anything, and you can easily – and delightfully – make an entire meal of them. Often you will be brought a tray from which you can choose those you want.

beyaz peynir	behy-ahz pehy-neer	white, sheep's milk cheese
börek	ber-rehk	flaky pastry filled with white cheese or meat
cacık	jah-jihk	beaten yoghurt with grated cucumber and garlic
patlıcan salatası	paht-lih-jahn sah-lah-tah-sih	aubergine/eggplant purée

| *pilaki/piyaz* | pee-lah-kee/ pee-yahz | cold white beans and onions vinagrette |
| *tarama salatası* | tah-rah-mah sah-lah-tah-sih | red caviar in mayonnaise |

hors d'oeuvre	err-dervr	*Ördövr*
one portion	beer-pohr-sih-yohn	*Bir porsiyon*
small sandwich	kyu-chyuk sahnd-weech	*Küçük sandviç*
normal-sized sandwich	nohr-mahl sahnd-weech	*Normal sandviç*

SELF-CATERING

bread	ehk-mehk	*ekmek*
butter	teh-reh-yah-ih	*tereyağı*
cheese (white, sheep's)	(beh-yahz) pehy-neer	*beyaz peynir*
cheese (yellow, cow's)	(kah-shahr) pehy-neer	*kaşar peynir*
cheese (aged yellow)	(ehs-skee kah-shahr) pehy-neer	*eski kaşar peynir*
eggs	yoo-moor-tah(lahr)	*yumuta(lar)*
flour	oon	*un*
ham (forbidden to Muslims)	zhahm-bohn	*jambon*
honey	bahl	*bal*
milk	syut	*süt*
pepper	bee-behr	*biber*
salami	sah-lahm	*salam*
salt	tooz	*tuz*
sugar	sheh-kehr	*şeker*
yoghurt	yoh-oort	*yoğurt*

AT THE MARKET
Meat & Poultry

beef	sih-ihr eh-tee	*sığır eti*
brain (sheep's)	behy-yeen	*beyin*
chicken (roasting)	pee-leech	*piliç*

chicken (stewing)	tah-vook	*tavuk*
goat	keh-chee- eh-tee	*keçi eti*
heart	yyu-rehk	*yürek*
kidneys	ber-brehk	*böbrek*
lamb (milk-fed)	(syut) koo-zoo	*(süt) kuzu*
liver	jee-ehr	*ciğer*
meat	eht	*et*
mutton	koh-yoon eh-tee	*koyun eti*
pork	doh-mooz eh-tee	*domuz eti*
quail	bihl-dihr-jihn	*bıldırcın*
testicles (ram's eggs)	koch yoo-moor-tah-sih	*koç yumurtası*
tongue	deel	*dil*
turkey	heen-dee	*hindi*
veal	dah-nah	*dana*

Fish & Seafood

Aegean tuna	trahn-chah	*trança*
anchovy (fresh)	hahm-see	*hamsi*
black bream	kah-rah-gerz	*karagöz*
bluefish	lyu-fehr	*lüfer*
grey mullet	keh-fahl	*kefal*
lobster	ihs-tah-kohz	*ıstakoz*
mackerel	oos-koom-roo	*uskumru*
mussels	meed-yeh	*midye*
plaice	pee-see	*pisi*
red coralfish	mehr-jahn	*mercan*
red mullet	bahr-boon-yah	*barbunya*
roe, red caviar	tah-rah-mah	*tarama*
sardine (fresh)	sahr-dahl-yah	*sardalya*
sea bass	lehv-rehk	*levrek*
shrimp	kah-ree-des	*karides*
sole	deel bah-lih-ih	*dil balığı*
swordfish	kih-lihch bah-lih-ih	*kılıç balığı*
trout	ah-lah-bah-lihk	*alabalık*
tuna/tunny/bonito	pah-lah-moot	*palamut*
turbot	kahl-kahn	*kalkan*

FOOD

Vegetables

beans	fah-sool-yeh	*fasulye*
green (French) beans	tah-zeh fah-sool-yeh	*taze fasulye*
red beans	bahr-boon-yeh	*barbunye*
white beans	koo-roo fah-sool-yeh	*kuru fasulye*
cabbage	lah-hah-nah	*lahana*
carrot	hah-vooch	*havuç*
cauliflower	kahr-nah-bah-hahr	*karnabahar*
chickpeas/garbanzos	noh-hoot	*nohut*
cucumber	sah-lah-tah-lihk	*salatalık*
green pepper/ pimiento (sweet)	yeh-sheel bee-behr	*yeşil biber*
marrow/squash	kah-bahk	*kabak*
okra	bahm-yah	*bamya*
onion	soh-ahn	*soğan*
peas	beh-zehl-yeh	*bezelye*
potato	pah-tah-tes	*patates*
spinach	ihs-spih-nahk	*ıspınak*
tomato	doh-mah-tes	*tomates*

Fruit

Turkish fruit (*meyva* – plural *meyve* or *meyvalar*) is wonderful, abundant, but very seasonal. It makes the perfect dessert if Turkish sweets are too syrupy for you.

apple	ehl-mah	*elma*
apricot	kah-yih-sih	*kayısı*
banana	mooz	*muz*
cherry	kee-rahz	*kiraz*
fig	een-jeer	*incir*
grapefruit	grehy-foo-root	*greyfurut*
grapes	yu-zyum	*üzüm*
orange	pohr-tahk-kahl	*portakkal*
peach	shef-tah-lee	*şeftali*
pear	ahr-moot	*armut*
strawberries	chee-lehk	*çilek*
tangerine/mandarin	mahn-dah-leen	*mandalin*

| watermelon | kahr-pooz | *karpuz* |
| yellow melon | kah-voon | *kavun* |

SPICES & CONDIMENTS

fruit jam	reh-chehl	*reçel*
garlic	sahr-mih-sahk	*sarmısak*
ginger	zen-jeh-feel	*zencefil*
lemon	lee-monh	*limon*
oil	yah	*yağ*
olive oil	zehy-teen-yah-ih	*zeytinyağı*
onions	soh-ahn	*soğan*
red pepper	kihr-mih-zih bee-behr	*kırmızıbiber*
salt	tooz	*tuz*
sugar	sheh-kehr	*şeker*
vinegar	seer-keh	*sirke*

DRINKS

When speaking of drinks, *içki* usually refers to alcoholic beverages, while *meşrubat* refers to soft drinks. If your waiters say *İçecek?* or *Ne içeceksiniz?*, they're asking what you'd like to drink. The most popular drink in Turkey is certainly *çay*, tea, served in little tulip-shaped glasses, with sugar. If you want milk, *süt*, in your tea, you'll have to ask for it, causing neighbouring tea-drinkers to puzzle on the exotic preferences of foreigners.

A very popular alternative to regular tea is apple tea, *elma çay*. In summer, try *ayran*, a tart, refreshing beverage made by beating yoghurt and mixing it with spring water and a little salt.

As for Turkish coffee, *türk kahvesi*, order it *sade*, bitter without sugar; *az*, with a little sugar; *orta*, middling sweet; or *çok şekerli*, very sweet.

FOOD

arrak (anise brandy)	rah-kih	*rakı*
coffee	kahh-veh	*kahve*
fruit juice	mehy-vah soo-yoo	*meyva suyu*
light/dark beer	behy-ahz/see-yahh	*beyaz/siyah*
	bee-rah	*bira*

milk	syut	*süt*
mineral soda (fizzy)	soh-dah/mah-dehn soh-dah-sih	*soda/maden sodası*
spring water (not fizzy)	mem-bah soo-yoo	*memba suyu*
red/white wine	kihr-mih-zih/ behy-ahz shah-rahp	*kırmızı/beyaz şarap*
yoghurt drink	ahy-rahn	*ayran*

There isn't a good equivalent for a single 'shot' in Turkish, but a double shot is called a *'duble'* (doo-bleh).

a beer	beer bih-rah	*bir bira*
a small glass of beer	beer kyu-chyuk bahr-dahk bee-rah	*bir küçük bardak biraa*
big glass of beer	beer byu-yyuk bahr-dahk bee-rah	*bir büyük bardak bira.*
a small bottle of beer	beer kyu-chyuk shee-sheh bee-rah	*bir küçük şişe bira*
a large bottle of beer	beer byu-yyuk shee-sheh bee-rah	*bir büyük şişe bira*
whiskey/rum	wees-kee/rohm	*viski/rom*
wine/sherry	shah-rahp/sheh-ree	*şarap/şeri*
a glass of wine/ sherry	beer bahr-dahk shah-rahp/sheh-ree	*bir bardak şarap/şeri*
a bottle of wine/ whiskey	beer shee-sheh shah-rahp/wees-kee	*bir şişe şarap/ viski*
a jug of wine/ sherry	beer tehs-tee shah-rahp/sheh-ree	*bir testi şarap/ şeri*

THEY MAY SAY ...

Eech-kee-lehr behn-dehn!   The drinks are on me!

PAYING THE BILL

By law, tax is supposed to be included in the price of every item on the menu, and thus you should not pay an extra charge for tax. You may see *KDV dahildir* (Value-Added Tax Included) on the price list. A service charge may be added, but is usually not. In very cheap restaurants, tips are not really expected but some people leave a few coins or small bills. For meals in a restaurant with white tablecloths and courteous waiters, 8% to 10% is normal. In international-class luxury places, 12% to 15% is expected, and 20% is not sniffed at.

May I have the bill, please?
  heh-sahp lyut-fehn?   *Hesap lütfen?*
Is service/tax included?
  sehr-vees/vehr-gee   *Servis/vergi dahil mi?*
  dah-heel mee?

bill/check	heh-sahp	*hesap*
service charge	sehr-vees yuj-reh-tee	*servis ücreti*
tax	vehr-gee	*vergi*
tip	bahh-sheesh	*bahşış*
error	yahn-lihsh	*yanlış*

USEFUL WORDS

black pepper	kah-rah/ see-yahh bee-behr	*kara/siyah biber*
bread	ehk-mek	*ekmek*
butter	teh-reh-yah-ih	*tereyağı*
cheese	pehy-neer	*peynir*
family/ladies' dining room	ah-ee-leh sah-loh-noo	*aile salonu*
fruit jam	reh-chehl	*reçel*
garlic	sahr-mih-sahk	*sarmısak*
honey	bahl	*bal*
ice	booz	*buz*

FOOD

lemon	lee-mohn	*limon*
macaroni/noodles	mah-kahr-nah	*makarna*
mild yellow cheese	kah-shahr pehy-neer	*kaşar peynir*
olive oil	zehy-teen-yah-ih	*zeytinyağı*
olive(s)	zehy-teen	*zeytin*
pizza/flat bread	pee-deh	*pide*
sugar/candy/sweets	sheh-kehr	*şeker*
vinegar	seer-keh	*sirke*
water	soo	*su*

| Waiter! | gahr-sohn behy! | *Garson bey!* |
| (Waiter) please come. | bah-kahr-mih-sih-nihz | *Bakarmısınız.* |

COOKING TERMS

rare	ahz peesh-meesh	*az pişmiş*
well done/very done	ee-yee peesh-meesh	*iyi pişmiş*
with cheese	pehy-neer-lee	*peynirli*
with ground lamb	kihy-mah-lih	*kıymalı*
without meat	eht-seez	*etsiz*
yoghurt	yoh-oort	*yoğurt*

FOOD

IN THE COUNTRY

CAMPING

Is there a camping place round here?
boo-rah-lahr-dah beer kamp
yeh-ree vahr mih?
Buralarda bir kamp yeri
var mı?

Can I/we camp here?
boo-rah-dah kamp yah-pah-
bee-leer mee-yeem/mee-yeez?
Burada kamp yapabilir
miyim/miyiz?

Can you make a fire here?
ah-tesh yahk-mahk
sehr-best-mee?
Ateş yakmak serbest mi?

Where's the electric hookup?
eh-lehk-treek ba-lahn-tih-sih
neh-reh-deh?
Elektrik bağlantısı nerede?

Where's the shower/toilet?
doosh/too-vah-leht ·
neh-reh-deh?
Duş/tuvalet nerede?

Where can I have my gas
cylinder filled?
gahz tyu-pyu-myu neh-reh-deh
dohl-doo-rah-bee-leer-eem?
Gaz tüpümü nerede
doldurabilirim?

Some Useful Words

tent	chah-dihr	*çadır*
caravan (trailer)	kah-rah-vahn	*karavan*
camping place	kamp yeh-ree	*kamp yeri*

HIKING

Are there any tourist attractions near here?
jee-vahr-dah too-rees-teek
yehr-lehr vahr mih?
Civarda turistik yerler
var mı?

Where's the nearest village?
ehn yah-kihn kery neh-reh-deh?
En yakın köy nerede?

Is it safe to climb this mountain?
  boo dah-ah tihr-mahn-mahk
  ehm-nee-yeht-lee mee?
Is there a hut up there?
  yoo-kahr-dah koo-lyu-beh
  vahr mih?
Do we need a guide?
  rehh-beh-reh
  eeh-tee-yah-jih-mihz vahr mih?

Bu dağa tırmanmak
emniyetli mi?

Yukarda kulübe var mı?

Rehbere ihtiyacımız var mı?

Where can I find hiking trails in the region?
 boo berl-geh-neen   *Bu bölgenin tırmanış*
 tihr-mah-nihsh pah-tee-   *patikasını nereden*
 kah-sih-nih neh-reh-dehn   *bulabilirim?*
 boo-lah-bee-leer-reem?

Can I find a guide for a climbing tour?
 tihr-mahn-mah too-roo   *tırmanma turu için*
 ee-cheen kih-lah-vooz   *kılavuz bulabilir miyim?*
 boo-lah-bee-leer mee-yeem?

I'd like to talk to someone who knows this area.
 berl-geh-yee bee-lehn bee-ree   *Bölgeyi bilen biri ile*
 ee-leh koh-noosh-mahk   *konuşmak istiyorum.*
 ees-tee-yohr-room

How long is the trail?
 pah-tee-kah oo-zoon-loo-oo   *Patika uzunluğu ne*
 neh kah-dahr?   *kadar?*

Is the track easy to follow?
 pah-tee-kah koh-lahy-jah   *Patika kolayca takip*
 tah-keep   *edilebilir mi?*
 eh-deel-leh-bee-leer mee?

What altitude does it reach?
 neh kah-dahr   *Ne kadar yükseklikte?*
 yyuk-sehk-leek-the?

Which is the shorter route?
 hahn-gee yohl dah-hah   *Hangi yol daha kısa?*
 kih-sah?

Which is the easier route?
 hahn-gee yohl dah-hah   *Hangi yol daha kolay?*
 koh-lahy?

Is the path open?
 pah-tee-kah ah-chihk mih?   *Patika açık mı?*

When does it get dark?
 kah-rahn-lihk neh   *Karanlık ne zaman basar?*
 zah-mahn bah-sahr?

Is it very scenic?
    mahn-zah-rah gyu-zehl mee?   *Manzara güzel mi?*

Where can I hire mountain gear?
    neh-reh-dehn dah tah-kih-mih   *Nereden dağ takımı*
    kee-rah-lah-yah-bee-leer-reem?   *kiralayabilirim?*

Where can we buy supplies?
    neh-reh-dehn mahl-zeh-meh   *Nereden malzeme*
    ah-lah-bee-leer-reez?   *alabiliriz?*

On the Path

Where have you come from?
    neh-reh-dehn gehl-dee-neez?   *Nereden geldiniz.*

How long did it take you?
    neh kah-dahr syu-dyu?   *Ne kadar sürdü?*

Does this path go to …?
    boo pah-tee-kah …'eh   *Bu patika …'e gidiyor*
    gee-dee-yohr-moo?   *mu?*

I'm lost.
    kahy-bohl-doom   *Kayboldum.*

Where can we spend the night?
    geh-jeh-yee neh-reh-deh   *Geceyi nerede*
    gehch-eer-eh-bee-leer-reez?   *geçirebiliriz?*

Can I leave some things here for a while?
    bah-zih shehy-leh-ree   *Bazı şeyleri bir süre*
    beer syu-reh boo-rah-dah   *burada bırakabilirmiyim?*
    bih-rah-kah-bee-leer-mee-yeem?

altitude	yyuk-sek-leek	*yükseklik*
backpack	sihrt chan-tah-sih	*sırt çantası*
binoculars	(ee-kee gerz-leh	*(iki gözle bakılabilen)*
	bah-kih-lah-bee-lehn)	*dürbün*
	dyur-byun	
candles	moom (lahr)	*mum(lar)*
to climb	tihr-mahn-mahk/	*tırmanmak/çıkmak*
	chihk-mahk	

CUTTING THE DONKEY'S TAIL

A worthless person doesn't suffer hardships.
  ah-jih paht-lih-jah-nih kih-rah-ih chahl-mahz
  Acı patlıcanı kırağı çalmaz.
  (lit: a bitter eggplant does not get frostbitten)

Everyone talks about the things they love.
  ah-yihn-nihn kihrk hee-kah-yeh-see vahr-mihsh
  hehp-see deh ah-laht yu-zeh-ree-neh
  Ayının kırk hikayesi varmış hepsi de ahlat üzerine.
  (lit: the forty stories known by the bear are all about
  wild pears)

It's impossible to satisfy everyone.
  eh-sheh-een kooy-roo-oo-noo kah-lah-bah-lihk-
  tah kehs-meh, kee-mee oo-zoon dehr kee-mee
  kih-sah
  *Eşeğin kuyruğunu kalabalıkta kesme, kimi uzun der
  kimi kısa.*
  (lit: don't cut off the donkey's tail in public, some will
  say it's too long, some too short)

Bad companions gradually corrupt a good person.
  yu-zyum yu-zyu-meh bah-kah bah-kah kah-rah-rihr
  Üzüm üzüme baka baka kararır.
  (lit: grapes become black upon seeing one another)

When a subordinate person is angry with his superior,
it probably goes unnoticed.
  tahw-shahn dah-ah kyus-myush, dah-ihn
  hah-beh-ree ohl-mah-mihsh
  Tavşan dağa küsmüş, dağın haberi olmamış.
  (lit: the hare was angry with the mountain, but the
  mountain was unaware of it)

compass	poo-soo-lah	*pusula*
downhill	yoh-koosh ah-shah-ih/ ah-shah-ih-yah	*yokuş aşağı/aşağıya*
first-aid kit	eelk yahr-dihm koo-too-soo	*ilk yardım kutusu*
gloves	ehl-dee-vehn	*eldiven*
guide	kih-lah-vooz/rehh-behr	*kılavuz/ rehber*
guided trek	rehh-behr-lee tihr-mahn-mah too-roo	*rehberli tırmanma turu*
hiking	oo-zoon veh zohr-loo yyu-ryu-yyush yahp-mah	*uzun ve zorlu yürüyüş yapma*
hiking boots	tihr-mahn-mah cheez-meh-see	*tırmanma çizmesi*
hunting	ahv-jih-lihk	*avcılık*
ledge	dyuz chih-kihn-tih	*düz çıkıntı*
lookout (place)	ger-zeht-leh-meh yeh-ree	*gözetleme yeri*
map	hah-ree-tah	*harita*
mountain climbing	dah tihr-mahn-mah/ dah chihk-mah/ dah-jih-lihk	*dağ tırmanma/ dağ çıkma/ dağcılık*
pick	kahz-mah	*kazma*
provisions	ehr-zahk/ah-zihk	*erzak/ azık*
rock climbing	kah-yah tihr-mahn-mah	*kaya tırmanma*
rope	hah-laht/eep	*halat/ ip*
signpost	yohl gers-teh-rehn lehv-hah/ee-shah-reht dee-reh-ee	*yol gösteren levha/işaret direği*
steep	deek	*dik*
trek	oo-zoon veh zohr-loo beer yohl-joo-look	*uzun ve zorlu bir yolculuk*
uphill	yoh-koosh yoo-kah-rih	*yokuş yukarı*
to walk	yyu-ryu-mehk	*yürümek*

AT THE BEACH

Can we swim here?
    boo-rah-dah
    yyu-zeh-bee-leer-mee-yeez?   *Burada yüzebilirmiyiz?*
Is it safe to swim here?
    boo-rah-dah yyuz-mehk
    ehm-nee-yeht-lee mee?   *Burada yüzmek emniyetli mi?*

coast/shore	sah-heel	*sahil*
fishing	bah-lihk toot-mah/	*balık tutma/*
	bah-lihk ahv-lah-mah	*balık avlama*
rock	kah-yah	*kaya*
sand	koom	*kum*
sea	deh-neez	*deniz*
snorkelling	shnohr-kehl	*şnorkel*
suncream/	gyu-nehsh kreh-mee/	*güneş kremi/*
sunblock	gyu-nehsh ehn-geh-lee	*güneş engeli*
sunglasses	gyu-nehsh gerz-lyu-yu	*güneş gözlüğü*
surf (waves)	dahl-gah-lahr	*dalgalar*
surfing	serf	*sörf*
surfboard	serf tah-tah-sih	*sörf tahtası*
swimming	yyuz-meh	*yüzme*
swimming pool	yyuz-meh hah-voo-zoo	*yüzme havuzu*
towel	hahv-loo	*havlu*
waterskiing	soo kah-yah-ih	*su kayağı yapma*
	yahp-mah	
waves	dahl-gah-lahr	*dalgalar*
windsurfing	ryuz-gahr ser-fyu	*rüzgar sörfü*

IN THE COUNTRY

Diving

scuba diving	skoo-bah dahl-mah	*scuba dalma*

Are there good diving sites here?
boo-rah-dah dah-lih-nah-jahk   *Burada dalınacak güzel yer*
gyu-zehl yehr vahr mih?   *var mı?*

Can we hire a diving boat/guide?
dahl-gihch boh-too/   *Dalgıç botu/kılavuzu*
kih-lah-voo-zoo kee-rah-lah-   *kiralayabilirmiyiz?*
yah-bee-leer-mee-yeez?

We'd like to hire diving equipment.
dahl-gihch   *Dalgıç malzemeleri*
mahl-zeh-meh-leh-ree   *kiralamak istiyoruz.*
kee-rah-lah-mahk ees-tee-yohr-rooz

I'm interested in sunken ships.
bah-tihk geh-mee-lehr-leh   *Batık gemilerle*
eel-gee-leh-nee-yohr-room   *ilgileniyorum.*

WEATHER

What's the weather report?
hah-vah rah-poh-roo nah-sihl?   *Hava raporu nasıl?*

The weather will be hot/cold.
hah-vah sih-jahk/   *Hava sıcak/soğuk olacak.*
soh-ook oh-lah-jahk

It's going to rain/snow.
yah-moor/kahr yah-ah-jahk   *Yağmur/kar yağacak.*

The weather is beautiful today.
boo-gyun hah-vah gyu-zehl   *Bugün hava güzel.*

GET IT?

Remember that in Turkish **g** is always hard as
in 'get', never soft as in 'giant'.

Some Useful Words

autumn	sohn bah-hahr	*son bahar*
cloud(y)	boo-loot(-loo)	*bulut(lu)*
freeze (verb)	dohn-mahk	*donmak*
ice	booz	*buz*
'Indian summer'	pahs-tihr-mah yah-zih	*pastırma yazı*
rain (noun)	yah-moor	*yağmur*
rain (verb)	yah-moor yah-mahk	*yağmur yağmak*
snow (noun)	kahr	*kar*
spring	eelk bah-hahr	*ilk bahar*
summer	yahz	*yaz*
sun	gyu-nehsh	*güneş*
weather ('air')	hah-vah	*hava*
wind	ryuz-gahr	*rüzgar*
winter	kihsh	*kış*

GEOGRAPHICAL TERMS

beach	plazh	*plaj*
cave	mah-ah-rah	*mağara*
field	tahr-lah	*tarla*
harbour	lee-mahn	*liman*
hill	teh-peh	*tepe*
house	ehv	*ev*
lake	gerl	*göl*
mountain	dah	*dağ*
mountaineer(ing)	dah-jih(lihk)	*dağcı(lık)*
mud	chah-moor	*çamur*
river	ihr-mahk/neh-heer	*ırmak/nehir*
road	yohl	*yol*
rock	tahsh	*taş*
sand	koom	*kum*
sea	deh-neez	*deniz*
summit	doh-rook/zeer-veh	*doruk/zirve*
trail	pah-tee-kah	*patika*
tree	ah-ahch	*ağaç*
valley	deh-reh	*dere*
waterfall	sheh-lah-leh	*şelale*

IN THE COUNTRY

SIGHTS

bridge	ker-pryu	*köprü*
church	kee-lee-seh	*kilise*
fortress	kah-leh/hee-sahr	*kale/hisar*
historical/renowned	tah-ree-hee	*tarihi*
mosque	jah-mee	*cami*
museum	myu-zeh	*müze*
old	es-kee	*eski*
ruin(s)	hah-rah-beh(lehr)	*harabe(ler)*
statue	hehy-kel	*heykel*
temple	tah-pih-nahk/ mah-behd	*tapınak/mabed*

ANIMALS

bull	boh-ah	*boğa*
camel	deh-veh	*deve*
cat	keh-dee	*kedi*
cow	ee-nehk	*inek*
dog	ker-pehk	*köpek*
donkey	eh-shehk	*eşek*
duck	er-dehk	*ördek*
goat	keh-chee	*keçi*
goose	kahz	*kaz*
horse	aht	*at*
sheep/ram	kohy-yoon/kohch	*koyun/koç*
water buffalo	mahn-dah	*manda*
wolf	koort	*kurt*

Insects & Pests

bug	ber-jehk	*böcek*
cockroach	hah-mahm ber-jeh-ee	*hamam böceği*
fly	see-nehk	*sinek*
mosquito	see-vree-see-nehk	*sivrisinek*
poison(ous)	zeh-heer(lee)	*zehir(li)*
scorpion	ah-krehp	*akrep*
snake	yih-lahn	*yılan*

FLORA & AGRICULTURE

agriculture	zee-rah-aht/tah-rihm	*ziraat/ tarım*
banana	mooz	*muz*
barley	ahr-pah	*arpa*
chickpea	noh-hoot	*nohut*
corn	mih-sihr	*mısır*
cotton	pah-mook	*pamuk*
crop/harvest	yur-yun	*ürün*
farmer	cheeft-chee	*çiftçi*
flower	chee-chehk	*çiçek*
grapes	yu-zyum	*üzüm*
greenhouse	seh-rah	*sera*
harvest (verb)	hah-saht eht-mehk/	*hasat etmek/*
	beech-mehk	*biçmek*
irrigation	soo-lah-mah	*sulama*
leaf	yah-prahk	*yaprak*
melon	kah-voon	*kavun*
millet	dah-rih	*darı*
opium poppy	hahsh-hahsh	*haşhaş*
orchard	mehy-veh	*meyve bahçesi*
	bahh-cheh-see	
planting/sowing	deek-mehk/ehk-mehk	*dikmek/ekmek*
potatoes	pah-tah-tes	*patates*
rice (plant)	chehl-teek	*çeltik*
rye	chahv-dahr	*çavdar*
sugar beets	sheh-kehr-pahn-jah-rih	*şekerpancarı*
sultana (raisin)	sool-tah-nee	*sultani*
sunflower	ahy-chee-cheh-ee	*ayçiçeği*
tobacco	tyu-tyun	*tütün*
tree	ah-ahch	*ağaç*
village(r)	kery(lyu)	*köy(lü)*
(grape)vine/	bah	*bağ*
vineyard		
watermelon	kahr-pooz	*karpuz*
wheat	boo-dahy	*buğday*

IN THE COUNTRY

CROSSWORD

Across

1. subaquatic ox?
5. can be done socially but this is more exciting (2nd word)
7. black & white and read all over
8. flesh of a calf cooked in an oven (2 words)
10. snug when there's two of them in a pod

Down

2. Marmara is a Turkish one
3. a Turkish mini one is called a dolmus
4. 'Weather's lovely, wish you were here.'
6. throbbing headache
9. Lady Godiva would have had to hitch without one

Answers on page 260

IN THE COUNTRY

Every Turkish city and town has a health facility. In the cities there are hospitals and clinics, both government-run and private; in the towns there are clinics and first-aid stations. All prices are quite low – even at the private hospitals and clinics they are controlled by the government, as are prices for medicines. To find a *hastane* (hospital), look for the standard blue road sign bearing a large 'H' in a white box; for a *klinik* (clinic) or a place providing *ilk yardım* (first aid), look for a blue highway sign bearing a red crescent in a white box. This is the symbol of the Red Crescent Society, the Muslim equivalent of the Red Cross – it's used to indicate any medical facility. You might also see signs pointing the way to the *sağlık memuru* (public health official).

For minor aches and pains, it's customary to go to an *eczane* (chemist or pharmacy) and explain your problem. The *eczacı* (chemist) will sell you a remedy on the spot.

As for doctors, there are general practitioners and specialists in all cities – the bigger the city, the better the health care. Some Turkish ladies observe the custom of having a female friend accompany them if a male doctor makes a physical examination. But as half of all the medical doctors in Turkey are women, choosing your physician by gender is the obvious alternative.

IN AN EMERGENCY

Many large hospitals have an *acil servis* (emergency service/room) where you can go for quick treatment. If an ambulance is not readily available, a taxi will get you there quickly, hooting the horn all the way, a signal understood by other drivers indicating a medical emergency.

Please call ...	... chah-ihr-ihn	... çağırın.
an ambulance	jahn-koor-tah-rahn/ ahm-boo-lahns	cankurtaran/ ambulans
a doctor	dohk-tohr/heh-keem	doktor/hekim
the police	poh-lees	polis

HEALTH

It's an emergency.	ah-jeel vah-kah vahr	*Acil vaka var.*
Is there ... around here?	boo-rah-lahr-dah ... vahr mih?	*Buralarda ... var mı?*
a hospital	beer hahs-tah-neh	*bir hastane*
a doctor	beer dohk-tohr/ heh-keem	*bir doktor/hekim*
a chemist/ pharmacy	beer ehj-zah-neh	*bir eczane*
a dentist	beer deesh-chee/ deesh heh-kee-mee	*bir dişçi/ dış hekimi*

AT THE DOCTOR

How do you feel?
  nah-sihl hee-seh-dee-
  yohr-soo-nooz?

Nasıl hissediyorsunuz?

I don't feel well.
  kehn-dee-mee ee-yee
  hees-seht-mee-yoh-room

*Kendimi iyi
hissetmiyorum.*

Can the doctor come here?
  dohk-tohr boo-rah-yah
  gheh-leh-bee-leer mee?

*Doktor buraya
gelebilir mi?*

HEALTH

Where's the nearest ...	ehn yah-kihn ... neh-reh-deh	*En yakın ... nerede?*
doctor	dohk-tohr	*doktor*
hospital	hah-stah-neh	*hastane*
chemist/pharmacy	ehj-zah-neh	*eczane*
dentist	deesh-chee/ deesh heh-kee-mee	*dişçi/diş hekimi*

I'm sick.
  hahs-tah-yihm

Hastayım.

My friend is sick.
  ahr-kah-dah-shihm hahs-tah

Arkadaşım hasta.

I need an English speaking doctor.
  een-ghee-leez-jeh
  koh-noo-shahn dohk-tohr-ah
  eeh-tee-yah-jihm vahr

*İngilizce konuşan
doktora ihtiyacım var.*

I've caught a cold.
  yu-shyu-dyum

Üşüdüm.

HEALTH

YOU MAY HEAR ...

neh-yeen vahr?	What's the matter?
Neyin var?	
ah-rih hees-seh-dee-yohr-moo-soo-nooz?	Do you feel any pain?
Ağrı hissediyormusunuz?	
neh-reh-see ah-rih-yohr?	Where does it hurt?
Neresi ağrıyor?	
ah-teh-shee-neez vahr mih?	Do you have a fever?
Ateşiniz var mı?	
neh zah-mahn-dahn beh-ree bery-leh-see-neez?	How long have you been like this?
Ne zamandan beri böylesiniz?	
dah-hah ern-jeh bery-leh ohl-doo-nooz moo?	Have you had this before?
Daha önce böyle oldunuz mu?	
ee-lahch ah-lih-yohr moo-soo-nooz?	Are you taking medication?
İlaç alıyor musunuz?	
see-gah-rah ee-chee-yohr moo-soo-nooz?	Do you smoke cigarettes?
Sigara içiyor musunuz?	
eech-kee ee-chee-yohr moo-soo-nooz?	Do you drink alcoholic beverages?
İçki içiyor musunuz?	
oo-yoosh-too-roo-joo kool-lah-nih-yohr-moo-soo-nooz?	Do you use narcotics?
Uyuşturucu kullanıyormusunuz?	
hehr han-gee beer sheh-yeh ah-lehr-zhee-neez vahr mih?	Are you allergic to anything at all?
Her hangi bir şeye alerjiniz var mı?	

AILMENTS

My head's spinning/I'm dizzy.
   bah-shihm der-nyu-yohr   *Başım dönüyor.*
I'm going to vomit/be sick.
   koos-ah-jah-ihm geh-lee-yohr   *Kusacağım geliyor.*
I'm on medication for ...
   ... ee-cheen ee-lahch   *... için ilaç alıyorum.*
   ah-lih-yohr-room

HEALTH

I have (a) ...	... vahr	... *var.*
AIDS	ahyds	*aids*
anaemia	kahn-sihz-lihk/ ah-neh-mee	*kansızlık/anemi*
appendicitis	ah-pahn-dee-seet	*apandisit*
burn	yah-nihk	*yanık*
cancer	kahn-sehr	*kanser*
cholera	koh-leh-rah	*kolera*
zcold	nehz-lehm	*nezlem*
constipation	ka-bihz	*kabız*
cough	erk-syur-yuk	*öksürük*
cramp	kah-sihnch/krahmp	*kasınç/kramp*
cystitis	sees-teet	*sistit*
diabetes	sheh-kehr hahs-tah-lih-ih	*şeker hastalığı*
diarrhoea	ees-hah-leem	*ishalim*
disease/illness	hahs-tah-lihk	*hastalık*
fever	ah-the-sheem	*ateşim*

HEALTH

gastroenteritis	gahs-treet	*gastrit*
headache	bahsh ah-rih-sih	*baş ağrısı*
heart condition	kahlp	*kalp hastalığı*
	hahs-tah-lih-ih	
hepatitis/jaundice	sah-rih-lihk	*sarılık*
indigestion	mee-deh feh-sah-dih	*mide fesadı*
infection	boo-lahsh-mah/	*bulaşma/*
	ehn-fehk-see-yohn	*enfeksiyon*
influenza	greep	*grip*
lice	beet	*bit*
malaria	siht-mah	*sıtma*
migraine	mee-grehn	*migren*
nausea	mee-deh	*mide bulantısı*
	boo-lahn-tih-sih	
pain	beer aah-rih	*bir ağrı*
pneumonia	zah-tyu-ree	*zatürree*
rabies	koo-dooz	*kuduz hastalığı*
	hahs-tah-lih-ih	
serious disease	jeed-dee	*ciddi hastalık*
	hahs-tah-lihk	
sore throat	ah-rih-yahn	*ağrıyan boğaz*
	boh-ahz	
sprain	boor-kool-mah	*burkulma*
stomachache	mee-deh ah-rih-sih	*mide ağrısı*
sunburn	gyu-nehsh	*güneş yanığı*
	yah-nih-ih	
thrush	oh-rahl mahn-tahr	*oral mantar*
	hahs-tah-lih-ih/ahft	*hastalığı/afti*
toothache	deesh ah-rih-sih	*diş ağrısı*
travel sickness	seh-yah-hat mee-deh	*seyahat mide*
	boo-lahn-tih-sih	*bulantısı*
urinary infection	see-deek-yoh-loo/	*sidikyolu/*
	ee-drahr-yoh-loo	*idraryolu*
	ehn-fehk-syohn	*enfeksiyon*
venereal disease	zyuh-reh-vee	*zührevi hastalık*
	hahs-tah-lihk	
worms	koort (lahr)	*kurt(lar)*

USEFUL PHRASES

I feel better/worse.
kehn-dee-mee dah-hah
ee-yee/ker-tyu
hees-seh-dee-yohr-room
*Kendimi daha
iyi/kötü hissediyorum.*

This is my usual medicine.
boo beh-neem
geh-nehl-deh
ahl-dih-ihm ee-lahch
*Bu benim genelde
aldığım ilaç.*

I have been vaccinated.
ah-shih-lahn-dihm
Aşılandım.

I don't want a blood transfusion.
kahn nah-klee
ees-teh-mee-yohr-room
Kan nakli istemiyorum.

Can I have a receipt for my insurance?
see-gohr-tahm
ee-cheen mahk-booz
ah-lah-bee-leer-mee-yeem?
*Sigortam için makbuz
alabilirmiyim?*

HEALTH

WOMEN'S HEALTH

I'm/You're pregnant.
geh-beh-yeem/
geh-beh-see-neez
Gebeyim/gebesiniz.

Could I be examined by a female doctor?
kahh-dihn dohk-tohr-
oon-dahn moo-ah-yeh-neh
eh-deh-bee-leer-mee-yeem?
*Kahdın doktorundan
muayene edebilirmiyim?*

I'm pregnant.
hah-mee-leh-yeem
Hamileyim.

I think I'm pregnant.
hah-mee-leh
ohl-doo-oo-moo
dyu-shyu-nyu-yohr-room
*Hamile olduğumu
düşünüyorum.*

HEALTH

I'm taking birth control medicine.
doh-oom kohn-trohl   *Doğum kontrol ilacı alıyorum.*
ee-lah-jih ah-lih-yohr-room

I haven't had my period for ... weeks.
... hahf-tah-dihr ah-deht   *... haftadır adet görmedim.*
ger-meh-deem

I'd like to get the morning-after pill.
ee-leesh-kee sohn-rah-sih   *İlişki sonrası kullanılabilen*
kool-lah-nih-lah-bee-lehn   *doğum kontol hapı istiyorum.*
doh-oom kohn-trohl hah-pih
ees-tee-yohr-room

I'd like to use birth control medicine.
doh-oom kohn-trohl   *Doğum kontrol hapı*
hah-pih kool-lahn-mahk   *kullanmak istiyorum.*
ees-tee-yohr-room

abortion	dyu-shyuk yahp-mahk/	*düşük yapmak/*
	kyur-tahzh	*kürtaj*
cystic fibrosis	leef-lée sees-teet	*lifli sistit*
cystitis	sees-teet	*sistit*
diaphragm	dee-yah-frahm	*diyafram*
IUD	spee-rahl	*spiral*
(intra-uterine device)		
mamogram	mehm-oh-grahm	*memogram*
menstruation	ah-deht/reh-glee	*adet/regli*
miscarriage	cho-jook dyu-shyu-meh	*çocuk düşürme*
Pap smear	pahp see-meer	*Pap simir*
period pain	ah-deht ah-rih-sih	*adet ağrısı*
the Pill	doh-oom kohn-trohl	*doğum kontrol hapı*
	hah-pih	
premenstrual	ah-deht-leh eel-gee-lee	*adetle ilgili gerilim*
tension	geh-ree-leem	
thrush	oh-rahl mahn-tahr	*oral mantar*
	hahs-tah-lih-ih/ahft	*hastalığı/aft*
ultrasound	ool-trah-soh-oond	*ultrasound*

HEALTH

USEFUL WORDS & PHRASES

Don't do it!	yahp-mah-yihn	*Yapmayın!*
bleeding	kah-nah-mah	*kanama*
blood pressure	(yyuk-sek/	*(yüksek/düşük)*
(high/low)	dyu-shyuk)	*tansiyon*
	tahn-see-yohn	
injection	ee-neh	*iğne*
('needle')		
operation	ah-meh-lee-yaht	*ameliyat*
pill	hahp	*hap*
vomit/to vomit	koos-mah/	*kusma/kusmak*
	koos-mahk	
x-ray	rernt-gehn	*röntgen*

HEALTH

SPECIAL HEALTH NEEDS

I'm ...	behn ...	*Ben ...*
diabetic	sheh-kehr hahs-tah-sih-yihm	*şeker hastasıyım*
asthmatic	ahs-tihm-lih-yihm	*astımlıyım*
anaemic	kahn-sih-zihm	*kansızım*

I'm allergic to ...	... ah-lehr-zheem vahr	*... alerjim var.*
antibiotics	ahn-tee-bee-yoh-tee-eh	*antibiyotiğe*
aspirin	ah-speer-reen-eh	*aspirine*
bees	ah-rih-lah-rah	*arılara*
codeine	koh-deh-yeen-neh	*kodeine*
dairy products	syut mahl-zeh-meh-leh-reen-neh	*süt malzemelerine*
penicillin	peh-nee-see-leen-neh	*penisiline*
pollen	poh-lehn-neh/ chee-chehk-toh-zoo-nah	*polene/ çiçektozuna*

I have a skin allergy.
deh-ree ah-lehr-zheem vahr — *Deri alerjim var.*
I've had my vaccinations.
ah-shih-lah-rih-mih ohl-doom — *Aşılarımı oldum.*
I have my own syringe.
kehn-dee shih-rihn-gahm vahr — *Kendi şırıngam var.*
I need a new pair of glasses.
yeh-nee beer gerz-lyu-eh eeh-tee-yah-jihm vahr — *Yeni bir gözlüğe ihtiyacım var.*

addiction	ah-lihsh-kahn-lihk/ teer-yah-kee-leek	*alışkanlık/tiryakilik*
bite	ih-sih-rihk	*ısırık*
blood test	kahn tahh-lee-lee	*kan tahlili*
condom	preh-zehr-vah-teef	*prezervatif*
contraceptive	geh-beh-lee-yeeh ern-leh-yee-jee	*gebeliği önleyici*

injection	ehn-zhehk-see-yohn	*enjeksiyon*
injury	zah-rahr/yah-rah	*zarar/yara*
vitamins	vee-tah-meen (lehr)	*vitamin(ler)*
wound	yah-rah	*yara*

HEALTH

ALTERNATIVE TREATMENTS

acupuncture	ah-koo-poonk-toor	*akupunktur*
herbalist	koh-jah-kah-rih heh-keem	*kocakarı hekim*
homeopathy	hoh-mee-oh-pah-tee	*homeopati*
massage	mah-sahzh	*masaj*
meditation	meh-dee-tah-syohn	*meditasyon*
yoga	yoh-gah	*yoga*

PARTS OF THE BODY

It hurts here.
boo-rah-sih ah-jih-yohr   *Burası acıyor.*

My ... hurts.	... ah-rih-yohr	... *ağrıyor.*
arm	koh-loom	*kolum*
back	sihr-tihm	*sırtım*
bone	keh-mee-yeem	*kemiğim*
breast	meh-mehm	*memem*
chest	ger-yus-yum	*göğüsüm*
ear	koo-lah-ihm	*kulağım*
eye	ger-zyum	*gözüm*
finger	pahr-mah-ihm	*parmağım*

LONG LIFE TO YOU!

Çok yaşa! Bless You! said to someone who has sneezed. Literally means 'long life!' and the sneezer should reply *Sen de gör!* (sehn deh gerr!) meaning 'And long life to you too!'

foot	ah-yah-ihm	*ayağım*
hand	eh-leem	*elim*
head	bah-shihm	*başım*
heart	kaal-beem	*kalbim*
knee(cap)	deez (kah-pah-ih)	*diz (kapağı)*
leg	bah-jaah-ihm	*bacağım*
neck	bohy-noom	*boynum*
nose	boor-noom	*burnum*
stomach	kahr-nihm	*karnım*
throat	boh-ah-zihm	*boğazım*
tooth	dee-sheem	*dişim*

AT THE CHEMIST

Most modern medicines are available in Turkey, made locally under license. Often the brand name is the same as in English or similar. The generic names of drugs are often similar as well – try the English word, and if that doesn't work, give it a French pronunciation. Modern medical terms often come into Turkish via French, as in **antibiotik** and **antijen**, or a favourite, **tantürdiyot** 'tincture d'iode' – tincture of iodine!

How many times a day?
    gyun-deh kach deh-fah?   *Günde kaç defa?*
Four times a day.
    gyun-deh dert deh-fah   *Günde dört defa.*
Once every six hours.
    hehr ahl-tih sah-aht-teh   *Her altı saatte bir defa.*
    beer deh-fah

GET WELL SOON!

ghehch-meesh ohl-soon!   Get well Soon.
Geçmiş olsun! (lit: let it pass)

You also use *geçmiş olsun* in any circumstance where
something unpleasant has happened to a friend.

Are there side effects?
    yahn eht-kee-see vahr mih?   *Yan etkisi var mı?*
I'm allergic to penicillin.
    Peh-nee-see-lee-neh   *Penisiline karşı alerjim var.*
    kahr-shih ah-lehr-zheem vahr

AT THE DENTIST

I have a toothache.
    dee-sheem ah-rih-yohr   *Dişim ağrıyor.*
I have a hole/cavity.
    dee-sheem-deh   *Dişimde çürük var.*
    chyu-ryuk vahr
I've lost a filling.
    dohl-goom dyush-tyu   *Dolgum düştü.*
I've broken my tooth.
    dee-sheem kih-rihl-dih   *Dişim kırıldı.*
My gums hurt.
    deesh eht-leh-reem   *Diş etlerim ağrıyor.*
    ah-rih-yohr
I don't want it extracted.
    dee-shee-mee   *Dişimi çektirmek istemiyorum.*
    chehk-teer-mehk
    ees-teh-mce-yohr-room
Please give me an anaesthetic.
    lyut-fehn nahr-kohz   *Lütfen narkoz verin.*
    veh-reen

| Ouch! | ahh | Ah! |

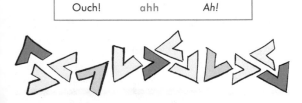

CROSSWORD

HEALTH

Across
2. keeps baby's food off baby's clothes (1st word)
5. conceited people have them on themselves
6. book for writing notes
7. that odd time of the day before night
8. cry for assistance

Down
1. wine, usually an aperitif
2. Mr T wore loads
3. someone you work with
4. packaging for letters home
5. pack them and go

Answers on page 260

DISABLED TRAVELLERS

I'm disabled/handicapped.
behn sah-kah-tihm

Ben sakatım

I need an assistant.
yahr-dihm-cih-yah
eeh-tee-yah-jihm vahr

Yardımcıya ihtiyacım var.

What services do you have for disabled people?
sah-kaht-lahr ee-cheen neh
sehr-vees-leh-ree-neez vahr?

Sakatlar için ne servisleriniz var?

Is there wheelchair access?
teh-kehr-lehk-lee
ees-kehm-leh gee-ree-shee
vahr mih?

Tekerlekli iskemle girişi var mı?

I'm deaf. Speak more loudly, please.
ah-eer doo-yoo-yohr-room.
lyut-fehn dah-hah yyuk-sehk
ses-leh koh-noo-shoo-nooz

Ağır duyuyorum. Lütfen daha yüksek sesle konuşunuz.

I can lipread.
doo-dahk oh-koo-yah-bee-lee-reem

Dudak okuyabilirim.

I have a hearing aid.
dooy-mah ah-leh-teem vahr

Duyma aletim var.

Does anyone here know sign language?
ee-shah-reht-leh koh-noosh-mah-sih-nih
bee-lehn vahr mih?

İşaretle konuşmasını bilen var mı?

| disabled person | sah-kaht een-sahn | *sakat insan* |
| wheelchair | teh-kehr-lehk-lee ees-kehm-leh | *tekerlekli iskemle* |

SPECIFIC NEEDS

GAY TRAVELLERS

Where are the gay hangouts?

gehy-leh-reen tehr-jeeh eh-dehn
yehr-leh-ree neh-reh-deh?

*Geylerin tercih eden
yerleri nerede?*

Are we/Am I likely to be harassed (here)?

beez/behn (boo-rah-dah)
tah-jeez eh-dee-leer-mee-yeez/
eh-dee-leer-mee-yeem?

*Biz/Ben (burada) taciz
edilirmiyiz/edilirmiyim?*

Is there a gay bookshop around here?

boo jee-vahr-dah gehy
kee-tahp-chih vahr mih?

*Bu civarda gey kitapçı
var mı?*

Is there a local gay guide?

mah-hahl-lee gehy
rehh-beh-ree vahr mih?

*Mahalli gey rehberi
var mı?*

Where can I find some gay/lesbian magazines?

neh-reh-dehn gehy/
lehz-bee-yehn dehr-gee-leh-ree
boo-lah-bee-lee-reem?

*Nereden gey/lezbiyen
dergileri bulabilirim?*

Is there a gay telephone emergency hotline?

gehy-lehr ee-cheen
ah-jeel yahr-dihm
haht-tih vahr mih?

*Geyler için acil yardım
hattı var mı?*

TRAVELLING WITH THE FAMILY

Are there facilities for babies?

beh-behk-lehr ee-cheen
koh-lah-yee-lihk vahr mih?

*Bebekler için kolaylıklar
var mı?*

Do you have a child minding service?

cho-jook bah-kihm
sehr-wee-see-neez vahr mih?

*Çocuk bakım servisiniz
var mı?*

Where can I find an (English)-speaking babysitter?

(een-gee-leez-jeh) koh-noo-shan
bah-kih-jih neh-reh-den
boo-lah-bee-leer-reem?

*(İngilizce) konuşan
bakıcı nereden
bulabilirim?*

Can you put an (extra) bed/cot in the room?
oh-dah-yah (eks-trah) beer
yah-tahk koh-yah-bee-
leer-mee-see-neez?
*Odaya (ekstra) bir
yatak Zkoyabilirmisiniz?*

I need a car with a child seat.
cho-jook kohl-took-loo
beer ah-rah-bah-yah
eeh-tee-yah-jihm vahr.
*Çocuk koltuklu bir
arabaya ihtiyacım var.*

Is it suitable for children?
cho-jook-lah-rah ooy-goon moo?
Çocuklara uygun mu?

Are there any activities for children?
cho-jook-lahr ee-cheen
ahk-tee-wee-teh-lehr vahr mih?
*Çocuklar için
aktiviteler var mı?*

Is there a family discount?
ah-yee-leh een-dee-ree-mee-neez
vahr mih?
Aile indiriminiz var mı?

Are children allowed to enter?
cho-jook-lahr
gee-reh-bee-leer mee?
Çocuklar girebilir mi?

Do you have a food suitable for children?
cho-jook-lah-rah
ooy-goon yeh-mehk vahr mih?
*Çocuklara uygun yemek
var mı?*

LOOKING FOR A JOB

Where can I find local job advertisements?
neh-reh-deh eesh-bool-mah
ee-lahn-lah-rih
boo-lah-bee-lee-reem?
*Nerede iş bulma
ilanları bulabilirim?*

Do I need a work permit?
chah-lihsh-mah eez-nee-neh
eeh-tee-yah-jihm vahr mih?
*Çalışma iznine
ihtiyacım var mı?*

I've had experience.
tehj-ryu-behm vahr
Tecrübem var.

I've come about the position advertised.
ee-lahn-dah-kee poh-zees-yohn
ee-cheen gehl-deem
*İlandaki pozisyon
için geldim.*

SPECIFIC NEEDS

I'm ringing about the position advertised.
ee-lahn-dah-kee poh-zees-yohn   *İlandaki pozisyon*
ee-cheen ah-rih-yoh-room   *için arıyorum.*

What is the wage?
neh mahsh   *Ne maaş veriyorsunuz?*
veh-ree-yohr-soo-nooz?

Will I have to pay tax?
vehr-gee   *Vergi ödeyecekmiyim?*
er-deh-yeh-jehk-mee-yeem?

I can start ...	... bahsh-lee-yah-bee-lee-reem	... *başlayabilirim*
today	boo-gyun	*Bugün*
tomorrow	yah-rihn	*Yarın*
next week	geh-leh-jehk hahf-tah	*Gelecek hafta*

Useful Words

casual	tehk-leef-seez	*teklifsiz*
employee	eh-leh-mahn	*eleman*
employer	pah-trohn	*patron*
full-time	fool-tahym/tahm-gyun	*fultaym/tamgün*
job, work	eesh	*iş*
occupation/trade	mehs-lehk/eesh	*meslek/iş*
part-time	pahrt-tahym	*parttaym*
resume/cv	er-zeht	*özet*
traineeship	stahzh/ee-sheh yeh-nee bahsh-lah-yahn keem-seh	*staj/işe yeni başlayan kimse*
work experience	eesh tehj-ryu-beh-see	*iş tecrübesi*

ON BUSINESS

We're attending a ...	... ee-cheen gehl-deek	... *için geldik.*
conference	tohp-lahn-tih	*toplantı*
lecture	kohn-feh-rahns	*konferans*
meeting	tohp-lahn-tih	*toplantı*
trade fair	tee-jah-reht foo-ah-rih	*ticaret fuarı*

I have an appointment with (Mr. Yılmaz).
(Bahy Yihl-mahz)'lah
rahn-deh-woom vahr
(Bay Yılmaz)'la randevum var.

Here's my business card.
eesh-teh beh-neem
kahrt-vee-zeet
İşte benim kartvizit

I need an interpreter.
tehr-jyu-mah-nah
ee-tee-yah-jihm vahr
Tercümana ihtiyacım var.

I need to use a computer.
beel-gee-sah-yahr
kool-lahn-mah-yah
ee-tee-yah-jihm vahr
Bilgisayar kullanmaya ihtiyacım var.

I want to send a fax/an email.
fahks/ee-mehyl
gern-dehr-mehk
ees-tee-yoh-room
Fax/E-meyl göndermek istiyorum.

Useful Words

cellular/mobile phone	jehp teh-leh-fohn	*cep telefon*
client	myush-teh-ree/	*müşteri/*
	myu-wehk-keel	*müvekkil*
colleague	mehs-lehk-tahsh/	*meslektaş/*
	eesh ahr-kah-dah-shih	*iş arkadaşı*
distributor	dah-ih-tih-jih/bah-yee	*dağıtıcı/bayi*
email	ee-mehyl	*e-meyl*
exhibition	sehr-gee	*sergi*
manager (director)	myu-dyur/	*müdür/*
	yer-neht-mehn/	*yönetmen/*
	meh-neh-zhehr	*menejer*
profit/earnings	kahr/kah-zahnch	*kar/kazanç*
proposal	er-neh-ree/tehk-leef	*öneri/teklif*

ON TOUR

We're touring with a group.
goo-roo-booy-leh	*Gurubuyle geziyoruz*
geh-zee-yohr-rooz	

We're on a tour.
toor-dah-yihz	*Tur'dayız.*

I'm ...	behn ...	*Ben ...*
with the group	goo-roo-booy-lah-yihm	*gurubuylayım.*
with the band	myu-zeek goo-roo-boo-lah-yihm	*müzik gurubuylayım.*
with the team	tah-kih-mih-yee-lah-yihm	*takımıylayım.*
with the crew (yacht, ship)	tahy-fah-sih-yee-lah-yihm	*tayfasıylayım.*
with the crew (film, etc.)	eh-kee-beey-leh-yeem	*ekibiyleyim.*

Please speak with our manager.

lyut-fehn meh-neh-zheh-ree-meez-leh koh-noo-shoo-nooz
Lütfen menejerimizle konuşunuz.

We've lost our equipment.

geh-rehch-leh-ree-mee-zee kahy-beht-teek
Gereçlerimizi kaybettik

We sent equipment on this ...	geh-rehch-leh-ree-mee-zee boo ... yohl-lah-dihk	*Gereçlerimizi bu ... yolladık.*
flight	oo-chahk-lah	*uçakla*
train	trehn-leh	*trenle*
bus	oh-toh-byus-leh	*otobüsle*

SPECIFIC NEEDS

PILGRIMAGE & RELIGION

Are you a ...?	... mih-sih-nihz?	*... mısınız?*
Christian	hrees-tee-yahn	*Hristiyan*
Buddhist	boo-deest	*Budist*
Catholic	kah-toh-leek	*Katolik*
Jew	moo-seh-vee	*Musevi*
Muslim	myu-slyu-mahn	*Müslüman*
Protestant	proh-tehs-tahn	*Protestan*

Can I participate in this service/mass?

boo ah-yee-neh/ee-bah-deh-teh kah-tih-lah-bee-leer-mee-yeem?
Bu ayine/ibadete katılabilirmiyim?

Can I pray here?

boo-rah-dah doo-ah eh-deh-bee-leer-mee-yee?
Burada dua edebilirmiyim?

Where can I pray/worship?

neh-reh-deh doo-ah ehj-deh-bee-lee-reem?
Nerede dua edebilirim?

Can I receive communion here?

boo-rah-dah koh-myun-yohn ah-lah-bee-leer-mee-yeem?
Burada komünyon alabilirmiyim?

religious procession	deen-dahr ah-lah-yih	*dindar alayı*
sacraments	koot-sahl eesh-lehm-lehr	*kutsal işlemler*
shrine	tah-pih-nahk	*tapınak*

TRACING ROOTS & HISTORY

I think my ancestors came from this area.
    beh-neem ah-tah-lah-rihm   *Benim atalarım*
    boo-rah-lahr-dahn   *buralardan gelmişler.*
    gehl-meesh-lehr

I'm looking for my relatives.
    ahk-rah-bah-lah-rih-mih   *Akrabalarımı arıyorum.*
    ah-rih-yoh-room

Is there anyone here by the name of ...?
    boo-rah-lahr-dah   *Buralarda ... soyadında*
    ... sohy-ah-dihn-dah   *birileri var mı?*
    bee-ree-leh-ree vahr mih?

I have/had a relative who lives/lived around here.
    boo-rah-lahr-dah   *Buralarda bir akrabam*
    beer ah-krah-bahm   *oturur/otururdu.*
    oh-too-roor/oh-toor-oor-doo

I think he fought/died near here.
    oh boo-rah-lahr-dah   *O buralarda*
    sah-vahsh-tih/erl-dyu   *savaştı/öldü.*

My father/grandfather fought/died here in WWI.
    bee-reen-jee dyun-yah   *Birinci dünya*
    sah-vah-shin-dah bah-bahm/   *savaşında babam/*
    byu-yyuk-bah-bahm boo-rah-   *büyükbabam burada*
    dah sah-vahsh-tih/erl-dyu   *savaştı/öldü.*

TIMES, DATES & FESTIVALS

TELLING THE TIME

Turks use both the 12-hour and 24-hour clocks, as in Europe. The 24-hour clock is the more formal system used in print and conversation. The 12-hour system is more casual. Time is easy if it's 'on the hour' or 'half past'. Just say *saat* (hour) and the number, or in the case of half past, the number plus *buçuk*. Other times are more complicated. For present time, use the hour, the minutes, and ... *geçiyor* (... is passing) or ... *kalıyor* (... is remaining). For a past or future time, use *geçe* and *kala* instead. Either *on beş* (15) or *çeyrek* (quarter) can be used to say 'fifteen past' or 'quarter to', etc. (See page 183 for numbers.)

What time is it? (lit: how many hours?)
    sah-aht kahch?   *Saat kaç?*

It's 8 o'clock.
    sah-aht seh-keez   *Saat sekiz.*

It's half past three. (hour three-one half)
    sah-aht yuch-boo-chook   *Saat üç buçuk.*

It's 14.15.
    sah-aht ohn der-dyu   *Saat on dördü*
    ohn-bhesh geh-chee-yohr   *on beş geçiyor.*

It's 20 to 12.
    sah-aht ohn ee-kee-yeh   *Saat on ikiye yirmi*
    yeer-mee kah-lih-yohr   *kalıyor.*

The bus leaves at 6.10.
    oh-toh byus sah-aht   *Otobüs saat altıyı on*
    ahl-tih-yih ohn geh-cheh   *geçe kalkar.*
    kahl-kahr

The train should arrive at 18 minutes to seven.
    trehn sah-aht yeh-dee-yeh   *Tren saat yediye on sekiz*
    ohn seh-keez kah-lah   *kala gelmeli.*
    gehl-meh-lee

DAYS

day	gyun	*gün*
week	hahf-tah	*hafta*
Sunday	pah-zahr	*pazar*
Monday	pah-zahr-teh-see	*pazartesi*
Tuesday	sah-lih	*salı*
Wednesday	char-shahm-bah	*çarşamba*
Thursday	pehr-shehm-beh	*perşembe*
Friday	joo-mah	*cuma*
Saturday	joo-mahr-teh-see	*cumartesi*

MONTHS

month	ahy	*ay*
year	seh-neh/yihl	*sene/yıl*
January	oh-jahk	*ocak*
February	shoo-baht	*şubat*
March	mahrt	*mart*
April	nee-sahn	*nisan*
May	mah-yihs	*mayıs*
June	hah-zee-rahn	*haziran*
July	tehm-mooz	*temmuz*
August	ah-oos-tohs	*ağustos*
September	ehy-lyul	*eylül*
October	eh-keem	*ekim*
November	kah-sihm	*kasım*
December	ah-rah-lihk	*aralık*

SEASONS

Spring	eelk-bah-hahr	*ilkbahar*
Summer	yahz	*yaz*
Autumn/Fall	sohn-bah-hahr	*sonbahar*
Winter	kihsh	*kış*

DATES

Note that the Muslim religious 'day', like the Jewish one, begins at sundown, not at midnight, so a festival to be held on the 25th of the month will run from sundown on the 24th to sundown on the 25th. Also, as with Jewish holidays, many shops and offices in Turkey close for the afternoon before the holiday, called the 'eve' (*arife*, ah-ree-feh).

What's today's date?
(lit: today the-month's how-many)
   boo-gyun ah-yihn kah-chih?   *Bugün ayın kaçı?*
Today is the eighteenth.
(lit: today the-month's-eighteenth)
   boo-gyun ah-yihn   *Bugün ayın onsekizinci.*
   ohn-seh-kee-zeen-jee
Today is 23 July.
(lit: today 23 July)
   boo-gyun yeer-mee-yuch   *Bugün yirmiüç temmuz.*
   tehm-mooz

PRESENT

When?
   neh zah-mahn?   *Ne zaman?*
What day is it today?
   boo-gyun hahn-gee gyun?   *Bugün hangi gün?*
Today is Tuesday.
(lit: Tuesday-day)
   boo gyun sah-lih gyu-nyu   *Bugün salı günü.*

TIMES, DATES
& FESTIVALS

now	sheem-dee	*şimdi*
today	boo-gyun	*bugün*
in the morning	sah-bahh-leh-yeen	*sabahleyin*
in the afternoon	er-leh-dehn sohn-rah	*öğleden sonra*
in the evening	ahk-shahm-dah	*akşamda*
at night	geh-jeh-leh-yeen	*geceleyin*
early/late	ehr-kehn/gech	*erken/geç*
this week	boo hahf-tah	*bu hafta*
this month	boo ahy	*bu ay*
every hour/	hehr sah-aht/	*her saat/*
day/month	gyun/ahy	*gün/ay*

PAST

five hours and 35	behsh sah-aht	*beş saat otuz*
minutes before	oh-tooz besh	*beş dakika*
	dah-kee-kah	*evvel*
	ehv-vehl	
nine hours	doh-kooz	*dokuz saattan*
afterwards	sah-aht-tahn	*sonra*
	sohn-rah	
yesterday	dyun	*dün*
last week	geh-chen hahf-tah	*geçen hafta*
last month	geh-chen ahy	*geçen ay*

FUTURE

In 20 minutes.
   yeer-mee dah-kee-kah-dah   *Yirmi dakikada.*
Nine hours from now.
   doh-kooz sah-aht sohn-rah   *Dokuz saat sonra.*
How many hours does it take?
   Kahch sah-aht syu-rehr?   *Kaç saat sürer?*
It takes ... hours.
   ... sah-aht syu-rehr   *... saat sürer.*
It takes ... minutes.
   ... dah-kee-kah/   *... dakika/dakka sürer.*
   dahk-kah syu-rehr

TIMES, DATES & FESTIVALS

When will you come (back)?
neh zah-mahn   *Ne zaman geleceksiniz?*
geh-leh-jehk-see-neez?
When will it be ready?
neh zah-mahn hah-zihr   *Ne zaman hazır olacak?*
oh-lah-jahk?
I'll stay for four days/weeks.
behn det gyun/hahf-tah   *Ben dört gün/hafta*
kah-lah-jah-ihm   *kalacağım.*

tomorrow
yahr-ihn   *yarın*
soon/right away
yah-kihn-dah/heh-mehn   *yakında/hemen*
next week/month
geh-leh-jehk hahf-tah/ahy   *gelecek hafta/ay*

During the Day

morning	sah-bahh	*sabah*
afternoon	er-leh-dehn sohn-rah	*öğleden sonra*
evening	ahk-shahm	*akşam*
night	geh-jeh	*gece*
hour	sah-aht	*saat*
minute	dah-kee-kah/dahk-kah	*dakika/dakka*
second (time)	sah-nee-yeh	*saniye*
sometimes	bah-zehn	*bazen*
fast/slow	chah-book/yah-wahsh	*çabuk/yavaş*

FESTIVALS (OFFICIAL NATIONAL HOLIDAYS)

- *Yılbaşı*

  yihl-bah-shih

  New Years Day always 1 January

- *Ramazan Bayramı* (rah-mah-zahn bahy-rah-mih) also known as *Şeker Bayramı* (sheh-kehr bahy-rah-mih)

  The 'Sweets' Bayram marks the end of the Islamic 'fasting' month of Ramazan. It occurs at a different time each year, due to the difference between the Islamic and Gregorian calendars.

- *Kurban Bayramı*

  koor-bahn bahy-rah-mih

  'Sacrifice' Festival.

  Like Ramazan/Şeker Bayramı, it occurs at a different time each year due to the difference between the Islamic and Gregorian calendars. Still, it always occurs two Islamic calendar months after Ramazan/Şeker Bayramı. This Festival has it's origin in the story of Abraham, Ishmael (Isaac in the Hebrew Bible) and the sacrificial lamb.

- *Ulusal Egemenlik ve Çocuk Bayramı*

  oo-loo-sahl eh-geh-mehn-leek weh cho-jook bahy-rah-mih

  National Independence and Children's Festival 23 April

• *Atatürk'ü Anma, Gençlik ve Spor Bayramı*
  ah-tah-tyu-kyu ahn-mah gehnch-leek weh spohr bahy-rah-mih
  A festival with a combined purpose – to honor Atatürk, Modern Turkey's Founder, and to celebrate Youth and Sports 19 May

• *Zafer Bayramı*
  sah-fehr bahy-rah-mih
  'Victory' Festival for the Turkish War of Independence on 30 August, 1922

• *Cumhuriyet Bayramı*
  joom-hoo-ree-yeht bahy-rah-mih
  Turkish Republic Day Festival 29 October

Festive Expressions

İyi Seneler
  ee-yee seh-neh-lehr

New Years –
Good wishes for the year

İyi Bayramlar
  ee-yee bahy-rahm-lahr

Ramazan and Kurban Festivals – Good wishes for the Festivals

Weddings

Congratulations!
  teh-breek-lehr!

Tebrikler!

Happiness to the groom and bride!
  dah-maht weh geh-lee-neh moot-loo-look-lahr!

Damat ve geline mutluluklar!

engagement	nee-shahn	*nişan*
honeymoon	bah-lah-yih	*balayı*
wedding	dyu-yun	*düğün*
wedding anniversary	ehw-lehn-meh yihl dyur-nyu-myu	*evlenme yıl dönümü*

| wedding cake | dyu-yun pahs-tah-sih | *düğün pastası* |
| wedding present | dyu-yun heh-dee-yeh-see | *düğün hediyesi* |

Toasts

To your honour! (sg)
   sheh-reh-feh!   *Şerefe!*

To your honour! (pl, pol)
   sheh-reh-fih-nee-zeh!   *Şerefinize!*

To your health! (pl, pol)
   sah-lih-ih-nih-zah!   *Sağlığınıza!*

While there is no 'baptism' in Islam, there is *sünnet* syun-neht, the celebration of circumcision when a boy reaches approximately 6 years of age. It marks his passing from early childhood.

NUMBERS & AMOUNTS

Once you learn the numbers from one to 10, plus 'hundred', 'thousand', and 'half', you can recognise or say any Turkish number, as all numbers are constructed simply of these building blocks.

CARDINAL NUMBERS

1	beer	*bir*
2	ee-kee	*iki*
3	yuch	*üç*
4	derrt	*dört*
5	besh	*beş*
6	ahl-tih	*altı*
7	yeh-dee	*yedi*
8	seh-keez	*sekiz*
9	doh-kooz	*dokuz*
10	ohn	*on*
11	ohn beer	*on bir*
12	ohn ee-kee	*on iki*
13	ohn yuch	*on üç*
20	yeer-mee	*yirmi*
30	oh-tooz	*otuz*
40	kihrk	*kırk*
50	ehl-lee	*elli*
60	ahlt-mihsh	*altmış*
70	yeht-meesh	*yetmiş*
80	sek-sehn	*seksen*
90	dohk-sahn	*doksan*
100	yyuz	*yüz*
101	yyuz beer	*yüz bir*
200	ee-kee yyuz	*iki yüz*
1000	been	*bin*
2000	ee-kee been	*iki bin*
10,000	ohn been	*on bin*
a million	meel-yohn	*milyon*

Turks tend to run the number words together into one huge word. In these examples the words are separated for easy recognition:

24	yeer-mee derrt	*yirmi dört*
159	yyuz ehl-lee doh-kooz	*yüz elli dokuz*
10,501	ohn been behsh yyuz beer	*on bin beş yüz bir*
346,217	yuch yyuz kihrk ahl-tih	*üç yüz kırk altı bin*
	been ee-kee yyuz ohn yeh-dee	*iki yüz on yedi*

ORDINAL NUMBERS

Ordinal numbers consist of the number plus the suffix *ıncı*, *-inci*, *-uncu* or *-üncü*, depending upon 'vowel harmony'. In writing an ordinal number, a full stop (.) abbreviates the suffix. Thus *birinci* and '1'. mean the same thing and are pronounced the same way, beer-een-jee.

first	beer-een-jee	*birinci*
second	ee-keen-jee	*ikinci*
sixth	ahl-tihn-jih	*altıncı*
thirteenth	ohn-yu-chyun-jyu	*onüçüncü*
fifty-eighth	ehl-lee-seh-keez-een-jee	*ellisekizinci*
hundredth	yyuz-yun-jyu	*yüzüncü*
hundred and	yyuz yeht-meesh-	*yüzyetmişyedinci*
seventy-seventh	yeh-deen-jee	

FRACTIONS

1/4	chehy-rehk	*çeyrek*
1/2 (when used alone, eg 'I want half')	yah-rihm	*yarım*
1/2 (with a number, eg 1 1/2)	boo-chook	*buçuk*

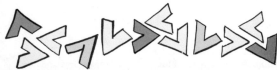

EMERGENCIES

Help!	eem-daht!	*İmdat!*
Watch out!	deek-kaht!	*Dikkat!*
Thief!	hihr-sihz!	*Hırsız!*

Stop!	doo-roon/door!	*Durun (pol)/Dur! (inf)*
Go away!	gee-deen/geet!	*Gidin (pol)/Git! (inf)*
It's an emergency.	ah-jeel doo-room	*Acil durum.*

Call (tell) the police!
  poh-lees-seh hah-behr veh-reen!   *Polise haber verin!*

(There's a) fire!
  yahn-gihn vahr!   *Yangın var!*
There's been an accident.
  beer kah-zah ohl-doo   *Bir kaza oldu.*

Could you help us please?
  bee-zeh yahr-dihm   *Bize yardım*
  eh-deh-bee-leer-mee-see-neez   *edebilirmisiniz lütfen?*
  lyut-fehn?
I'm lost.
  kahy-bohl-doom   *Kayboldum.*
Where are the toilets?
  too-vah-leht neh-reh-deh?   *Tuvalet nerede?*

HEALTH EMERGENCIES
I'm ill.
  rah-haht-sih-zihm   *Rahatsızım.*
My friend is ill.
  ahr-kah-dah-shihm rah-haht-sihz   *Arkadaşım rahatsız.*
I have medical insurance.
  sah-lihk see-gohr-tahm vahr   *Sağlık sigortam var.*

EMERGENCIES

Call an ambulance/a doctor!
> beer-jahn-koor-tah-rahn/
> dohk-tohr cha-ihr-ihn!

Bir cankurtaran/
doktor çağırın!

Find a doctor!
> dohk-toh-roo
> ah-rah-yihn/ah-rah!

Doktoru arayın (pol)/
ara! (inf)

Could I please use the telephone?
> teh-leh-foh-noo
> kool-lah-nah-bee-leer-
> mee-yeem lyut-fehn?

Telefonu
kullanabilirmiyim
lütfen?

DEALING WITH THE POLICE

Call the police!
> poh-lee-see chah-ihr-rihn!

Polisi çağırın!

Where is the police station?
> poh-lees kah-rah-koh-loo
> neh-reh-deh?

Polis karakolu nerede?

We want to report an offence.
> sooch eeh-bahr eht-mehk
> ees-tee-yohr-rooz

Suç ihbar etmek
istiyoruz.

I've been raped/assaulted.
> teh-jah-vyu-zeh/sahl-dih-rih-yah
> oo-rah-dihm

Tecavüze/Saldırıya
uğradım.

I've been robbed.
> sohy-ool-doom

Soyuldum.

My ... was/were stolen.	beh-neem ... chah-lihn-dih	Benim ... çalındı.
backpack	sihrt chahn-tahm	sırt çantam
bags	bah-gah-zhihm	bagajım
camera	kah-meh-rahm	kameram
handbag	ehl chahn-tahm	el çantam
guidebook	rehh-behr kee-tah-bihm	rehber kitabım

money	pah-rahm	*param*
papers	doh-kyu-mahn-lah-rihm	*dokümanlarım*
travellers cheques	seh-yah-haht chehk-lehr-reem	*seyahat çeklerim*
passport	pah-sah-pohr-toom	*pasaportum*
wallet	jyuz-dah-nihm	*cüzdanım*

My possessions are insured.
  ehsh-yah-lahr-rihm
  see-gohr-tah-lih-dihr

Eşyalarım sigortalıdır.

I'm sorry/I apologise.
  yuz-gyu-nyum/er-zyur
  dee-leh-reem

Üzgünüm/Özür dilerim.

I didn't realise I was doing
anything wrong.
  yahn-lihsh beer shehy
  yahp-tih-ih-mihn fahr-
  kihn-dah deh-eel-deem

*Yanlış bir şey yaptığımın
farkında değildim.*

I didn't do it.
  yahp-mah-dihm

Yapmadım.

We are innocent.
  mah-soo-mooz

Masumuz.

We are foreigners.
  yah-bahn-jih-yihz

Yabancıyız.

EMERGENCIES

I wish to contact my embassy/consulate.

ehl-chee-lee-eem-leh/
kohn-soh-lohs-loo-oom-lah
teh-mah-sah gehch-mehk
ees-tee-yohr-room

*Elçiliğimle/Konsolosluğumla
temasa geçmek istiyorum.*

Can I call someone?

bee-ree-see-nee ah-rah-
yah-bee-leer-mee-yeem?

Birisini arayabilirmiyim?

I want a lawyer who speaks English.

een-gee-leez-jeh koh-noo-
shahn ah-voo-kaht
ees-tee-yohr-room

*İngilizce konuşan
avukat istiyorum.*

I'd like to pay a fine to resolve this matter.

boo ee-shee hahl-leht-mehk
ee-cheen jeh-zah-sih-nih
er-deh-mehk ees-tee-yohr-room

*Bu işi halletmek için
cezasını ödemek istiyorum.*

Can we pay an on-the-spot fine?

jeh-zah-yih boo-rah-dah
er-deh-yeh-bee-leer-mee-yeez?

*Cezayı burada
ödeyebilirmiyiz?*

I understand.

ahn-lih-yohr-room

Anlıyorum.

I don't understand.

ahn-lah-mih-yohr-room

Anlamıyorum

I know my rights.

hahk-lah-rih-mih
bee-lee-yohr-room

Haklarımı biliyorum.

arrested	too-took-lahn-mihsh	*tutuklanmış*
cell	hyuj-reh	*hücre*
embassy/consulate	ehl-chee-leek/ kohn-soh-lohs-look	*Elçilik/Konsolosluk*
fine (payment)	pah-rah jeh-zah-sih	*para cezası*
guilty	sooch-loo	*suçlu*
lawyer	ah-voo-kaht	*avukat*

not guilty	sooch-sooz	*suçsuz*
police officer	poh-lees meh-moo-roo	*polis memuru*
police station	poh-lees kah-rah-koh-loo	*polis karakolu*
prison	hah pees-hah-neh/ jeh-zah-eh-vee	*hapishane/cezaevi*
trial	yahr-gih-lah-mah	*yargılama*

What am I accused of?
  neh ee-cheen
  sooch-lah-nee-yohr-room   *Ne için suçlanıyorum?*

The Police May Say

...-dehn doh-lah-yih yahr-gih-lah-nah-jahk-sih-nihz
  ...-den dolayı yargılanacaksınız.
  You will be charged with ...
oh ...-dehn doh-lay-yih yahr-gih-lah-nah-jahk
  O ...-den dolayı yargılanacak.
  She/He will be charged with ...

hyu-kyu-meht ah-lehy-hee-neh ger-steh-ree/hyu-kyu-meht
kahr-shih faah-lee-yeh-tee
  Hükümet aleyhine gösteri/hükümet karşı faaliyeti
  anti-government activity

bah-rih-shih bohz-mah/hoo-zoor vehr-meh-meh
  barışı bozma/huzur vermeme
  disturbing the peace

kah-chahk oo-yoosh-too-roo-joo sah-heep-leek
  kaçak uyuşturucu sahiplik
  possession of illegal substances

syu-reh-see gehch-meesh vee-zeh
  süresi geçmiş vize
  overstaying your visa

EMERGENCIES

trah-fee-eh kahr-shih gehl-meh
trafiğe karşı gelme
traffic violation

ee-zeen-seez chah-lihsh-mah
izinsiz çalışma
working with no permit

sahl-dih-rih	*saldırı*	assault
kah-chahk gee-reesh	*kaçak giriş*	illegal entry
jee-nah-yeht	*cinayet*	murder
vee-zeh-seez-leek	*vizesizlik*	no visa
teh-jah-vyuz	*tecavüz*	rape
hihr-sihz-lihk	*hırsızlık*	theft/shoplifting

A

able (to)
(verbal-suffix)
-eh-beel/ -ah-beel — *-ebil/ -abil*

Can I take your photo?
Rehs-mee-nee chehk-ch-bee-leer-mee-yeem?
Resmini çekebilirmiyim?

Can you show me on the map?
hah-ree-tah-dah ger-steh-reh-bee-leer-mee-seen?
Haritada gösterebilirmisin?

aboard	-deh/-dah/ -the/-tah	*-de/-da/ -te/-ta* (suffix)
above	yoo-kah-rih	*yukarı*
abroad	ohr-tah-lihk-tah	*ortalıkta*
accept	kah-bool eht-mehk	*kabul etmek*
accident	kah-zah	*kaza*
ache	ah-rih	*ağrı*
accommodation	kah-lah-jahk yehr	*kalacak yer*
across	kahr-shih kahr-shih-sihn-dah	*karşı karşısında*
addiction	ah-lihsh-kahn-lihk	*alışkanlık*
address	ah-dres	*adres*
admission	ee-tee-rahf	*itiraf*
to admit	ee-tee-rahf eht-meck	*itiraf etmek*
adult	yeh-teesh-keen	*yetişkin*
advice	nah-see-haht	*nasihat*
aeroplane	oo-chahk	*uçak*
afraid (of)	(-dehn) kork-mahk	*(-den) korkmak*
after	sohn-rah	*sonra*
afternoon	er-leh-dehn sohn-rah	*öğleden sonra*

this	boo	*bu*
afternoon	er-leh-dehn sohn-rah	*öğleden sonra*
again	tek-rahr	*tekrar*
against	kahr-shih	*karşı*
age	yahsh	*yaş*
(a while)	beer-ahz	*(biraz)*
ago	ern-jeh	*önce*
to agree	rah-zih	*razı*
	ohl-mahk	*olmak*
ahead	ee-leh-ree	*ileri*
AIDS	aidz	*AIDS*
air	hah-wah	*hava*
air-conditioning	klee-mah	*klima*
air mail	oo-chahk-lah	*uçakla*
airport	hah-wah-ah-lah-nah	*havaalanı*
airport tax	hah-wah-ah-lah-nah wehr-gee-see	*havaalanı vergisi*
alarm clock	chah-lahr sah-aht	*çalar saat*
all	hehp-see	*hepsi*
allergy	ah-lehr-zjee	*alerji*
allow	ee-zeen wehr-mehk	*izin vermek*
it's allowed	yah-sahk deh-eel (deer)	*yasak değil(dir)*
it's not allowed	yah-sahk-tihr	*yasaktır*
almost	heh-men	*hemen*
	heh-men	*hemen*
alone	yahl-nihz	*yalnız*
already	sheem-dee-dehn	*şimdiden*
also	dah-hee beer deh	*dahi bir de*
altitude	yyuk-sehk-leek	*yükseklik*
always	hehr-zah-mahn	*her zaman*

amateur	ah-mah-terr	amatör
ambassador	byyuk-ehl-chee	büyükelçi
America	ah-meh-ree-kah	Amerika
among	ah-rah-sihn-dah	arasında
ancient	ahn-teek	antik
and	weh	ve
angry	erf-keh-lee	öfkeli
animal	hahy-wahn	hayvan
annual	yihl-lihk	yıllık
another one	beer dah-hah	bir daha
answer	jeh-wahp	cevap
answering	jeh-wahp weh-rehn	cevap veren
antibiotics	ahn-tee-bee-yoh-teek	antibiyotik
antique	ahn-tee-kah	antika
antiseptic	ahn-tee-sehp-teek	antiseptik
any	hehr-hahn-gee beer	herhangi bir
appointment	rahn-deh-woo	randevu
archaeological	ahr-keh-oh-lo-zjeek	arkeolojik
architecture	mee-mahr-lihk	mimarlık
argue	tahr-tish-mahk	tartışmak
arm	kohl	kol
arrive	wahr-mahk	varmak
arrivals	geh-lehn-lehr	gelenler
art	sah-naht	sanat
art gallery	sah-naht gah-leh-ree-see	sanat galerisi
artist	sah-naht-chih	sanatçı

artwork	(gyu-zehl) sah-naht-lahr	(güzel) sanatlar
ashtray	kyul tah-blah-sih	kül tablası
Asia	ahs-yah	Asya
ask (for something)	ee-steh-meck	istemek
(question)	sohr-mahk	sormak
asthmatic	ah-stihm-lah eel-gee-lee	astımla ilgili
atmosphere	aht-mohs-fehr	atmosfer
aunt (maternal)	tehy-zeh	teyze
(paternal)	hah-lah	hala
Australia(n)	ah-woo-strahl-yah (-lih)	Avustralya (lı)
automatic teller machine	bahnk-ah-mah-teek	banka-matik
autumn	sohn-bah-hahr	sonbahar
avenue	soh-kahk	sokak
awful	kohr-koonch	korkunç

B

baby	beh-behk	bebek
baby food	beh-behk mah-mah-sih	bebek maması
babysitter	choh-juk bah-kih-jih-sih	çocuk bakıcısı
back (body)	sihrt	sırt
at the back (behind)	ahr-kah-dah	arkada
backpack	sihrt chan-tah-sih	sırt çantası

bad	feh-nah	*fenah*
bag	chahn-tah	*çanta*
baggage	bah-gazh	*bagaj*
baggage claim	eh-mah-net	*emanet*
bakery	fih-rihn	*fırın*
balcony	bahl-kohn	*balkon*
ball	tohp	*top*
band (musical)	myu-zeek goo-roo-boo	*müzik gurubu*
bandage	sahr-hih	*sargı*
bank	bahn-kah	*banka*
banknotes	kah-iht pah-rah	*kağıt para*
bar	bahr	*bar*
barber	behr-behr	*berber*
basket	seh-peht	*sepet*
bath	bahn-yoh	*banyo*
bathe	bahn-yoh yahp-mak	*banyo yapmak*
bathing suit	mah-yoh	*mayo*
bathroom	bahn-yoh	*banyo*
battery (dry)	peel	*pil*
battery (car)	ah-kyu ah-kyum-yyu-lah-tuer	*akü akümülatör*
be	ohl-mahk	*olmak*
beach	plazh	*plaj*
beans	fah-sool-yeh	*fasulye*
beautiful	gyu-zehl	*güzel*
because	chyun-kyu	*çünkü*
bed	yah-tahk	*yatak*
bedroom	yah-tahk oh-dah-sih	*yatak odası*
beef	sih-ihr	*sığır*
beer	bee-rah	*bira*
before	ehv-weh	*evvel*
beggar	dee-lehn-jee	*dilenci*
begin	bahsh-lah-mahk	*başlamak*

behind	peh-sheen-dehn	*peşinden*
below	ah-shah-ih-dah	*aşağıda*
beside	yah-nihn-dah	*yanında*
best	ehn ee-yee	*en iyi*
better	dah-hah ee-yee	*daha iyi*
between	ah-rah-sihn-dah	*arasında*
bicycle	bee-seke-leht	*bisiklet*
big	byu-yyuk	*büyük*
bill	heh-sahp	*hesap*
bird	koosh	*kuş*
birth certificate	nyu-foos kah-ih-dih	*nüfus kağıdı*
birthday	doh-oom gyu-nyu	*doğum günü*
bite	ih-sih-rihk	*ısırık*
black	see-yahh	*siyah*
B&W film	see-yahh beh-yahz fee-lm	*siyah beyaz film*
blanket	bah-tah-nee-yeh	*battaniye*
bleed	kah-nah-mah	*kanama*
Bless you! (sneeze)	chohk yah-shah	*Çok yaşa!*
blind	kerr	*kör*
blood	kahn	*kan*
blood group	kahn groo-boo	*kan grubu*
blood pressure	tahn-see-yohn	*tansiyon*
blood test	kahn tah-lee-lee	*kan tahlili*
blue	mah-wee	*mavi*
to board	been-mehk	*binmek*
boat	kah-yihk	*kayık*
boat (motor)	moh-tohr	*motor*

body	wyu-joot	vücut
to boil	kah-yee-nah-mahk	kaynamak
Bon appétit!	ah-fee-yeht ohl-soon!	Afiyet olsun!
Bon voyage!	ee-yee yohl-joo-look-lahr!	İyi yolculuklar!
book	kee-tahp	kitap
to book	reh-zehr-wah-see-yohn yahp-mahk	rezervasyon yapmak
bookshop	kee-tah-beh-wee	kitabevi
boots	cheez-meh	çizme
border (frontier)	sih-nihr	sınır
bored	jahn sih-kihn-tih-sih	can sıkıntısı
boring	jahn sih-kih-jih	can sıkıcı
borrow	er-dyunch ahl-mahk	ödünç almak
both	ee-kee-see	ikisi
bottle	shee-sheh	şişe
bottle opener	shee-she ah-chah-jah-ih	şişe açacağı
bottom (location)	deep-teh	dipte
bowl	tahs	tas
box	koo-too	kutu
boy	oh-lahn	oğlan
boyfriend	ehr-kehk ahr-kah-dahsh	erkek arkadaş
bread	ehk-mehk	ekmek
to break	kihr-mahk	kırmak
breakfast	kahh-wahl-tih	kahvaltı
breathe	soh-look ahl-mahk	soluk almak

bribe	ryush-weht	rüşvet
to bribe	ryush-weht wehr-mehk	rüşvet vermek
bridge (n)	ker-pryu	köprü
bring	geh-teer-mehk	getirmek
Bring ...!	... geh-tee-reen	... getirin!
broken	kih-rihk	kırık
brother	ehr-kehk kahr-dehsh	erkek kardeş
brown	kah-weh-rehn-gee	kahve-rengi
bruise (n)	chyu-ryuk	çürük
bucket	koh-wah	kova
bug	ber-jehk	böcek
build (yah-pih)	yahp-mahk	(yapı) yapmak
building	bee-nah	bina
burn	yah-nihk	yanık
to burn	yahn-mahk	yanmak
bus	oh-toh-byus	otobüs
bus station	oh-toh-byus tehr-mee-nah-lee	otobüs terminali
bus stop	oh-toh-byus doo-rah-ih	otobüs durağı
business	eesh	iş
busker	soh-kahk myu-zees-yehn-ee	sokak müzisyeni
busy	mehsh-gyul	meşgül
but	ah-mah/ fah-kaht	ama/ fakat
butter	teh-reh-yah-ih	tereyağı
buttons	dyu-meh	düğme

buy — sah-tihn ahl-mahk — *satın almak*

I'd like to buy (a book).
(kee-tahp) ahl-mahk ee-stee-yoh-room
(Kitap) almak istiyorum.

Where can I buy a ticket?
neh-reh-dehn bee-leht ah-lah-bee-lee-reem?
Nereden bilet alabilirim?

C

café	kah-feh	*kafe*
calendar	tahk-weem	*takvim*
camera	kah-meh-rah	*kamera*
camera shop	foh-toh-rahf-chih	*fotoğrafçı*
to camp	kahmp yahp-mahk	*kamp yapmak*

Can we camp here?
boo-rah-dah kahmp yah-pah-bee-leer-mee-yeez
Burada kamp yapabilirmiyiz?

campsite	kahmp yeh-ree	*kamp yeri*
can (able to)	-eh-beel, -ah-beel	-ebil, -abil *(verbal suffixes)*

We can do it.
yah-pah-bee-leer-eez
Yapabiliriz.

I can't do it.
yah-pah-mahm
Yapamam.

can (aluminium)	(ah-lyu-meen-yoom) koo-too	*(alüminyum) kutu*
Canada	kah-nah-dah	*Kanada*

can opener	kohn-sehr-weh ah-chah-jah-ih	*konserve açacağı*
cancel	eep-tahl eht-mehk	*iptal etmek*
candle	moom	*mum*
car	ah-rah-bah	*araba*
cards	oh-yoon kah-ih-dih	*oyun kağıdı*
to care (about)	oo-moo-roon-dah ohl-mahk	*umurunda olmak*
(for someone)	-eh bahk-mahk	-e *bakmak*
Careful!	deek-kaht	*Dikkat!*
caring	bah-kahn	*bakan*
carpet	hah-lih	*halı*
carry	tah-shih-mahk	*taşımak*
carton	kahr-tohn koo-too	*karton kutu*
cash register	kah-sah	*kasa*
cashier	wehz-neh-dahr	*veznedar*
cassette	kah-seht	*kaset*
castle	kah-leh	*kale*
cat	keh-dee	*kedi*
cathedral	kah-teh-drahl	*katedral*
caves	mah-ah-rah	*mağara*
CD	see-dee	*CD*
celebrate	koot-lah-mahk	*kutlamak*
centimetre	sahn-tee-meh-treh	*santimetre*
ceramic	seh-rah-meek	*seramik*
chair	sahn-dahl-yeh	*sandalye*
champagne	shahm-pahn-yah	*şampanya*
chance	shahns	*şans*
to change	deh-eesh-teer-mehk	*değiştirmek*

change (money)	kahm-bee-yoh	kambiyo
changing room	soh-yoon-mah oh-dah-sih	soyunma odası
charming	hohsh	hoş
cheap	oo-jooz	ucuz
cheat (n)	yuch kah-iht-chih	üç kağıtçı
Cheat!	beh-nee doh-lahn-dihr-dihn!	Beni dolandırdın!
to check	kohn-trohl eht-mehk	kontrol etmek
check-in (reception)	reh-sehp-see-yohn	resepsiyon
Checkmate!	maht	Mat!
checkpoint	kohn-trohl nohk-tah-sih	kontrol noktası
Cheers!	sheh-reh-feh	Şerefe!
cheese	pehy-neer	peynir
chemist (pharmacy)	ej-zah-neh	eczane
chess	saht-rahnch	satranç
chest	ger-yus	göğüs
chicken	tah-wook	tavuk
child	choh-jook	çocuk
child-minding	choh-jook bah-kahn	çocuk bakan
children	choh-jook-lahr	çocuklar
chocolate	chee-koh-lah-tah	çikolata
choose	sehch-mehk	seçmek
Christian name	eelk ees-mee	ilk ismi
cigarette	see-gah-rah	sigara
cigarette papers	see-gah-rah kah-iht-lah-rih	sigara kağıtları
cinema	see-neh-mah	sinema
citizenship	wah-tahn-dahsh-lihk	vatandaşlık

city	sheh-heer	şehir
city centre	sheh-heer mehr-keh-zee	şehir merkezi
city walls	sheh-heer doo-wahr-lahr-ih	şehir duvarları
civil rights	een-sahn hahk-lahr-ih wah-tahn-dahsh-lihk hahk-lahr-ih	insan hakları
classical art	klah-seek sah-naht	klasik sanat
clean (adj)	teh-meez	temiz
cliff	ooch-oo-room	uçurum
climb	tihr-mahn-mahk	tırmanmak
cloakroom	wehs-tee-yehr	vestiyer
clock	sah-aht	saat
to close	kah-pah-mahk	kapamak
closed	kah-pah-lih	kapalı
clothing	geey-see-lehr	giysiler
clothing store	gee-yeem eh-wee	giyim evi
cloudy	boo-loot-loo	bulutlu
coast	sah-heel	sahil
coat	pahl-toh	palto
coffee	kahh-weh	kahve
coins	mah-deh-nee pah-rah	madeni para
cold (temperature) (ailment)	soh-ook nehz-leh	soğuk nezle
colleague	mehs-lehk-tahsh	meslektaş
college	koh-lejz	kolej
colour	rehnk	renk
comb	tah-rahk	tarak
Come!	geh-leen (-eez)	Gelin(iz)!

comedy	koh-meh-dee	komedi
comfortable	rah-haht	rahat
commerce	tee-jah-reht	ticaret
communist	koh-myyun-eest	komünist
companion	ahr-kah-dahsh/ yohl-dahsh	arkadaş/ yoldaş
company (business)	sheer-keht	şirket
(guests)	mees-ah-fihr	misafir
compass	poo-soo-lah	pusula
complaint	shee-kyah-yeht	şikayet
concert	kohn-sehr	konser
confirm (booking)	doh-roo-lah-mahk	doğrulamak
Congratulations!	teh-breek-lehr	Tebrikler!
conservative	too-too-joo	tutucu
constipated	kahb-zeh-teel-mehk	kabze tilmek
construction work	yah-pih eesh-ee	yapı işi
consulate	kohn-soh-lohs-look	konsolosluk
contact lenses	kohn-tahk-lehns	kontak-lens
contraception	geh-beh-leek-tehn koh-roon-mah	gebelikten korunma
contraceptives	geh-beh-lee-ee ern-leh-yee-jee kohn-sehr-wah-teef	gebeliği önleyici konservatif
contract	kohn-traht	kontrat
to cook	pee-sheer-mehk	pişirmek
cool	seh-reen	serin
cool (colloquial)	beer- sheh	bir şey

corner	ker-sheh	köşe
corrupt	ah-lahk-sihz	ahlaksız
to cost	fih-yah-tih	fiyatı
	ohl-mahk	olmak

How much does it cost to go to ...?
(eez-meer)'eh kah-cha gee-deh-bee-leer-eez?
(İzmir)'e kaça gidebiliriz?

It costs a lot.
chohk pah-hah-lih
Çok pahalı

cotton	pah-mook	pamuk
country (nation)	mehm-leh-keht	memleket
countryside	kihr	kır
a cough	erk-syu-ryuk	öksürük
count	sahy-mahk	saymak
court (legal)	mah-keh-meh	mahkeme
cow	ee-nehk	inek
crab	yehn-gech	yengeç
crafts	ehl sah-naht-lah-rih	el sanatları
crazy	deh-lee	deli
credit card	kreh-dee kar-tih	kredi kartı
creep (slang)	ah-shah-ih-lihk heh-reef	aşağılık herif
cricket	jihr-jihr-ber-jeh-ee	cırcır-böceği
cross (angry)	erf-keh-lee	öfkeli
crossroads	kahw-shahk	kavş\,ak
cuddle (n)	koo-jahk	kucak
cup	feen-jahn	fincan
cupboard	doh-lahp	dolap
curator	myu-zeh	müze
current affairs	gyun-jehl oh-lahy-lahr	güncel olaylar
customs (traditions)	gee-leh-nehk-lehr	gelenekler
(at airport)	gyum-ryuk	gümrük
to cut	kehs-mehk	kesmek

to cycle	bee-seek-leh-teh	bisiklete
cycling	bee-seek-leh-teh	bisiklete
cyclist	bee-seek-leht-jee	bisikletci
cystitis	sees-teet	sistit

D

daily	gyun-deh-leek	gündelik
dairy products	syut yu-ryun-leh-ree	süt ürünleri
damp	nehm-lee	nemli
to dance	dahns eht-mehk	dans etmek
dangerous	teh-lee-keh-lee	tehlikeli
dark (colour)	koh-yoo	koyu
darkness	kah-rahn-lihk	karanlık
date (appointment)	rahn-deh-woo	randevu
(in history)	tah-reeh	tarih
to date (someone)	flert eht-mehk	flört etmek
date of birth	doh-oom gyun-yu	doğum günü
daughter	kihz	kız
dawn	tahn	tan
day	gyun	gün
dead	erl-myush	ölmüş
deaf	sah-ihr	sağır
to deal	eesh yahp-mahk	iş yapmak
death	er-lyum	ölüm
decide	kah-rahr wehr-mehk	karar vermek
deep	deh-rehn	derin
deforestation	ohr-mahn-sihz-lahsh-tihr-mah	ormansızlaştırma
degree	deh-reh-jeh	derece
delay	geh-jeek-meh	gecikme
delicatessen	shar-kyut-teh-ree	şarküteri
delicious	neh-fees	nefis
delirious	sah-yihk-lah-yahn	sayıklayan
democracy	deh-moh-krah-see	demokrasi
dentist	deesh heh-kee-mee	diş hekimi
deny	een-kahr eht-mehk	inkâr etmek
deodorant	deh-oh-doh-rahn	deodoran
depart	hah-reh-keht eht-mehk	hareket etmek
department stores	(byu-yuk) mah-ah-zah	(büyük) mağaza
departure	gee-deesh kahl-kihsh	gidiş kalkış
desert	cherl	çöl
design	tah-sahr-rihm	tasarım
dessert	taht-lih	tatlı
destination	gee-dee-leh-jehk yehr	gidilecek yer
destroy	yohk eht-mehk	yok etmek
detail	ahy-rihn-tih	ayrıntı
diabetic	dee-yah-beh-teek	diyabetik
dial tone	(teh-leh-fohn-dah) cheh-weer seh-see	(telefonda) çevir sesi
diarrhoea	ees-hahl	ishal
diary	gyun-jeh	günce
dictionary	serz-lyuk	sözlük
to die	erl-mehk	ölmek
different	fahrk-lih	farklı
difficult	zohr	zor
dinner	ahk-shahm yeh-meh-yee	akş\,am yemeği

direct	dee-rehkt	*direkt*
dirty	pees	*pis*
disabled	sah-kaht	*sakat*
discount	een-deer-eem	*indirim*
discover	kehsh-feht-mehk	*keşfetmek*
discrimination	ah-yih-rihm	*ayırım*
disease	hah-stah-lihk	*hastalık*
disembark	een-mehk	*inmek*
to dive	dahl-mahk	*dalmak*
diving	dahl-gihch	*dalgıç*
equipment	tehch-hee-zaht	*teçhizat*
dizzy	bah-shih der-nehn	*başı dönen*
do	eht-mehk yahp-mahk	*etmek yapmak*

What are you doing?
neh yah-pih-yohr-soon?
Ne yapıyorsun?

I didn't do it.
yahp-mah-dihm
Yapmadım.

doctor	dohk-tohr heh-keem	*doktor hekim*
dog	ker-pehk	*köpek*
door	kah-pih	*kapı*
dormitory	yah-tahk-hah-neh	*yatakhane*
double	ee-kee mees-lee	*iki misli*
double bed	ee-kee kee-shee-leek yah-tahk	*iki kişilik yatak*
double room	(oh-tell-deh) cheeft yah-tahk-lih oh-dah	*(otelde) çift yataklı oda*
dozen	dyu-zee-neh	*düzine*
drama	drahm	*dram*
to dream	ryu-yah gerr-mehk	*rüya görmek*

dress (n)	ehl-bee-seh	*elbise*
drink (alcoholic)	eech-kee	*içki*
to drink	eech-mehk	*içmek*
to drive	(ah-rah-bah) soor-mehk	*(araba) sürmek*
driver's licence	eh-lee-yeht	*ehliyet*
drug (legal)	ee-lahch	*ilaç*
(illegal)	oo-yoosh-too-roo-joo	*uyuşturucu*
drug dealer	oo-yoosh-too-roo-joo sah-tih-jih-sih	*uyuşturucu satıcısı*
to be drunk	sahr-hohsh ohl-mahk	*sarhoş olmak*
dry (adj)	koo-roo	*kuru*
to dry	koo-root-mahk	*kurutmak*
dry cleaning	koo-roo teh-meez-leh-meh	*kuru temizleme*
dummy (pacifier)	ehm-zeek	*emzik*

E

each	hehr bëer-ee	*herbiri*
ear(s)	koo-lahk (-lahr)	*kulak(lar)*
early	ehr-kehn	*erken*
Earth	Dyun-yah	*Dünya*
earth (soil)	tohp-rahk	*toprak*
east	doh-oo	*doğu*
easy	koh-lah-yee	*kolay*
eat	yeh-mehk	*yemek*
economy	eh-koh-noh-mee	*ekonomi*
education	eh-ee-tihm	*eğitim*
egg	yoo-moor-tah	*yumurta*
electricity	eh-lehk-treek	*elektrik*

elevator	ah-sahn-serr	asansör
embarassed	oo-tahn-mihsh	utanmış
embassy	byu-yyuk-ehl-chee-leek	büyük-elçilik
emergency	ah-jeel doo-room	acil durum
employee	eh-leh-mahn	eleman
employer	pah-trohn	patron
empty	bohsh	boş\,
end	sohn	son
to end	bee-teer-mehk sohn wehr-mehk	bitirmek son vermek
endangered species	teh-lee-keh-yeh ah-tahn tyur	tehlikeye atan tür
engagement (marriage)	nee-shahn-lahn-mah	nişanlanma
engine	moh-tohr loh-koh-moh-teef	motor lokomotif
England	een-geel-teh-reh	ingiltere
to enjoy (oneself)	zehwk ahl-mahk	zevk almak
enough	yeh-tehr	yeter
to enter	geer-mehk	girmek
envelope	zahrf	zarf
environment	chehw-reh	çevre
epileptic	sah-rah-lih	saralı
equal opportunity	fihr-saht eh-sheet-lee-ee	fırsat eşitliği
equality	eh-sheet-leek	eşitlik
equipment	tehch-hee-zaht	teçhizat
Europe	ahw-roo-pah	Avrupa
evening	ahk-shahm	akş\,am
every day	hehr gyun	her gün

example	er-nehk	örnek
For example, ...		
... er-neh-een		
... örneğin		
excellent	myu-kehm-mehl	mükem-mel
exchange	deh-eesh-teer-meh	değiş-tirme
to exchange	deh-eesh-teer-mehk	değiş-tirmek
exchange rate	der-weez koo-roo	döviz kuru
excluded	-een dih-shihn-dah bih-rahk-mihsh	in dışında bırakmış
Excuse me.		
ah-feh-dehr-see-neez		
Afedersiniz.		
to exhibit	sehr-gee-leh-mehk	sergi-lemek
exhibition	sehr-gee	sergi
exit	chik-ihsh	çıkış
expensive	pah-hah-lih	pahalı
too expensive	chohk pah-hah-lih	çok pahalı
exploitation	serm yur-meh (kehn-dee chih-kahr-ih-nah) kool-lahn-mah	sömürme (kendi çıkarına) kullanma
express	ehk-spres	ekspres
express mail	ah-jeh-leh pohs-tah	acele posta
eye	gerz	göz

face (n)	yyuz	yüz
factory	fah-bree-kah	fabrika
to faint	bah-yihl-mahk	bayılmak

ENGLISH – TURKISH

English	Pronunciation	Turkish
fall (autumn)	sohn bah-hahr	son bahar
family	ahy-leh	aile
	ah-krah-bah-lahr	akrabalar
fan	wahn-tee-lah-ter	vantilatör
far	oo-zahk	uzak
farm	cheeft-leek	çiftlik
fast		
(speed)	chah-book	çabuk
(abstain from eating)	oh-rooch	oruç
fat		
(adj)	sheesh-mahn	şişman
(for cooking)	yah	yağ
father	bah-bah	baba
father-in-law	kah-yihn-peh-dehr	kayınpeder
faucet (tap)	moos-look	musluk
fault (someone's)	kah-bah-haht	kabahat
faulty	koo-soor-loo	kusurlu
fear	kohr-koo	korku
to fear	kohrk-mahk	korkmak
to feel		
(touch)	doh-koon-mahk	dokunmak
(emotion)	hees-seht-mehk	hissetmek
feelings	hees-lehr	hisler
fence	pahr-mahk-lihk	parmaklık
festival	feh-stee-wahl	festival
	bahy-rahm	bayram
	shehn-leek	şenlik
fever	ah-tehsh	ateş
few	ahz	az
fiancée/ fiancé	nee-shahn-lih	nişanlı
fiction	roh-mahn	roman
fight	kahw-gah	kavga
	der-wyush	dövüş
to fight	kahw-gah eht-mehk	kavga etmek
fill	dohl-door-mahk	doldurmak
film (negatives)	fee-lm neh-gah-teef	film negatif
(cinema)	fee-lm	film
(camera)	fee-lm	film
film speed	fee-lm hih zih	film hızı
filtered	fihl-treh-dehn geh-cheer-meesh	filtreden geçirmiş
to find	bool-mahk	bulmak
fine (n)	pah-rah	para
	jeh-zah-sih	cezası
finger	pahr-mahk	parmak
fire	ah-tehsh	ateş
firewood	oh-doon	odun
first	eelk	ilk
first-aid kit	eelk yahr-dihm koo-too-soo	ilk yardım kutusu
fish (n)	bah-lihk	balık
fish shop	bah-lihk-chih	balıkçı
flashlight	ehl feh-neh-ree	el feneri
flat (land etc)	dyuz	düz
flea	pee-reh	pire
flight (aeroplane)	oo-choosh	uçuş\,
floor	yehr	yer
floor (storey)	kaht	kat
flour	oon	un
flower	chee-chehk	çiçek
'flu	greep	grip

to follow		
(movement)	tah-keep eht-mehk	takip etmek
(comprehend)	ahn-lah-mahk	anlamak
food	yeh-mehk	yemek
foot	ahy-ahk	ayak
foot (measurement)	foot	fut
football (soccer)	foot-bohl	futbol
footpath	yah-yah yoh-loo	yaya yolu
for ...	ee-cheen	... için
foreign	dihsh	dış
foreigner	yah-bahn-jih	yabancı
forest	ohr-mahn	orman
forever	sohn-soo-zah kah-dahr	sonsuza kadar
to forget	oo-noot-mahk	unutmak
I forget.	oo-noo-toom	Unuttum
Forget about it!		
oo-noot geet-seen		
Unut gitsin		
forgive	ah-feht-mehk	affetmek
fork (utensil)	chah-tahl	çatal
fortnight	ee-kee hahf-tah	iki hafta
foyer	foo-ah-yeh	fuaye
free (not bound)	sehr-behst	serbest
(of charge)	beh-dah-wah	bedava
to freeze		
(something)	dohn-mahk	donmak
(feel cold)	dohn-door-mahk	dondurmak
fresh	tah-zeh	taze
friend	ahr-kah-dahsh	arkadaş\,

in front of	er-nyun-deh	önünde
frozen foods	dohn-doo-rool-moosh yee-yeh-jek-lehr	dondurulmuş yiyecekler
fruit picking	meh-weh tohp-lah-mah	meyve toplama
full	doh-loo	dolu
fun	eh-lehn-jeh	eğlence
for fun	zehwk ee-cheen	zevk için
have fun	zehwk ahl-mahk	zevk almak
make fun of	ah-lahy eht-mehk	alay etmek
funeral	jeh-nah-zeh ter-reh-nee	cenaze töreni
future	geh-leh-jehk	gelecek

G

game (sport)	mahch	maç
garage	gah-rahj	garaj
garbage	cherp	çöp
garden	bahh-cheh	bahçe
gate	kah-pih	kapı
gay	gehy	gey
	ehsh-jeen-sehl	eşcinsel
general	gehn-ehr-ahl	general
genuine	gehr-chehk	gerçek
German	ahl-mahn	Alman
Get lost!	tohz ohl	Toz ol!
gift	heh-dee-yeh	hediye
gig	beer eesh	bir iş
girl	kihz	kız
girlfriend	kihz ahr-kah-dahsh	kız arkadaş

give	wehr-mehk	vermek

Could you give me
(a glass of water)...?
(beer bahr-dahk soo)
wehr-eehr mee-see-neez?
(Bir bardak su) verir misiniz?

glass
(window)	jahm	cam
(drinking)	bahr-dahk	bardak
glasses (eye)	gerz-lyuk	gözlük
go	geet-mehk	gitmek

Let's go.
gee-deh-leem
gidelim

We'd like to go to ...
(eez-meer)'eh geet-mehk
ees-tee-yoh-rooz
(İzmir)'e gitmek istiyoruz

Go straight ahead.
doh-roo gee-dee-neez
Doğru gidiniz.

go out with.
ee-leh chihk-mahk
ile çıkmak

Go!	gee-deen	Gidin!
goal (score)	gohl	gol
goat	keh-chee	keçi
God	tahn-rih	Tanrı
	ahl-lah	Allah
good	ee-yee	iyi

Goodbye. (by person leaving)
ahl-lah-hah ihs-mahr-lah-dihk
allaha ısmarladık

Goodbye. (to person leaving)
gyu-leh gyu-leh hohsh chah-kahl
güle güle hoşça kal

Good afternoon.
ee-yee gyun-lehr tyun-ahy-dihn
İyi günler tünaydın

Good luck!
ee-yee shahns-lahr
İyi şanslar!

Good morning.		
gyun-ahy-dihn		
Günaydın.		
Good night.		
ee-yee ahk-shahm-lahr		
İyi akşamlar		
government	hyu-kyu-meht	hükümet
gram	grahm	gram
grandchild	toh-roon	torun
grandfather	deh-deh	dede
grandmother	ahn-neh-ahn-neh	anneanne
	neh-neh	nene
graphic art	grah-feek suh-naht	grafik sanat
grass	cheem	çim
Great!	hah-ree-kah!	Harika!
green	yeh-sheel	yeşil
greengrocer	mah-nahw	manav
guess	tah-meen eht-mehk	tahmin etmek
guest	mees-ah-feer	misafir
guide (n)	meeh-mahn-dahr	mihmandar
guide (person)	reh-behr kih-lah-wooz	rehber kılavuz
guide (audio)	serz-lyu rehh-behr	sözlü rehber
guidebook	reh-behr kee-tah-bih	rehber kitabı
guidedog	yohl ger-steh-rehn ker-pehk	yol gösteren köpek
guided trek	reh-behr-lee toor	rehberli tur
guitar	gee-tahr	gitar

H

hair	sahch	saç
hairbrush	sahch fihr-chah-sih	saç fırçası

half	yah-rihm	yarım
hallucinate	hah-yahl eht-mehk	hayal etmek
ham	jzahm-bohn	jambon
hammer	cheh-keech	çekiç
hammock	hah-mahk	hamak
hand	ehl	el
handbag	ehl chahn-tah-sih	el çantası
handmade	ehl ee-shee	el is\,i
handsome	yah-kih-shihk-lih	yakışıklı
happy	moot-loo	mutlu
Happy birthday!	moot-loo yihl-lahr	Mutlu yıllar!
harbour	lee-mahn	liman
hard	sehrt	sert
harrassment	tah-jeez-leek	tacizlik
hash (drug)	hah-sheesh	haşiş
hat/cap	shahp-kah	şapka
have	wahr	var
	sah-heep	sahip
	ohl-mahk	olmak

Do you have ...?
...wahr mih?
...var mı?

I have ...
beh-neem ... wahr
Benim ... var.

hayfever	bah-hahr ah-lehr-jee-see	bahar alerjisi
he	oh	o
head (n)	bahsh	baş\,
headache	bahsh ah-rih-sih	baş ağrısı
health	sah-lihk	sağlık
hear	dooy-mahk	duymak
hearing aid	koo-lahk-lih	kulaklı
heart	yyu-rehk	yürek
heat (n)	sih-jahk-lihk	sıcaklık
heater	soh-bah	soba

heavy	ah-ihr	ağır
Hello!	mehr-hah-bah	Merhaba
Hello! (answering telephone)	eh-fehn-deem	Efendim!
help	yahr-dihm	yardım
Help!	eem-daht	İmdat!
Help yourself.	boo-yoo-roon-(ooz)	buyurun (uz)
herbalist	beet-kee-jee	bitkici
here	boo-rah-dah	burada
heroin	eh-roh-een	eroin
heroin addict	eh-roh-een bah-ihm-lih-sih	eroin bağımlısı
high	oo-yoosh-too-roo-joo	uyuşturucu
to hike	oo-zoon yoo-roo-yoosh yahp-mahk	uzun yürüyüş yapmak
hiking	oo-zoon yyu-ryu-yyush yah-pahn	uzun yürüyüş yapan
hiking boot(s)	oo-zoon yyu-ryu-yyush ee-chin chiz-meh(lehr)	uzun yürüyüş için çizme(ler)
hiking route(s)	oo-zoon yyu-ryu-yyush ee-chin yohl(lahr)	uzun yürüyüş için yol(lar)
hill	teh-peh	tepe
to hire	kee-rah-lah-mahk	kiralamak
hitchhike	oh-toh-stohp yahp-mahk	otostop yapmak

204

HIV positive	aich-eye-wee poh-see-teef	HIV positif
holiday	tah-teel	tatil
homeless	ehw-seez	evsiz
homosexual	esh-jeen-sehl gehy	eşcinsel gey
honest	dyu-ryust	dürüst
honeymoon	bahl-ah-yih	balayı
horrible	myut-heesh	müthiş
horse	aht	at
hospital	hahs-tah-neh	hastane
hot	sih-jahk	sıcak
	soh-ook	sıcak

It's hot.
sih-jahk
Sıcak.

hotel	oh-tehl	otel
hour	sah-aht	saat
house	ehw	ev
housework	ehw eesh-ee	ev işi
How?	nah-sihl	Nasıl?

How do I get to (Istanbul)?
(ee-stahn-bool)'ah nah-sihl gee-deh-reem?
(Istanbul)'a nasıl giderim?

How do you say ...?
...'ee nah-sihl ser-leh-neer?
...'i nasıl söylenir?

How many?
kahch?
Kaç?

How much?
neh kah-dahr?
Ne kadar?

hug	koo-jahk-lah-mah	kucaklama
human rights	seen-sahn hahk-lah-rih	insan hakları
hungry	ah-jihk-mahk	acıkmak
husband (my)	koh-jah(m)	koca(m)

I	behn	Ben
ice	booz	buz
ice cream	dohn-door-mah	dondurma
identification (document)	keem-leek	kimlik
idiot	ah-mahk	ahmak
if	-seh/ -sah	se/ -sa (verbal suffix)
ill	hah-stah	hasta
immediately	heh-mehn	hemen

It's important.
er-nehm-lee
Önemli.

It's not important.
er-nehm-lee deh-eel
Önemli değil.

in a hurry
ah-jeh-leh ee-leh
acele ile

included	dah-heel	dahil
incomprehensible	ahn-lahsh-ihl-mahz	anlaşılmaz
India	heen-dee-stahn	Hindistan
indicator	gers-tehr-geh	gösterge
indigestion	hah-zihm-sihz-lihk	hazımsızlık
inequality	eh-sheet-seez-leek	eşitsizlik
infection	boo-lahsh-mah	bulaş\,ma
injection	ee-neh	iğne
injury	zah-rahr	zarar
insect	ber-jehk	böcek
inside	ee-chehr-deh	içerde
instructor	er-reht-mehn	öğretmen
insurance	see-gohr-tah	sigorta

intense	shee-deht-lee	şiddetli
interesting	eel-ginch ehn-teh-reh-sahn	ilginç enteresan
intermission	ah-rah	ara
international	oo-loos-lahr-ah-rah-sih	uluslararası
interview	gerr-ryush-meh	görüşme
itch	kah-shihn-tih	kaşıntı
itinerary	pee-lahn	plan

J

jail	jeh-zah-eh-wee hah-pees-hah-neh	cezaevi hapishane
jar	kah-wah-nohz	kavanoz
jealous	kihs-kahnch	kıskanç
jeans	jeen	cin
jeep	jeep	cip
jewellery	myu-jehw-heh-raht	mücevherat
job	eesh	iş
joke	shah-kah	şaka
to joke	shah-kah	şaka yapmak
journalist	gahz-teh-jee	gazeteci
journey	yohl-joo-look	yolculuk
judge	yahr-gihch	yargıç
... juice	soo-yoo	... suyu
jump	aht-lah-mahk	atlamak
jumper (sweater)	kah-zahk	kazak
justice	ah-dah-leht	adalet

K

key	ah-nah-tahr	anahtar
kick	tehk-meh	tekme
kill	erl-dyur-mehk	öldürmek
kilogram	kee-loh-grahm	kilogram
kilometre	kee-loh-meh-treh	kilometre
kind	cheh-sheet tyur	çeşit türtür
king	krahl	kral
kiss	er-pyu-jyuk	öpücük
to kiss	erp-mehk	öpmek
kitchen	moot-fahk	mutfak
knee	deez	diz
knife	bih-chahk	bıçak
to know (something)	beel-mehk	bilmek
(someone)	tah-nih-mahk	tanımak

I don't know.
beel-mehm
Bilmem.

L

lake	gerl	göl
lamp	lahm-bah	lamba
land	ahr-sah	arsa
language	deel lee-sahn	dil lisan
large	byu-yyuk	büyük
last	sohn	son
last night	geh-chehn geh-jeh	geçen gece
late	gehch	geç
later	sohn-rah	sonra
laugh	gyul-meh	gülme
laundry (clothes)	chah-mah-shihr	çamaşır

law	kah-noon	*kanun*
lawyer	ah-woo-kaht	*avukat*
laxatives	lahk-sah-teef myus-heel	*laxatif müshil*
lazy	tehm-behl	*tembel*
loaded (petrol/gas)	koor-shoon-loo behn-zeen	*kurşunlu benzin*
leader	lee-dehr	*lider*
learn	er-rehn-mehk	*öğrenmek*
leather	deh-ree	*deri*
ledge	rahf gee-bee dyuz chih-kihn-tih	*raf gibi düz çıkıntı*
to be left (behind/over)	bih-rahk-ihl-mahk	*bırakılmak*
left (not right)	sohl	*sol*
left-wing	sohl-joo	*solcu*
leg	bah-jahk	*bacak*
legislation	kah-noon yahp-mah	*kanun yapma*
lens	mehr-jehk	*mercek*
lesbian	lehz-bee-yehn	*lezbiyen*
less	dah-hah kyu-chyuk	*daha küçük*
letter (mail)	mehk-toop	*mektup*
liar	yah-lahn-jih	*yalancı*
library	kyu-tyu-pah-neh	*kütüphane*
lice	beet(lehr)	*bit(ler)*
to lie	yah-lahn sery-leh-mehk	*yalan söylemek*
life	hah-yaht yah-shahm	*hayat yaşam*
lift (elevator)	ah-sahn-serr	*asansör*
light(s)	ih-shihk (-lahr)	*ışık(lar)*
light (weight)	hah-feef	*hafif*
light bulb	ahm-pyul	*ampül*

lighter (cigarette)	chahk-mahk	*çakmak*
to like	beh-yehn-mehk	*beğenmek*
like (similar)	behn-zehr	*benzer*
line	chooz-gee	*çizgi*
lips	doo-dahk-lahr	*dudaklar*
listen	deen-leh-mehk	*dinlemek*
Listen!	deen-leh-yeen	*Dinleyin!*
little (amount)	ahz	*azaz*
(size)	kyu-chyuk	*küçük*
a little bit	bee-rahz	*biraz*
to live (life)	yahsh-ah-mahk	*yaşamak*
(somewhere)	oh-toor-mahk	*oturmak*
Long live ...!	yahsh-ah-sihn	*Yaşasın!*
local	yeh-rehl	*yerel*
local bus	beh-leh-dee-yeh oh-toh-byu-syu	*belediye otobüsü*
location	yehr mah-hahl	*yer mahal*
lock (n)	kee-leet	*kilit*
to lock	kee-leet-leh-mehk	*kilitlemek*
long	oo-zoon	*uzun*
long distance	sheh-heer-lehr-ah-rah-sih	*şehirlerarası*
long-distance bus	sheh-heer-lehr-ah-rah-sih oh-toh-byus	*şehir lerarası otobüs*
to look	bahk-mahk	*bakmak*
(after)	-eh bahk-mahk	*e bakmak*
(for)	-ee ah-rah-mahk	*i aramak*

loose change	boh-zook pah-rah	bozuk para
to lose	kahy-beht-mehk	kaybetmek
loser	kahy-beh-dehn keem-seh	kaybeden kimse
loss	zah-rahr	zarar
a lot	chohk	çok
loud	gyu-ryul-tyu-lyu	gürültülü
love (affectionate)	sehw-gee	sevgi
(romantic)	ahshk	aşk
lover	ah-shihk	aşık
	sehw-gee-lee	sevgili
low (price)	dyu-shyuk	düşük
loyal	sah-dihk	sadık
luck	tah-lee	talih
lucky	tah-lee-lee	talihli
luggage	bah-gahzh	bagaj
luggage	bah-gajz rah-fih	bagaj rafı
lockers	bah-gajz doh-lahp-lah-rih	bagaj dolapları
lump	pahr-chah	parça
lunch	er-leh yeh-meh-yee	öğle yemeği
lunchtime	er-lee tah-tee-lee	öğle tatili
luxury	lyuks shehy	lüks şey

M

mad (crazy)	deh-lee	deli
(angry)	erf-keh-lee	öfkeli
made (of)	dehn yah-pihl-mihsh	'den yapılmış
magazine	dehr-gee	dergi
mail	pohs-tah	posta
mailbox	pohs-tah koo-too-soo	posta kutusu

main road	ah-nah-yohl	anayol
main square	mehy-dahn	meydan
majority	choh-oon-look	çoğunluk
to make	yahp-mahk	yapmak
man/person	ah-dahm	adam
	een-sahn	insan
manager	myu-dyur	müdür
many	chohk	çok

Many happy returns!
moot-loo yihl-lahr, nee-jeh seh-neh-leh-reh!
Mutlu yıllar, nice senelere!

map	hah-ree-tah	harita

Can you show me on the map?
hah-ree-tah-dah ger-steh-reh-bee-leer-mee-seen?
Haritada gösterebilirmisin?

marijuana	mahr-ee-huu-ah-nah keh-neh-weer	marihuana kenevir
marital status	mey-dehn-ee hahl	medeni hal
market	pah-zahr	pazar
	mahr-keht	market
marriage	ehw-lehn-meh	evlenme
married	ehw-lee	evli

Are you married?
ehw-lee-mee-see-neez?
Evli misiniz?

I'm married.
ehw-lee-yeem
Evliyim.

marry	ehw-lehn-mehk	evlenmek
massage	mah-sazj	masaj
mat	hah-sihr	hasır
match (sport)	mahch	maç
matches	kee-breet	kibrit

208

It doesn't matter.
fahr-keht-mehz
Farketmez.

What's the matter?
neh wahr?
Ne var?

Just a minute.
beer dah-kee-kah
Bir dakika.

in (five) minutes
behsh dah-kee-kah sohn-rah
beş dakika sonra

mattress	der-shehk	döşek
maximum	ehn chohk	en çok
maybe	behl-kee	belki
mayor	beh-leh-dee-yeh bahsh-kah-nih	belediye başkanı
mechanic	mah-kee-neest	makinist
medicine	ee-lahch	ilaç
meditation	meh-dee-tahs-yohn	meditasyon
to meet		
(chance)	-eh rahst-lah-mahk	e rastlamak
(planned)	kahr-shih-lah-mahk	karşı lamak
member	yu-yeh	üye
menstruation	ah-deht	âdet
menu	meh-nyu	menü
message	meh-sazj	mesaj
metre	meh-treh	metre
midnight	geh-jeh yah-rih-sih	gece yarısı
migraine	mee-grehn	migren
military service	ahs-kehr-leek	askerlik
milk	syut	süt
millimetre	meel-ee-meh-treh	milimetre
million	meel-yohn	milyon
mind	ah-kihl	akıl
mineral water	mah-dehn-soo-yoo	maden-suyu
minimum	ehn ahz	en az
minute	dah-kee-kah	dakika

mirror	ahy-nah	ayna
miscarriage	choh-jook dyu-shyur-meh	çocuk düşürme
miss (some-one)	erz-leh-mehk	özlemek
mistake	yahn-lihsh	yanlış
mobile phone	jehp-teh-leh-foh-noo	cep telefonu
modem	moh-dehm	modem
moisturising cream	nehm-lehn-dee-ree-jee krehm	nemlendirici krem
money	pah-rah	para
month	ahy	ay
this month	boo ahy	bu ay
monument	ah-beh-deh ah-niht	abide anıt
moon	ahy	ay
more	dah-hah	daha
morning	sah-bahh	sabah
mosque	jah-mee	cami
mother	ahn-neh	anne
mother-in-law	kah-yihn-wah-lee-deh	kayın-valide
motorcycle	moh-tohr-seek-leht	motor-sikleto
to motorcycle	moh-tohr-seek-leh-teh been-mehk	motor-siklete binmek
motorway (tollway)	oh-toh-bahn	otoban
mountain	da	dağ
mountain hut	dah koo-lyu-beh-see	dağ kulübesi

mountain path	dah yoh-loo	dağ yolu
mountain range	dah seel-see-leh-see	dağ silsilesi
mountain-eering	dah-jih-lihk	dağcılık
mouth	ah-ihz	ağız
movie	fee-lihm	film
mud	chah-moor	çamur
Mum	ahn-neh-jee-eem	anneciğim
muscle	kahs	kas
museum	myu-zeh	müze
music	myu-zeek	müzik
musician	myu-zees-yehn	müzisyen
Muslim	myus-lyu-mahn	Müslüman
mutton	koh-yoon eh-tee	koyun eti

name (n)	ahd	ad
nappy	choh-jook beh-zee	çocuk bezi
nappy rash	choh-jook beh-zee ee-see-leek	çocuk bezi isilik
national park	meel-lee pahrk	milli park
nationality	meel-lee-yeht	milliyet
nature	doh-ah	doğa
nausea	boo-lahn-tih	bulantı
near	yah-kihn	yakın
necessary	geh-rehk-lee	gerekli
to need	-eh ee-htee-yah-jih ohl-mahk geh-rehk-lee ohl-mahk	e ihtiyacı olmak gerekli olmak

needle (sewing)	ee-neh dee-keesh	iğne dikiş
	ee-neh-see	iğnesi
(syringe)	shihr-ihn-gah	şırınga
neither ... nor ...	neh ... neh ...	ne ... ne ...
net	ah	ağ
never	heech beer zah-mahn	hiç bir zaman
new	yeh-nee	yeni
news	hah-behr	haber
newsagency	hah-behr ah-zjahn-sih	haber ajansı
newspaper(s)	gah-zeh-teh (lehr)	gazete (ler)
New Year's Day	yihl-bah-shih	Yılbaşı
New Year's Eve	yihl-bah-shih geh-jeh-see	Yılbaşı gecesi
New Zealand	yeh-nee zeh-lahn-dah geh-leh-jehk	Yeni Zelanda gelecek
next to	-een yah-nihn-dah	in yanında
next week	geh-leh-jehk hahf-tah	gelecek hafta
nice	hohsh	hoş
nickname	tahk-mah ahd	takma ad
night	geh-jeh	gece
no	hah-yihr	hayır
noise	gyur-yul-tyu	gürültü
noisy	gyur-yul-tyu-lyu	gürültülü
none	yohk	yok
noon	er-leh	öğle
north	koo-zehy	kuzey
nose	boo-roon	burun(-nu)
not ...	... deh-eel	... değil
notebook	dehf-tehr	defter

nothing	heech beer shehy	hiç bir şey
not yet	heh-nyuz deh-eel	henüz değil
novel (book)	roh-mahn	roman
now	sheem-dee	şimdi
number	noo-mah-rah	numara
nurse	hehm-shee-reh	hemşire

O

obvious	behl-lee	belli
offence	kah-bah-haht	kabahat
office	dah-ee-reh	daire
offside	ohf-sahyt	ofsayt
often	sihk sihk	sık sık

(note: make sure to pronounce the short ih instead of an ee sound in this word-sik sik (*seek seek*) means 'prick')

oil (cooking)	sih-wih-yah	sıvıyağ
oil (crude)	peh-trohl	petrol
OK	peh-kee tah-mahm	peki tamam
old (adj)	ehs-kee	eski
old (person)	yahsh-lih	yaşlı
olive oil	zehy-teen-yah	zeytinyağ
olive(s)	zehy-teen (lehr)	zeytin(ler)
on	-deh/ -dah	-de/ -da (suffix)
on time	zah-mah-nihn-dah	zamanında
once (one time)	beer deh-fah	bir defa
one-way (ticket)	tehk yern-lyu (bee-leht)	tek yönlü (bilet)
only	yahl-nihz	yalnız
open (adj)	ah-chihk	açık
to open	ahch-mahk	açmak

opening	ah-chih-lihsh	açılış
opera	oh-peh-rah	opera
operation (surgical)	ah-meh-lee-yaht	ameliyat
operator	oh-peh-rah-terr	operatör
opinion	ger-ryush	görüş
opposite	kahr-shih	karşı
or	weh-yah	veya
oral	oh-rahl	oral
orange (colour)	too-roon-joo	turuncu
to order (food)	ihs-mahr-lah-mahk	ısmarlamak
ordinary	sih-rah-dahn	sıradan
organise	dyu-zehn-leh-mehk	düzenlemek
orgasm	ohr-gah-zm	orgazm
original	oh-ree-zjee-nahl	orijinal
(the) other	er-byur	öbür
(an) other	bahsh-kah	baş\,ka
outer space	oo-zahy	uzay
outside	dih-shahr-dah	dış\,arda
over	yu-zehr-een-deh	üzerinde
overcoat	pahl-toh	palto
overdose	ah-shih-rih dohz	aşırı doz
to owe	bohr-joo ohl-mahk	borcu olmak
owner	sah-heep	sahip
oxygen	ohk-see-zjehn	oksijen

P

pacifier (dummy)	ehm-zeek	emzik
package	pah-keht ahm-bahl-azj	paket ambalaj
packet (cigarettes)	pah-keht (see-gah-rah)	paket (sigara)

padlock	ahs-mah kee-leet	asma kilit
page (book)	sahy-fah (kee-tahp)	sayfa (kitap)
pain	ah-jih	acı
painful	ah-rih-lih	ağrılı
pain in the neck	bahsh beh-lah-sih	baş belası
painkiller(s)	ah-rih kehs-ee jee(lehr)	ağrı kesici (ler)
to paint	boh-yah-mahk	boyamak
painter(artist)	rehs-sahm	ressam
painting(s)	reh-seem (-lehr)	resim(ler)
pair (n)	cheeft	çift
palace	sah-rahy	saray
pan	tehp-see	tepsi
paper	kah-iht	kâğıt
parcel	koh-lee	koli
pardon me	ahf-feh-dehr-see-neez	affedersiniz
pardon	pahr-dohn	pardon
parents	ah-nah bah-bah	ana baba
park (n)	pahrk	park
to park	pahrk eht-mehk	park etmek
parliament	pahr-lah-mehn-toh	parlamento
part	pahr-chah	parça
party (fiesta!)	pahr-tee	parti
(political)	pahr-tee	parti
pass	geh-cheesh	geçiş
passenger	yohl-joo	yolcu
passport	pah-sah-pohrt	pasaport
passport number	pah-sah-pohrt noo-mah-rah-sih	pasaport numarası
past	gehch-meesh	geçmiş

path	yohl	yol
to pay	er-deh-mehk	ödemek
payment	er-deh-meh	ödeme
peace	bah-rihsh	barış
pedestrian	yah-yah	yaya
pen	kah-lehm	kalem
penis	peh-nees	penis
penknife	chah-kih	çakı
people	een-sahn-lahr	insanlar
pepper	bee-behr	biber
percent	yyuz-deh	yüzde
performance	ger-steh-ree	gösteri
period pain	ah-deht ah-rih-sih	adet ağrısı
permanent	kah-lih-jih	kalıcı
permanent collection	kah-lih-jih koh-lehk-see-yohn	kalıcı koleksiyon
permission	ee-zeen	izin
permit	ee-zeen behl-gehy-see	izin belgesi
person	keem-seh kee-shee	kimse kişi
personality	kee-shee-leek	kişilik
to perspire	tehr-leh-mehk	terlemek
petrol	behn-zeen	benzin
pharmacy (chemist)	ehdj-zah-neh	eczane
phone book	teh-leh-fohn reh-beh-ree	telefon rehberi
phone box	teh-leh-fohn koo-loo-beh-see	telefon kulübesi
phonecard	teh-leh-fohn kahr-tih	telefon kartı

photo	foh-toh-rahf	fotoğraf
Can/May I take a photo?		
foh-toh-rahf chehk-eh-bee-leer-mee-yeem		
Fotoğraf çekebilirmiyim?		
photography	foh-toh-rahf-chih-lihk	fotoğrafçılık
to pick up	kahl-dihr-mahk	kaldırmak
pie	toor-tah	turta
piece	pahr-chah	parça
pig	doh-mooz	domuz
pill	hahp	hap
the Pill	doh-oom kohn-trohl hah-pih	doğum kontrol hapı
pillow	yah-stihk	yastık
pillowcase	yah-stihk yyu-zyu	yastık yüzü
pine	chahm	çam
pink	pehm-beh	pembe
pipe	boh-roo	boru
place	yehr	yer
place of birth	doh-oom yeh-ree	doğum yeri
plane (air)	uu-chahk	uçak
planet	geh-zeh-gehn	gezegen
plant	beet-kee	bitki
plastic	plah-steek	plastik
plate	tah-bahk	tabak
plateau	plah-toh	plato
platform (train/bus)	peh-rohn	peron
play (theatre)	sah-neh oh-yoon-oo	sahne oyunu
to play (a game)	ohy-nah-mahk	oynamak
(music)	chahl-mahk	çalmak
please	lyut-fehn	lütfen
plug (bath)	tih-pah	tıpa

plug (electric)	feesh	fiş
pocket	jehp	cep
poetry	shee-eer	şiir
poison (ous)	zeh-heer (-lee)	zehir(li)
police	poh-lees	polis
police officer	poh-lees meh-moo-roo	polis memuru
politics	see-yah-seht	siyaset
politicians	poh-lee-tee-kah-jih (-lahr)	politikacı (lar)
pollen	poh-lehn	polen
pollution	keer-leht-meh	kirletme
pool (swimming)	yyuz-meh hah-woo-zoo	yüzme havuzu
(game)	bee-lahr-doh	bilardo
poor	yohk-sool	yoksul
popular	poh-pyu-lehr	popüler
pork	doh-mooz eh-tee	domuz eti
port (sea)	lee-mahn	liman
possible	oh-lah-sih	olası
It's not possible.		
oh-lah-sih deh-eel		
Olası değil.		
to post	pohs-tah-lah-mahk	posta-lamak
post office	pohs-tah-neh	postane
postcard	kahrt-pohs-tahl	kartpostal
post code	pohs-tah koh-doo	posta kodu
postage	pohs-tah yuj-reh-tee	posta ücreti
post office	poh-stah-neh	postane

pot		
(ceramic)	cherm-lehk	çömlek
(drug)	mah-ree-hoo-ah-nah	marihuana
pottery	chah-nahk	çanak
	cherm-lehk	çömlek
poverty	yohk-sool-look	yoksulluk
power	gyuch	güç
prayer	doo-ah	dua
to prefer	tehr-jee eht-mehk	tercih etmek
pregnant	hah-mee-leh	hamile
prehistoric art	preh-hee-stoh-reek sah-naht	prehistorik sanat
pre-menstrual tension	ah-deht-leh eel-gee-lee geh-ree-leem	âdetle ilgili gerilim
to prepare	hah-zihr-lahn-mahk	hazırlanmak
prescription	reh-cheh-teh	reçete
present		
(gift)	heh-dee-yeh	hediye
(time)	shim-dee-kee (zah-mahn)	şimdiki (zaman)
president	bahsh-kahn	başkan
pressure	bah-sihnch	basınç
pretty	gyu-zehl	güzel
prevent	ern-leh-mehk	önlemek
price	fih-yaht	fiyat
pride	goo-roor	gurur
prime minister	bahsh-bah-kahn	başbakan
prison	hahp-ees-hah-neh jeh-zah-eh-wee	hapishane cezaevi

prisoner	too-took-loo	tutuklu
private	er-zehl	özel
private hospital	er-zehl hah-stah-neh	özel hastane
privatisation	er-zehl-lehsh-teer-meh	özelleştirme
to produce	mehy-dah-nah geh-teer-mehk	meydana getirmek
profession	mehs-lehk	meslek
profit	kahr	kâr
profitability	kahr-lih-lihk	kârlılık
program	proh-grahm	program
promise	serz	söz
proposal	er-neh-ree	öneri
prostitute	oh-rohs-poo	orospu
protect	koh-roo-mahk	korumak
protected forest	koh-roon-mah-lih ohr-mahn	korunmalı orman
protected species	koh-roon-mah-lih tyur	korunmalı tür
province	eel	il
public toilet	oo-moo-mee too-wah-leht	umumi tuvalet
pull	chehk-mehk	çekmek
puncture	paht-lahk	patlak
punish	jeh-zah-lahn-dihr-mahk	cezalandırmak
pure	sahf	saf
push	eet-mehk	itmek
put	kohy-mahk	koymak

Q

qualifications	nee-teh-leek-lehr	nitelikler
quality	nee-teh-leek	nitelik

214

quarantine	kahr-ahn-tee-nah	*karantina*
quarrel	kahw-gah	*kavga*
quarter (amount)	dett-teh beer	*dörtte bir*
(to/after the hour)	chehy-rehk	*çeyrek*
question (n)	soh-roo	*soru*
to question	soh-roo sohr-mahk	*soru sormak*
question (topic)	koh-noo	*konu*
queue	sih-rah	*sıra*
quick	chah-book	*çabuk*
quiet (adj)	sah-keen	*sakin*
quit	bih-rahk-mahk	*bırakmak*

R

rabbit	tahw-shan	*tavşan*
race (ancestry)	ihrk	*ırk*
	sohy	*soy*
racism	ihrk-chih-lihk	*ırkçılık*
radiator	rahd-yah-terr	*radyatör*
railroad	deh-meer-yoh-loo	*demiryolu*
railway	deh-meer-yoh-loo	*demiryolu*
railways	deh-meer-yoh-lah-rih	*demiryolları*
rain (n)	yah-moor	*yağmur*
rape	teh-jah-wyuz	*tecavüz*
rare (meat)	ahz peesh-meesh	*az pişmiş*
rash (n)	der-kyun-tyu	*döküntü*
rat	sih-chahn	*sıçan*
rate of pay	mah-ahsh	*maaş*
raw	chee	*çiğ*
razor	oos-too-tah	*ustura*

razor (electric)	trahsh-mah-kee-nah-eh-dehn	*neden*
receipt	mahk-booz	*makbuz*
to receive	ahl-mahk	*almak*
recent	yeh-nee	*yeni*
recently	sohn zah-mahn-lahr-dah	*son zamanlarda*
recognise	tah-nih-mahk	*tanımak*
recommend	tahw-see-yeh eht-mehk	*tavsiye etmek*
recording (audio)	kah-yiht	*kayıt*
recyclable	yeh-nee-dehn eesh-leh-meh soh-koo-lah-bee-leer	*yeniden işleme sokulabilir*
red	kihr-mih-zih	*kırmızı*
refrigerator	booz doh-lah-bih	*buz dolabı*
refugee	myul-teh-jee	*mülteci*
refund	geh-ree er-deh-meh	*geri ödeme*
to refund	geh-ree er-deh-mehk	*geri ödemek*
to refuse	kah-bool eht-meh-mehk	*kabul etmemek*
regional	berl-geh-sehl	*bölgesel*
registered mail	tah-ahh-hyut-lyu mehk-toop	*taahhütlü mektup*
to regret	peesh-mahn-lihk dooy-mahk	*pişmanlık duymak*
relationship (family only)	ee-leesh-kee ahk-rah-bah-lihk bah-ih	*ilişki akrabalık bağı*
relax	gehw-shehy-mehk	*gevşemek*

religion	deen	din
remember	hah-teer-lah-mahk	hatırlamak
remote	oo-zahk	uzak
rent	kee-rah pah-rah-sih	kira parası
to rent	kee-rah-lah-mahk	kiralamak
repairs	tah-mee-raht	tamirat
to repair	tah-meer eht-mehk	tamir etmek
to repeat	tehk-rahr-lah-mahk	tekrarlamak
Repeat!	tehk-rahr-lah-yihn!	Tekrarlayın!
reservation	reh-zehr-wahs-yohn	rezervasyon
to reserve (booking)	ah-yihrt-mahk reh-zehr-wahs-yon yahp-mahk	ayırtmak rezervasyon yapmak
respect	sahy-gih	saygı
the rest	kah-lahn meek-tahr	kalan miktar
to rest	deen-lehn-mehk	dinlenmek
restaurant	loh-kahn-tah	lokanta
return (comeback)	dern-mehk gee-deesh	dönmek gidiş
(ticket)	dern-yush bee-leht-ee	dönüş bileti
review (of book etc)	yeh-nee-dehn eh-lehsh-tee-ree	eleştiri
rhythm	ree-teem	ritim
rice (uncooked)	pee-reench	pirinç
(cooked)	pee-lahw	pilav
rich (wealthy)	zehn-geen	zengin
(food)	yah-lih	yağlı

to ride (a horse)	(aht) been-mehk	(at) binmek
right (correct)	doh-roo	doğru
right (side)	sah	sağ
to be right	hahk-lih	haklı

(followed by personal suffixes)

You're right.
hahk-lih-sih-nihz
Haklısınız.

Right now.
tahm sheem-dee
Tam şimdi.

right-wing	sah-jih	sağcı
ring (finger)	yyu-zyuk	yüzük
(sound)	chihn-lah-mah seh-see	çınlama sesi
(phone)	(teh-leh-foh-noon) chahl-mah seh-see	(telefonun) çalma sesi

I'll give you a ring.
sah-nah teh-leh-fohn eh-deh-jeh-eem
Sana telefon edeceğim.

rip-off	-ee doh-lahn-dihr-mahk	-i dolandırmak
risk	tehy-lee-keh	tehlike
river	neh-heer	nehir
road	yohl	yol
road map	yohl hah-ree-tah-sih	yol haritası
road sign	lehw-hah	levha
rob	sohy-mahk	soymak
rock	kah-yah	kaya
rock	kah-yah-yah	kayaya
climbing	tihr-mahn-mah	tırmanma
rock face	kah-yah-dahn bee doo-wahr	kayadan bir duvar

rock group	rohk myu-zeek goo-roo-boo	rock müzik gurubu
romance	ahshk	aşk
roof	chah-tih	çatı
room	oh-dah	oda
room number	oh-dah noo-mah-rah-sih	oda numarası
rope	hah-laht	halat
round	yoo-wahr-lahk	yuvarlak
route	yohl	yol
rubbish	cherp	çöp
rug	hah-lih	halı
ruins	hah-rah-beh	harabe
rules (of game)	koo-rahl-lahr	kurallar
run	kohsh-mahk	koşmak

S

sad	keh-dehr-lee	kederli
safe (adj)	ehm-nee-yeht-lee	emniyetli
safe (n)	kah-sah	kasa
safe sex	gyu-wehn-lee sex	güvenli seks
salary	mah-ahsh	maaş
(be on) sale	een-dee-reem wahr	indirim var
sales department	sah-tihsh deh-pahrt-mahn	satış departman
salt	tooz	tuz
same	ahy-nih tihp-kih	aynı/tıpkı
sand	koom	kum
sandal	sahn-dah-leht	sandalet
sanitary napkins	kah-dihn pehd-lehr	kadın pedler
save	koor-tahr-mahk	kurtarmak

say	sery-leh-mehk	söylemek
scarves	eh-sharp-lahr	eşarplar
scenery	mahn-zah-rah	manzara
school	oh-kool	okul
science	fehn	fen
scissors	mah-kahs	makas
to score	poo-ahn sahy-mahk	puan saymak
Scotland	ees-kohch-yah	I\.skoçya
sculpture	hehy-kehl	heykel
sea	deh-neez	deniz
seasick	deh-neez toot-mah-sih	deniz tutması
seaside	sah-heel	sahil
seat (bus/train)	yehr	yer
seat (safety) belt	ehm-nee-yeht keh-meh-ree	emniyet kemeri
second (time)	sah-nee-yeh	saniye
see	ger-mehk	görmek

We'll see!
ger-reh-jeh-eez!
Göreceğiz!

I see (understand).
ahn-lih-yoh-room ahn-lah-dihm
Anlıyorum anladım.

See you later.
ger-ryu-shyu-ryuz
Görüşürüz.

See you tomorrow.
yah-rihn ger-ryu-shyu-ryuz
Yarın görüşürüz.

selfish	behn-jeel	bencil
self-service	sehlf-sehr-wees	selfservis
sell	saht-mahk	satmak
send	gern-dehr-mehk	göndermek

sensible	mahn-tihk-lih	*mantıklı*
sentence		
(words)	jyum-leh	*cümle*
(prison)	hyu-kyum	*hüküm*
to separate	ah-yihr-mahk	*ayırmak*
serious	jeed-dee	*ciddi*
service (assistence)	heez-meht	*hizmet*
several	beer-kahk	*birkaç*
sew	deek-mehk	*dikmek*
sex	sex	*seks*
sexism	jeen-see-yeht	*cinsiyet*
	ah-yih-rih-mih	*ayırımı*
sexy	sehk-see	*seksi*
shade	gerl-geh	*gölge*
shadow	gerl-geh	*gölge*
shampoo	shahm-poo-ahn	*şampuan*
shape (form)	bee-cheem	*biçim*
share (with)	pahy-lahsh-mahk	*paylaşmak*
share a dorm	oh-dah pahy-lahsh-mahk	*oda paylaşmak*
shave	trahsh eht-mehk	*traş etmek*
she	oh	*o*
sheep	koh-yoon	*koyun*
sheet (bed)	chahr-shahf	*çarşaf*
sheet (of paper)	kah-iht-tahn beer	*kâğıttan bir*
	yahp-rahk	*yaprak*
ship	geh-mee	*gemi*
to ship	gern-dehr-mehk	*göndermek*
shirt	germ-lehk	*gömlek*
shoe lace	ay-yahk-kab-bih bah-ih	*ayakkabı bağı*
shoes	ah-yah-kah-bih	*ayakkabı*
shop	dyuk-kahn	*dükkan*
go shopping	ah-lishsh weh-ree-sheh cihk-mahk	*alış verişe çıkmak*

short		
(length)	kih-sah	*kısa*
(height)	kih-sah	*kısa*
	bohy-loo	*boylu*
shortage	ehk-seek-leek	*eksiklik*
shorts	shohrt	*şort*
shoulder(s)	oh-mooz(-lahr)	*omuz(lar)*
to shout	bah-ihr-mahk	*bağırmak*
to show	gerr-stehr-mehk	*göstermek*

Can you show me on the map?
hah-ree-tah-dah ger-steh-reh-bee-leer-mee-see-neez?
Haritada gösterebilirmisiniz?

shower	doosh	*duş*
shut (closed)	kah-pah-lih	*kapalı*
shy	oo-tahn-gahch	*utangaç*
sick	hahs-tah	*hasta*
a sickness	hahs-tah-lihk	*hastalık*
side	tah-rahf	*taraf*
sign (on) road	lehw-hah	*levha*
to sign	eem-zah-lah-mahk	*imzalamak*
signal (n)	ee-shah-reht	*işaret*
signature	eem-zah	*imza*
silk	ee-pehk	*ipek*
of silver	gyu-myush-tehn yah-pihl-mihsh	*gümüşten yapılmış*
similar	behn-zehr	*benzer*
simple	bah-seet	*basit*
since (May)	(mahy-ihs)	*(mayıs)*
	'tahn beh-ree	*'tan beri*
sing	shahr-kih	*şarkı*
	sery-lehl-mehk	*söylemek*
singer	shahr-kih-jih	*şarkıcı*
single		
person	beh-kahr	*bekâr*
room	tehk oh-dah-lih	*tek odalı*

sister	kihz kahr-dehsh	kız kardeş
sit	oh-toor-mahk	oturmak
size (clothes)	byu-yyuk-lyuk	büyüklük
(clothes)	beh-dehn	beden
(shoes)	noo-mah-rah	numara
skin	jeelt	cilt
sky	gerk	gök
to sleep	oo-yoo-mahk	uyumak
sleeping bag	ooy-koo too-loo-moo	uyku tulumu
sleeping car	yah-tahk-lih wah-gohn	yataklı vagon
sleeping pills	ooy-koo hah-pih	uyku hapı
sleepy	ooy-koo-loo	uykulu
slide (film)	slahyt	slayt
slowly	yah-wahsh yah-wahsh	yavaş yavaş
small	kyu-chyuk	küçük
a smell	koh-koo	koku
to smell	kohk-lah-mahk	koklamak
to smile	gyu-lyum-seh-mehk	gülümsemek
to smoke	eech-mehk	içmek
to smoke a cig-arette	see-gah-rah eech-mehk	sigara içmek
soap	sah-boon	sabun
soccer	fuut-bohl	futbol
socialist	sohs-yah-leest	sosyalist
social welfare	sohs-yahl reh-fah	sosyal refah
solid	kah-tih	katı
some (ina-nimate)	bah-zih	bazı
(animate)	kee-mee	kimi
someone	bee-ree beer-ee-see	biri birisi
something	beer-shehy	birşey
sometimes	bah-zehn	bazen
son	oh-ool (loo)	oğul (lu)
song	shahr-kih	şarkı
soon	yah-kihn-dah	yakında
I'm sorry.	yuz-gyu-nyum	Üzgünüm.
sound	sehs	ses
south	gyu-nehy	güney
South Africa	gyu-nehy ahf-ree-kah	Güney Afrika
souvenir	hah-tih-rah	hatıra
souvenir shop	hah-tih-rah dyuk-kah-nih	hatıra dükkanı
space	yehr	yer
speak	sery-leh-mehk	söylemek
special	er-zehl	özel
specialist	ooz-mahn	uzman
speed	hihz	hız
speed limit	ahz-ah-mee syu-raht	azami sürat
spicy (hot)	ah-jeh	acı
spoon	kah-shihk	kaşık
sport	spohr	spor
a sprain	boor-kool-mah	burkulma
spring (season)	eelk bah-hahr	ilk bahar
square (shape)	kah-reh	kare
(town)	mehy-dahn	meydan
stage	sahh-neh	sahne
stairway	mehr-dee-wehn	merdiven
stale	bah-yaht	bayat
stamp(s)	pool(-lahr)	pul(lar)
standard (usual)	nohr-mahl	normal
standard of living	yah-shahm stahn-dahr-dih	yaşam standardı
star(s)	yihl-dihz(lahr)	yıldız(lar)
start	bahsh-lah-mahk	başlamak
station	ee-stahs-yohn gahr oh-toh gahr	istasyon gar otogar
stationers	kihr-tah-see-yeh-jee	kırta-siyeci
statue	hehy-kehl	heykel

to stay		
(remain)	kahl-mahk	kalmak
(some-where)	oh-toor-mahk	oturmak
to steal	chahl-mahk	çalmak
steam	boo-hahr	buhar
steep		
(incline)	deek	dik
(price)	yyuk-sehk	yüksek
step	ah-dihm	adım
stomach	mee-deh	mide
	kah-rihn	karın
stomach-ache	mee-deh ah-rih-sih	mide ağrısı
stone	tahsh	taş
stoned	zohm	zom
(drugged)	oo-yoosh-too-roo-joo eht-kee-seen-deh oh-lahn	uyuş-turucu etkisinde olan
to stop	door-mahk	durmak
Stop!	doo-roon!	Durun!
storm	fihr-tih-nah	fırtına
story	hee-kah-yeh	hikâye
stove	fih-rihn	fırın
straight	doh-roo	doğru
strange	too-hahf	tuhaf
stranger	yah-bahn-jih	yabancı
stream	deh-reh	dere
street	soh-kahk	sokak
	jahd-deh	cadde
strength	koow-weht	kuvvet
string	eep	ip
stroll/walk	doh-lahsh-mah	dolaşma
strong	koow-weht-lee	kuvvetli
stubborn	ee-naht-chih	inatçı
student	er-rehn-jee	öğrenci
studio	styud-yoh	stüdyo
stupid	ahp-tahl	aptal
style (fashion)	moh-dah	moda

subtitles	ahlt-yah-zih	altyazı
suburb	wah-rohsh	varoş
suburbs of	bahn-lee-yer	banliyö
subway station	meh-troh ee-stahs-yoh-noo	metro istasyonu
success	bahsh-ah-rih	başarı
suffer	ih-stih-rahp chehk-mehk	ıstırap çekmek
sugar	sheh-kehr	s\,eker
suitcase	bah-wool	bavul
summer	yahz	yaz
sun	gyu-nehsh	güneş
sunblock	gyu-nehsh ehn-geh-lee	güneş engeli
sunburn	gyu-nehsh yah-nih-ih	güneş yanığı
sunglasses	gyu-nehsh gerz-lyu-yu	güneş gözlüğü
sunny	gyu-nehsh-lee	güneşli
sunrise	gyu-neh-sheen doh-mah-sih	güneşin doğması
sunset	gyu-neh-sheen baht-mah-sih	güneşin batması
I'm sure.	eh-meen-eem	Eminim.
surface mail	oo-chahk-lah ohl-mah-yahn pohs-tah	uçakla olmayan posta
surname	sohy-ah-dah	soyadı
surprise (n)	syur-preez	sürpriz
survive	hahy-aht-tah kahl-mahk	hayatta kalmak
sweet	taht-lih	tatlı
swim	yurz-mehk	yüzmek
swimming	yyuz-meh	yüzme
pool	hah-woo-soo	havuzu
swimsuit	mah-yoh	mayo
switch-board	teh-leh-fohn sahn-trah-lih	telefon santralı
sympathetic	sehm-pah-teek	sempatik
syringe	shih-rihn-gah	şırınga

T

table	mah-sah	masa
tablet (medicine)	hahp	hap
tailor	tehr-zee	terzi
to take	trehn ee-leh	tren ile
(train)	geet-mehk	gitmek
(photos)	foh-toh-raf chehk-mehk	fotoğraf çekmek
talk	koh-noosh-mahk	konuşmak
tall	oo-zoon	uzun
	bohy-loo	boylu
tampons	tahm-pohn	tampon
tap (faucet)	moos-look	musluk
taste	taht	tat
tasty	taht-lih	tatlı
tax	wehr-gee	vergi
taxi stand	tahk-see doo-rah-ih	taksi durağı
tea	chahy	çay
teacher	uer-reht-mehn	öğretmen
teeth	deesh(-lehr)	diş(ler)
telegram	tehl-grahf	telgraf
telephone	teh-leh-fohn	telefon
to tele-phone	teh-leh-fohn eht-mehk	telefon etmek
telephone ex-change	teh-leh-fohn sahn-trah-lih	telefon santralı
telephone office	teh-leh-fohn oh-fees	telefon ofis
television	teh-leh-weez-yohn	televizyon
tell	sery-leh-mehk	söylemek
temperature (fever)	ah-tehsh	ateş
(weather)	deh-reh-jeh	derece
temple	tah-pih-nahk	tapınak
tent	chah-dihr	çadır
terrible	kohr-koonch	korkunç
thank	tesh-ehk-kyur eht-mehk	teşekkür etmek

thank you (informal)	sah ohl	sağ ol
(polite)	tesh-ehk-kyur eh-deh-reem	tes\,ekkür ederim
thanks	mehr-see	mersi
that (one)	shoo(noo)	s\,u(nu)
the other (one)	oh(noo)	o(nu)
there	oh-rah-dah	orada
they	ohn-lahr	onlar
thick	kah-lihn	kalın
thief	hihr-sihz	hırsız
thin	een-jeh	ince
think	dyu-shyun-mehk	düşünmek
thirsty	soo-sah-mihsh	susamış
this (one)	boo(noo)	bu(nu)
thought	dyu-shyun-jeh	düşünce
throat	boh-ahz	boğaz
ticket(s)	bee-leht(-lehr)	bilet(ler)
ticket collector	bee-leht-chee	biletçi
ticket machine	bee-leht mah-kee-nah-sih	bilet makinası
ticket office	bee-leht gee-sheh-see	bilet gişesi
tide	gehl-geet	gelgit
tight	sihk-ihsh-mihsh	sıkışmış
time	wah-keet	vakit
timetable	tah-ree-feh	tarife
tin (can)	koo-too	kutu
tin opener	kohn-sehr-weh ah-cha-jah-ih	konserve açacağı
tip (gratuity)	bah-seesh	bahşiş
tired	yohr-goon	yorgun
tissues	mehn-deel	mendil
toast	kih-zahrt-mihsh ek-mehk	kızart-mıs\, ekmek
tobacco	tyu-tyun	tütün
today	boo-gyun	bugün
toilet(s)	too-wah-leht (-lehr)	tuvalet (ler)
toilet paper	too-wah-keht kah-ih-dih	tuvalet kağıdı

tomorrow	yahr-ihn	*yarın*
tonight	boo geh-jeh	*bu gece*
tooth	deesh	*diş*
toothache	deesh ah-rih-sih	*diş ağrısı*
toothbrush	deesh fihr-chah-sih	*diş fırçası*
toothpaste	deesh mah-joo-noo	*diş macunu*
torch(flash-light)	ehl feh-neh-ree	*el feneri*
to touch	doh-koon-mahk	*dokunmak*
tour	toor	*tur*
tourist	too-reest	*turist*
tourist infor-mation office	too-ree-zm byu-roh-soo	*turizm bürosu*
towards	-eh doh-roo	*-e doğru*
towel	hahw-loo	*havlu*
toy (n)	oy-oon-jahk	*oyuncak*
track (path)	pah-tee-kah	*patika*
traffic	trah-feek	*trafik*
traffic lights	trah-feek lahm-bah-sih	*trafik lambası*
trail	yohl	*yol*
train (n)	trehn	*tren*
train station	gahr ee-stahs-yohn	*gar istasyon*
tram	trahm-wahy	*tramvay*
transit	trahn-seet	*transit*
lounge	yohl-joo sah-lohn-oo	*yolcu salonu*
translate	cheh-weer-mehk	*çevirmek*
travel (n)	seh-yah-haht	*seyahat*
travel	seh-yah-haht eht-mehk	*seyahat etmek*
travel (books)	seh-yah-haht (kee-tahp-lah-rih)	*seyahat (kitapları)*
travel sickness	seh-yah-haht mee-deh boo-lahn-tih-sih	*seyahat mide bulantısı*
travellers cheques	seh-yah-haht cheh-kee	*seyahat çeki*
tree	ah-ahch	*ağaç*

trek	oo-zoon weh zohr-loo beer yohl-joo-look	*uzun ve zorlu bir yolculuk*
trip	yohl-joo-look	*yolculuk*
trousers	pahn-tah-lohn	*pantolon*
truck	kahm-yohn	*kamyon*
It's true.	doh-roo	*Doğru*
trust	gyu-wehn	*güven*
truth	gehr-chehk	*gerçek*
to try	chah-lihsh-mahk	*çalışmak*
T-shirt	tee-sherrt	*tişört*
tune	meh-loh-dee	*melodi*
Turkish bath	hah-mahm	*hamam*
to turn	dern-dyur-mehk	*döndür-mek*
Turn left. (pol/inf) soh-lah der-nyu-nyuz/ *Sola dönünüz./* soh-lah der-nyun *Sola dönün.*		
television	teh-leh-weez-yohn	*televizyon*
twice	ee-kee deh-fah	*iki defa*
twin beds	cheeft yah-tahk(-lahr)	*çift yatak(lar)*
typical	tee-peek	*tipik*
tyre(s)	lah-steek(lehr)	*lastik(ler)*

U

umbrella	shem-see-yeh	*şemsiye*
understand	ahn-lah-mahk	*anlamak*
unique	tehk	*tek*
universe	ehw-rehn	*evren*
university	yu-nee-wehr-see-teh	*üniversite*
unleaded (petrol)	koor-shoon-sooz	*kurşunsuz*
unsafe	teh-lee-keh-lee	*tehlikeli*

until (June)	hah-zee-rah-nah kah-dahr	*Hazirana kadar*
unusual (unique) (abnormal)	ger-ryul-meh-deek ah-jah-yee	*görülmedik acayip*
up	yoo-kah-rih-yah	*yukarıya*
up(stairs)	yoo-kah-rih	*yukarı*
uphill	yohk-oosh yoo-kah-ih	*yokuş yukarı*
urgent	ah-jeel	*acil*
useful	yah-rahr-lih	*yararlı*

V

vacant	bohsh	*boş*
vacation	tah-teel	*tatil*
vaccination	ah-shih-lah-mah	*aşılama*
valley	wah-dee	*vadi*
valuable	deh-ehr-lee	*değerli*
van	mee-nee-byus	*minibüs*
vegetables	sehb-zeh	*sebze*
vegetarian	weh-zjeh-tahr-yehn eht-yeh-mehz	*vejetaryen etyemez*

I'm vegetarian.
weh-zjeh-tahr-yehn-eem
Vejetaryenim.

village	kery	*köy*
vine	ahs-mah	*asma*
vineyard	bah	*bağ*
vein	dah-mahr	*damar*
venereal disease	zyuh-reh-wee hahs-tah-lihk	*zührevi hastalık*
to visit	zee-yah-reht eht-mehk	*ziyaret etmek*
vitamins	wee-tah-meen	*vitamin*
voice	sehs	*ses*
volume (amount) (sound)	hah-jeem sehs gyu-jyu	*hacim ses gücü*

to vomit	koos-mahk	*kusmak*
very	chohk	*çok*
video tape	wee-deh-oh-tehyp	*videoteyp*
view	mahn-zah-rah	*manzara*
virus	wee-ryus	*virüs*
visa	wee-zeh	*vize*

W

wage (n)	mahsh	*maaş\,*
wait	behk-leh-mehk	*beklemek*
waiter	gahr-sohn	*garson*
to walk	yyu-ryu-mehk	*yürümek*
wall (external)	(dihsh) doo-wahr	*(dış) duvar*
want	ees-teh-mehk	*istemek*
war	sah-wahsh	*savaş*
warm	ih-lihk	*ılık*
wash (something) (oneself)	yih-kah-mahk yih-kahn-mahk	*yıkamak yıkanmak*
washing machine	chah-mah-shihr mah-kee-neh-see	*çamaşır makinesi*
watch (n)	sah-aht	*saat*
to watch	bahk-mahk	*bakmak*
water	soo	*su*
water bottle	soo shee-sheh-see	*su şişesi*
wave (n)	dahl-gah	*dalga*
way	yohl	*yol*

Please tell me the way to (Izmir).
(eez-mihr)'eh nah-sihl gee-deh-bee-lee-reem
(İzmır)'e nasıl gidebilirim?

Which way?
hahn-gee yohl-dahn?
Hangi yoldan?

| Way Out | chih-kihsh | *Çıkış* |

we	beez	biz
weak	zah-yihf	zayıf
wear	gee-mehk	giymek
weather	hah-wah	hava
wedding	dyu-yun	düğün
week	hahf-tah	hafta
weekend	hahf-tah soh-noo	hafta sonu
weigh	tahrt-mahk	tartmak
weight	ah-ihr-lihk	ağırlık
welcome	hohsh gehl-dee-neez	hoş geldiniz
well	ee-yee	iyi
west	bah-tih	batı
wet	ihs-lahk	ıslak
What?	neh	Ne?

What is he saying?
eh sery-lyu-yohr?
Ne söylüyor?

What time is it?
Sah-aht kahch?
Saat kaç?

What does it mean?
neh deh-mehk?
Ne demek?

What's this?
boo neh?
Bu ne?

wheel	tehk-ehr-lehk	tekerlek
wheelchair	teh-kehr-lehk-lee sahn-dahl-yeh	tekerlekli sandalye
When?	neh zah-mahn?	Ne zaman?

When does it leave?
neh zah-mahn kahl-kee-yohr?
Ne zaman kalkıyor?

| Where? | neh-reh-deh? | Nerede? |

Where is the bank?
bahn-kah neh-reh-deh?
Banka nerede?

| Which? | hahn-gee? | Hangi? |

Which one?
hahn-gee-see?
Hangisi?

| white | beh-yahz | beyaz |
| Who? | keem? | Kim? |

Who is it?
keem oh?
Kim o?

Who are they?
ohn-lahr keem?
Onlar kim?

whole	byu-tyun	bütün
Why?	nee-cheen	Niçin?
	neh-dehn	Neden?
wife	kah-rih	karı
win	kah-zahn-mahk	kazanmak
wind	ryuz-gahr	rüzgâr
window	pehn-jeh-reh	pencere
wine	shah-rahp	şarap
winery	bah-jih	bağcı
winter	kihsh	kış
wire	tehl	tel
wine	shah-rahp	s\,arap
wise	ah-reef	arif
to wish	dee-leh-mehk	dilemek
with	-ee-leh	-ile
within	ee-cheh-ree-deh	içeride

Within an hour.
beer-sa-ah-teh kah-dahr
Bir saate kadar.

without	-seez/-sihz/-syuz/-sooz	-siz/-sız/-süz/-suz
woman	kah-dihn hah-nihm	kadın hanım
wonderful	shah-hah-neh	şahane
wood (n)	oh-doon	odun
wool	yyun	yün
word	keh-lee-meh	kelime
work	eesh	iş
to work	chah-lihsh-mahk	çalışmak

working	chal-ush-mah	çalışma
hours	sahaht-leh-ree	saatleri
work	chah-lihsh-	çalışma
permit	mah eez-nee	izni
world	dyun-yah	dünya
worried	tah-sah-lih	tasalı
worth	deh-ehr	değer
wound	yah-rah	yara
write	yahz-mahk	yazmak
writer	yah-zahr	yazar
wrong	yahn-lihsh	yanlış

I'm wrong (at fault).
yahn-lihsh-ihm
Yanlışım.

I'm wrong (incorrect).
yahn-lihsh-ihm
Yanlışım.

X

x-ray	rernt-gehn	*röntgen*

Y

year	yihl	yıl
	seh-neh	sene
yes	eh-weht	evet
yesterday	dyun	dün
yet		dah-hah
daha		
you (polite)	seez	siz

You're welcome.
beer shehy deh-eel
Bir şey değil.

young	gehnch	genç
youth	er-rehn-jee	öğrenci
hostel	yoor-doo	yurdu

Z

zodiac	zohd-yahk	Zodyak
zoo	hahy-wah-	hayva-
	naht bah-	nat
	cheh-see	bahçesi

A

Note that in the Turkish alphabet, the letters ç, ğ, ş, ö, ü and the undotted ı are listed separately. Alphabetical order is as follows:

a b c ç d e f g ğ h ı i j k l m n o o ö p q r s ş t u u v w x y z

So, for example, when searching for a word with a ü in it, remember that it will appear after all words containing u in the same position. Thus, küçük (small) appears after Kuzey (north), and not after kucaklama (hug).

A

abide	ah-bee-deh	monument
acayip	ah-jah-yeep	strange
acele ile	ah-jeh-leh ee-leh	in a hurry
acele posta	ah-jeh-leh pohs-tah	express mail
acı	ah-jih	pain/spicy
acıkmak	ah-jihk-mahk	to be hungry
acil	ah-jeel	urgent
acil durum	ah-jeel doo-room	emergency
açık	ah-chihk	open (adj)
açılış	ah-chih-lihsh	opening (opera)
açmak	ahch-mahk	to open
ad	ahd	name (n)
adalet	ah-dah-leht	justice
adam	ah-dahm	man
adet ağrısı	ah-dcht ah-rih-sih	period pain
âdet	ah-deht	menstruation
âdetle ilgili	ah-deht-leh eel-gee-lee	premenstrual
gerilim	gehr-ee-leem	tension
adım	ah-dihm	step
adres	h-dres	address

Afedersiniz.
ah-feh-dehr-see-neez
Excuse me.

affetmek	ahf-feht-mehk	to forgive
afiş	ah-fees	poster

Afiyetolsun!
ah-fee-yeh-tohl-soon!
Bon appétit!

ağ	ah	net
ağaç	ah-ahch	tree
ağırlık	ah-ihr-lihk	weight
ağız	ah-ihz	mouth
ağrı	ah-rih	ache
ağrı kehsee-jee(-lehr)	ah-rih kehs-ee-jee (-lehr)	painkiller(s)
ahlaksız	ah-lahk-sihz	corrupt
ahmak	ah-mahk	idiot
ahşap	ah-shahp	wood (adj)
AIDS	AIDZ	AIDS
aile	ah-ee-leh	family
akıl	ah-kihl	mind
akrabalar	ah-krah-bah-lahr	family
aksetme		
akşam	ahk-shahm	evening
akşam yemeği	ahk-shahm yeh-meh-yee	dinner
akümülatör (akü)	ah-kyu/ah-kyum-yu-lah-ter	car battery
alayetmek	ah-lahy-eht-mehk	to make fun of
alerji	ah-lehr-zjee	allergy
Allah	ahl-lah	God

Allaha ısmar-ladık.
ahl-lah-hah ihs-mahr-lah-dihk
goodbye (said to person leaving)

almak	ahl-mahk	to receive
Alman	ahl-mahn	German

altyazı	ahlt-yah-zih	subtitles
ama	ah-mah	but
amatör	ah-mah-terr	amateur
ambalaj	ahm-bahl-azj	package
ameliyat	ah-meh-lee-yaht	operation (surgery)
Amerika	ah-meh-ree-kah	America
ampül	ahm-pyul	bulb
ana baba	ah-nah bah-bah	parents
anahtar	ah-nahh-tahr	key
anayol	ah-nah-yohl	main road
anıt	ah-niht	monument
anlamak	ahn-lah-mahk	to realise/understand
anlaşılmaz	ahn-lahsh-ihl-mahz	incomprehensible
Anlaştık!	ahn-lahsh-tihk!	Agreed!
anne	ahn-neh	mother
anneanne	ahn-neh-ahn-neh	grandmother
anneciğim	ah-neh-jee-eem	Mum
antik	ahn-teek	ancient
antika	ahn-tee-kah	antique
aptal	ahp-tahl	stupid
ara	ah-rah	intermission
araba	ah-rah-bah	car/wagon
arasında	ah-rah-sihn-dah	between
arasında	ah-rah-sihn-dah	among
arkada	ahr-kah-dah	at the back (behind)
arkadaş	ahr-kah-dahsh	friend/companion
arkeolojik	ahr-keh-oh-loh-zjeek	archaeological
arsa	ahr-sah	land
asansör	ah-sahn-ser	lift (elevator)
askerlik	ahs-kehr-leek	military service
asma kilit	ahs-mah kee-leet	padlock
asma	ahs-mah	vine
astımla ilgili	ah-stihm-lah eel-gee-lee	asthmatic
Asya	ahs-yah	Asia
aşağıda	ah-shah-ih-dah	below
aşağıdaki	ah-shah-ih-dah-kee	low (place)
aşağılık herif	ah-shah-ih-lihk heh-reef	creep (slang)
aşık	ah-shihk	lover
aşılama (aşı)	ah-shih-lah-mah (ah-shih)	vaccination
aşırı doz	ah-shih-rih dohz	overdose
aşk	ahshk	romance
at	aht	horse
ateş	ah-tehsh	fire
ateş	ah-tehsh	temperature (fever)
atlamak	aht-lah-mahk	to jump
Avrupa	ahw-roo-pah	Europe
avukat	ah-woo-kaht	lawyer
ay	ahy	moon/month
ayak	ahy-ahk	foot
ayakkabı bağı	ah-yahk-kah-bih bah-ih	shoelace
ayakkabı	ah-yah-kah-bih	shoes
aybaşı	ahy-bah-shih	menstruation
ayırım	ah-yih-rihm	discrimination
ayırtmak	ah-yihrt-mahk	to reserve
ayna	ah-yee-nah	mirror
aynı	ahy-nih	same
ayrılmak	ahy-rihl-mahk	to separate
ayrıntı	ahy-rihn-tih	detail
az	ahz	a little/few
azami	ah-zah-mee	maximum (adj)
azami sürat	ahz-ah-mee syu-raht	speed limit
az pişmiş	ahz peesh-meesh	rare (meat)

B

baba	bah-bah	father
bagaj	bah-gajz	luggage
bagaj	bah-gahjz	luggage
dolapları	doh-lahp-lah-rih	lockers
bagaj rafı	bah-gahjz rah-fih	luggage lockers
bağ	bah	vineyard
bağcı	bah-jih	winery
bağırmak	bah-ihr-mahk	to shout
bahar alerjisi	bah-hahr ah-lehr-jee-see	hayfever
bahçe	bahh-cheh	garden
bahis (bahsi)	bah-hees (bahh-see)	a bet
bahşiş	bahh-seesh	tip (gratuity)
bakan	bah-kahn	caring
bakmak	bahk-mahk	to look/ to watch
balayı	bahl-ah-yih	honeymoon
balık	bah-lihk	fish (n)
balıkçı	bah-lihk-chih	fish shop
balkon	bahl-kohn	balcony
banka	bahn-kah	bank
banka-matik	bahnk-ah-mah-teek	automatic teller machine
banliyö	bahn-lee-yer	suburbs of
banyo	bahn-yoh	bath/ bathroom
banyo yapmak	bahn-yoh yahp-mak	to bathe
bardak	bahr-dahk	glass (drinking)
barış	bah-rihsh	peace
basınç	bah-sihnch	pressure
basit	bah-siht	simple
baş	bahsh	head (n)
baş ağrısı	bahsh ah-rih-sih	headache
başarı	bahsh-ah-rih	success
başbakan	bahsh-bah-kahn	prime minister

baş belası	bahsh beh-lah-sih	pain in the neck
başı dönen	bah-shih der-nehn	dizzy
başka	bahsh-kah	(an)other
başkan	bahsh-kahn	president
başlamak	bahsh-lah-mahk	to begin/ to start
batı	bah-tih	west
battaniye	baht-tah-nee-yeh	blanket
bavul	bah-wool	suitcase
bayat	bah-yaht	stale
bayılmak	bah-yihl-mahk	to faint
bayram	bahy-rahm	festival
bazen	bah-zehn	sometimes
bazı	bah-zih	some (inanimate)
bebek	beh-behk	baby
bebek maması	beh-behk mah-mah-sih	baby food
bedava	beh-dah-wah	free (of charge)
beden	beh-dehn	size (of clothes)
bilet gişesi	bee-leht gee-sheh-see	ticket office
beğenmek	beh-ehn-mehk	to like
bekâr	beh-kahr	single (person)
beklemek	behk-leh-mehk	to wait
bekleme odası	behk-leh-meh oh-dah-sih	waiting room
belediye başkanı	beh-leh-dee-yeh bahsh-kah-nih	mayor
belediye otobüsü	beh-leh-dee-yeh oh-toh-byu-syu	local bus
belgesel	behl-geh-sehl	documentary
belki	behl-kee	maybe

belli	behl-lee	obvious
ben	behn	selfish
bencil	behn-jeel	
Beni dolan-dırdın!		
beh-nee doh-lahn-dihr-dihm!		
Cheat!		
benzer	behn-zehr	like (similar)
benzin	behn-zeen	petrol
berber	behr-behr	barber
beyaz	beh-yahz	white
bıçak	bih-chahk	knife
bırak-	bih-rahk-	to be left
ılmak	ihl-mahk	(behind/ over)
bırakmak	bih-rahk-mahk	to quit
biber	bee-behr	pepper
biçim	bee-cheem	shape
bilardo	bee-lahr-doh	pool (game)
bilen	bee-lehn	wise
bilet maki-	bee-leht	ticket
nası	mah-kee-nah-sih	machine
bilet(ler)	bee-leht (-lehr)	ticket(s)
biletçi	bee-leht-chee	ticket collector
bilmek	beel-mehk	to know (something)
bina	bee-nah	building
binmek	been-mehk	board (embark)
(at)	(aht)	to ride
binmek	been-mehk	(a horse)
bir daha	beer dah-hah	another one
Bir dakika.		
beer dah-kee-kah		
Just a minute.		
bir de	beer deh	also
bir defa	beer deh-fah	once/ one time
bir iş	beer eesh	gig
bir saate	beer-sa-	within
kadar	ah-teh kah-dahr	an hour

bir şey	beer shehy	cool (coll)
birşey	beer-shehy	something
Bir şey değil.		
beer shehy deh-eel		
You're welcome.		
bira	bee-rah	beer
biraz	bee-rahz	a little bit
biraz önce	beer-ahz ern-jeh	a while ago
biri	bee-ree	somebody
birisi	beer-ee-see	someone
birkaç	beer-kahch	several
bisiklet	bee-seek-leht	bicycle
bisikletçi	bee-seek-leht-jee	cyclist
bisiklete	bee-seek-	to cycle
binmek	leh-teh been-mehk	
bitler	beetlehr	lice
bitirmek	bee-teer-mehk	to end
bitki	beet-kee	plant
bitkici	beet-kee-jee	herbalist
biz	beez	we
boğaz	boh-ahz	throat
borcu	bohr-joo	to owe
olmak	ohl-mahk	
boru	boh-roo	pipe
boş	bohsh	empty
boyamak	boh-yah-mahk	to paint
bozuk	boh-zook	broken
bozuk	boh-zook	loose
para	pah-rah	change
böcek	ber-jehk	insect
bölgesel	berl-geh-sehl	regional
bu ay	boo ahy	this month
Budist	boo-deest	Buddhist
bu gece	boo geh-jeh	tonight
bugün	boo-gyun	today
buhar	boo-hahr	steam
bulantı	boo-lahn-tih	nausea
bulaşma	boo-lahsh-mah	infection
bulutlu	boo-loot-loo	cloudy

C

bu(nu)	boo(noo)	this (one)
bu öğle-	boo er-leh	this
den	-dehn	afternoon
sonra	sohn-rah	
burada	boo-rah-dah	here
burçlar	boorch-lahr	zodiac
kuşağı	koosh-ah-ih	
burkulma	boor-kool-	a sprain
	mah	
burun(-nu)	boo-roon	nose
bu yıl	boo yihl	this year
buyurun	boo-yoo-roon	help
(uz)	(-ooz)	yourself
buz	booz	ice
buzdolabı	booz doh-	refrigerator
	lah-bih	
büyük	byu-yyuk	big
büyükelçi	byuk-yyu-	ambass-
	kehl-chee	ador
büyü-	byu-yyu-kehl-	embassy
kelçilik	chee-leek	
büyüklük	byu-yyuk-lyuk	size

C

cadde	jahd-deh	street
cam	jahm	glass (window)
cami	jah-mee	mosque
can sıkıcı	jahn sih-kih-jih	boring
can sıkıntısı	jahn sih-kihn-tih-sih	bored
cenaze töreni	jeh-nah-zeh ter-reh-nee	funeral
cep	jehp	pocket
cep telefonu	jehp-teh-leh-foh-noo	mobile phone
cesur	jeh-soor	brave
cevap veren	jeh-vahp veh-rehn	answering
cevap	jeh-vahp	answer
cezaevi	jeh-zah-eh-vee	jail

cezaland-ırmak	jeh-zah-lahn-dihr-mahk	to punish
cırcırbö-ceği	jihr-jihr-ber-jeh-ee	cricket
ciddi	jeed-dee	serious
cilt	jeelt	skin
cin	jeen	jeans
cinsel	jeen-sehl	gay
cinsiyet ayırımı	jeen-see-yeht ah-yih-rih-mih	sexism
cip	jeep	jeep
cümle	jyum-leh	sentence (words)
çabuk	chah-book	quick
çabuk	chah-book	fast
çadır	chah-dihr	tent
çakı	chah-kih	penknife
çakmak	chahk-mahk	cigarette lighter
çalar saat	chah-lahr sah-aht	alarm clock
çalışma izni	chah-lihsh-mah eez-nee	work permit
çalışmak	chah-lahsh-mahk	to try/ to work
çalışma saatleri	chal-ush-mah sah-aht-leh-ree	working hours
(telefonun) çalma sesi	(teh-leh-foh-noon) chahl-mah seh-see	ring (of phone)
çalmak	chahl-mahk	to play (music)
çam	chahm	pine
çamaşır	chah-mah-shihr	laundry (dirty clothes)
çamaşır maki-nesi	chah-mah-shihr mah-kee-neh-see	washing machine
çamur	chah-muur	mud
çanak çömlek	chah-nahk cherm-lehk	pottery

çanta	chahn-tah	bag
çarşaf	chahr-shahf	sheet (bed)
çarşı	char-shih	market
çatal	chah-tahl	fork (utensil)
çatı	chah-tih	roof
çay	chah-yee	tea
çekiç	cheh-keech	hammer
çekmek	chehk-mehk	to pull
çeşit	cheh-sheet	kind/type
çevirme	cheh-veer-mehk	translate
çevre	chehv-reh	environment
çeyrek	chehy-rehk	quarter (to/after the hour)
Çıkış	chih-kihsh	Way Out
çıkış	chih-kihsh	exit
çınlama sesi	chihn-lah-mah seh-see	ring (sound)
çiçek	chee-chehk	flower
çift	cheeft	pair
çift yataklar	cheeft yah-tahk-lahr	twin beds
çiftlik	cheeft-leek	farm
çiğ	chee	raw
çiklet	cheek-leht	chewing gum
çikolata	chee-koh-lah-tah	chocolate
çim	cheem	grass
çizgi	cheez-gee	line
çizme	cheez-meh	boots
çocuk	choh-jook	child
çocuk bakan	choh-jook bah-kahn	child-minding
çocuk bakıcısı	choh-juk bah-kih-jih-sih	babysitter
çocuk bezi	choh-jook beh-zee	nappy
çocuk bezi isilik	choh-jook beh-zee ee-see-leek	nappy rash

çocuk düşürme	choh-jook dyu-shyur-meh	miscarriage
çocuklar	choh-jook-lahr	children
çoğunluk	choh-oon-look	majority
çok	chohk	very/many
çok fazla	chohk fahz-lah	many/too much
Çok yaşa! chohk yah-shah! Bless you! (when sneezing)		
çöl	cherl	desert
çömlek	cherm-lehk	pot (ceramic)
çöp	cherp	garbage/rubbish
çünkü	chyun-kyu	because
çürük	chyu-ryuk	a bruise

D

dağ	dah	mountain
dağ bisikleti	dah bee-seek-leh-tee	mountain bike
dağ kulübesi	dah koo-lyu-beh-see	mountain hut
dağ silsilesi	dah seel-see-leh-see	mountain range
dağ yolu	dah yoh-loo	mountain path
dağcılık	dah-jih-lihk	mountaineering
dağıtıcı	dah-ih-tih-jih	distributor
daha	dah-hah	more/yet
daha az	dah-hah ahz	less
daha iyi	dah-hah ee-yee	better
dahi	dah-hee	also
dahil	dah-heel	included
daire	dah-ee-reh	office
dakika	dah-kee-kah	minute (time)

(beş) dakika sonra	(behsh) dah-kee-kah sohn-rah	in (five) minutes
dalga	dahl-gah	wave (n)
dalgıç teçhizat	dahl-gihch tehch-hee-zaht	diving equipment
dalmak	dahl-mahk	to dive
damar	dah-mahr	vein
dans eden	dahns eh-dehn	dancing
dans etmek	dahns eht-mehk	to dance
davullar	dah-wool-lahr	drums
dahi	dah-hee	also
dede	deh-deh	grandfather
dik	deek dik	steep
defter	dehf-tehr	notebook
değerli	deh-ehr-lee	valuable
değiştirmek	deh-eesh-teer-mehk	to change/exchange
deli	deh-lee	mad/crazy
demiryolları	deh-meer-yohl-lah-rih	railways
demiryolu	deh-meer-yoh-loo	railway
demokrasi	deh-moh-krah-see	democracy
deniz	deh-neez	sea
deniz tutması	deh-neez toot-mah-sih	seasick
dere	deh-reh	stream
derece	deh-reh-jeh	temperature (weather)
dergi	dehr-gee	magazine
deri	deh-ree	leather
derin	deh-rehn	deep
dış	dihsh	foreign
dışarda	dih-shahr-dah	outside
dikiş iğnesi	dee-keesh ee-neh-see	needle (sewing)

Dikkat! deek-kaht!		Careful!
dil	deel	language
dilemek	dee-leh-mehk	to wish
dilenci	dee-lehn-jee	beggar
din	deen	religion
dindar	deen-dahr	religious
dinlemek	deen-leh-mehk	to listen
dinlenme	deen-lehn-meh	rest (relaxation)
dinlenmek	deen-lehn-mehk	to rest
Dinleyin! deen-leh-yeen!		Listen!
dipte	deep-teh	at the bottom
direkt	dee-rehkt	direct
diş	deesh	tooth
diş ağrısı	deesh ah-rih-sih	toothache
dişçi	deesh-chee	dentist
diş fırçası	deesh fihr-chah-sih	toothbrush
diş hekimi	deesh heh-kee-mee	dentist
diş ipliği	deesh eep-lee-yee	dental floss
dişler	deesh-lehr	teeth
diş macunu	deesh mah-joo-noo	toothpaste
diyabetik	dee-yah-beh-teek	diabetic
diz	deez	knee
doğa	doh-ah	nature
doğru	doh-roo	straight/correct
Doğru. doh-roo		It's true.
doğrulamak	doh-roo-lah-mahk	to confirm (a booking)

D
I
C
T
I
O
N
A
R
Y

233

doğu	doh-oo	east
doğum günü	doh-oom gyu-nyu	birthday/ date of birth
doğum kontrol hapı	doh-oom kohn-trohl hah-pih	the Pill
doğum yeri	doh-oom yeh-ree	place of birth
dokunmak	doh-koon-mahk	to touch
dolap	doh-lahp	cupboard
dolaşma	doh-lahsh-mah	stroll/ walk
doldurmak	dohl-door-mahk	to fill
dolu	doh-loo	full
domuz eti	doh-mooz eh-tee	pork
domuz	doh-mooz	pig
dondurma	dohn-door-mah	ice cream
dondurulmuş yiyecekler	dohn-doo-rool-moosh yee-yeh-jehk-lehr	frozen foods
dondurmak	dohn-door-mahk	to freeze
donmak	dohn-mahk	to freeze
döküntü	der-kyun-tyu	a rash
döndürmek	dern-dyu-mehk	to turn
dönmek	dern-mehk	return (comeback)
dörtte bir	dert-teh beer	quarter
döşek	der-shehk	mattress
döviz kuru	der-weez koo-roo	exchange rate
dövüş	der-wyush	fight
dramatik	drah-mah-teek	dramatic
dua	doo-ah	prayer
dudaklar	doo-dahk-lahr	lips
durmak	door-mahk	to stop (somewhere)

Durun!
doo-roon!
Stop!

duş	doosh	shower
(iç) duvar	(eech) doo-wahr	wall (interior)
duymak	dooy-mahk	to hear
düğme	dyu-meh	buttons
düğün	dyu-yun	wedding
dükkân	dyuk-kahn	shop
dün	dyun	yesterday
Dünya	dyun-yah	Earth
dünya	dyun-yah	world
düşük	dyu-shyuk	low (price)
düşünce	dyu-shyun-jeh	thought
düşünmek	dyu-shyun-mehk	to think
dürüst	dyu-ryust	honest
düz	dyuz	flat (adj)
düzenlemek	dyu-zehn-leh-mehk	organise
düzine	dur-zee-neh	dozen

E

eczane	edj-zah-neh	pharmacy/ chemist

Efendim!
eh-fehn-deem!
Hello! (answering telephone)

eğitim	eh-ee-teem	education
eğlence	eh-lehn-jeh	fun
ehliyet	eh-lee-yeht	driver's licence
ekmek	ehk-mehk	bread
ekonomi	eh-koh-noh-mee	economy
eksiklik	ehk-seek-leek	shortage
ekspres	ehk-spres	express
el	ehl	hand
el çantası	ehl chahn-tah-sih	handbag

el feneri	ehl feh-neh-ree	torch
el işi	ehl ee-shee	handmade
elbise	ehl-bee-seh	dress(noun)
elektrik	oh-lehk-treek	electricity
eleman	eh-leh-mahn	employee
eleştiri	eh-lehsh-tee-ree	review (book/film)
emanet	eh-mah-net	baggage claim

Eminim.
eh-meen-eem
I'm sure.

emniyet kemeri	ehm-nee-yeht keh-meh-ree	seat (safety) belt
emniyetli	ehm-nee-yeht-lee	safe (adj)
emzik	ehm-zeek	dummy/pacifier
en az	ehn ahz	minimum (adj)
engellemek	ern-leh-mehk	prevent
en iyi	ehn ee-yee	best
enteresan	ehn-teh-reh-sahn	interesting
erkek arkadaş	ehr-kehk ahr-kah-dahsh	boyfriend
erkek kardeş	ehr-kehk kahr-dehsh	brother
erken	ehr-kehn	early
eroin	eh-roh-een	heroin
eroin bağımlısı	eh-roh-een bah-ihm-lih-sih	heroin addict
eski	es-kee	old (adj)
eşarplar	eh-sharp-lahr	scarves
eşcinsel	esh-jeen-sehl	homosexual
eşitlik	eh-sheet-leek	equality
eşitsizlik	eh-sheet-seez-leek	inequality
etmek	eht-mehk	to do

etyemez	eht-yeh-mehz	vegetarian
ev	ehw	house
evet	eh-weht	yes
ev işi	ehw eesh-ee	housework
evlenme	ehw-lehn-meh	marriage
evlenmek	ehw-lehn-mehk	marry
evli	ehw-lee	married

Evli misiniz?
ehw-lee mee-see-neez?
Are you married?
Evliyim.
ehw-lee-yeem
I'm married.

evsiz	ehw-seez	homeless
evvel	ehw-wehl	before
evvelki gün	ehw-wehl-kee gyun	day before yesterday

F

fabrika	fah-bree-kah	factory

Farketmez.
fahr-keht-mehz
It doesn't matter.

farklı	fahrk-lih	different
fasulye	fah-sool-yeh	beans
faydalı	fahy-dah-lih	useful
fen	fehn	science
fenah	feh-nah	bad
festival	feh-stee-wahl	festival
fırın	fih-rihn	bakery/stove
fırsat eşitliği	fihr-saht eh-sheet-lee-ee	equal opportunity
fırtına	feer-tee-nah	storm
filim	fee-leem	film
film	fee-lm	film (for camera)
film hızı	fee-lm hih-zih	film speed
film negatif	fee-lm neh-gah-teef	film (negatives)

filtreden geçirmiş	feel-treh-dehn geh-cheer-meesh	filtered
fincan	feen-jahn	cup
fiş	feesh	plug (electrical)
fiyat	fee-yaht	price
fiyatı olmak	fee-yah-tih ohl-mahk	to cost
flört etmek	flert eht-mehk	to date (someone)
fotoğraf çekmek	foh-toh-raf chehk-mehk	to take photographs
fotoğraf	foh-toh-rahf	photo
fotoğrafçı	foh-toh-rahf-chih	camera shop
fotoğraf-çılık	foh-toh-rahf-chih-lihk	photo-graphy
fuaye	foo-ah-yeh	foyer
fut	foot	measure-ment
futbol	foot-bohl	football (soccer)

G

gar	gar	train station
garaj	gah-rahj	garage
garson	gahr-sohn	waiter
gazete(ler)	gah-zeh-the (lehr)	news-paper(s)
gazeteci	gahz-teh-jee	journalist
gebeliği önleyici	geh-beh-lee-ee ern-leh-ee-jee	contra-ceptives
gebelikten korun-ma	geh-beh-leek-tehn koh-roon-mah	contra-ception
gece yarısı	geh-jeh yah-rih-sih	midnight
gece	geh-jeh	night
gecikme	geh-jeek-meh	delay
geç	gehch	late

geçen gece	geh-chehn geh-jeh	last night
geçiş	geh-cheesh	pass
geçmiş	gehch-meesh	past
gelecek	geh-leh-jehk	next/future
gelecek hafta	geh-leh-jehk hahf-tah	next week
gelenekler	geh-leh-nehk-lehr	customs (traditions)
gelenler	geh-lehn-lehr	arrivals
gelgit	gehl-geet	tide
Gelin(iz)! geh-leen(-eez)! Come!		
gemi	geh-mee	ship
genç	gench	young/ a youth
general	gen-ehr-ahl	general
gerçek	gehr-chehk	genuine/ truth
gerekli	geh-rehk-lee	necessary
geri ödeme	geh-ree er-deh-meh	refund
geri ödemek	geh-ree er-deh-mek	to refund
getirmek	geh-teer-mehk	to bring
gevşemek	gehw-sheh-mehk	to relax
gey	gehy	homosexual
gezegen	geh-zeh-gehn	planet
gidilecek yer	gee-dee-leh-jehk yehr	destination
Gidin! gee-deen Go!		
gidiş	gee-deesh	departure
gidiş dönüş bileti	gee-deesh dern-yush bee-leht-ee	return (ticket)
girmek	geer-mehk	to enter
gitar	gee-tahr	guitar
gitmek	geet-mehk	to go

giyim evi	gee-yeem eh-wee	clothing store
giymek	gee-mehk	to wear
giysiler	gee-see-lehr	clothing
gol	gohl	goal (n) (sport)
göğüs	gery-yus	chest
gök	gerk	sky
göl	gerl	lake
gölge	gerl-geh	shade/shadow
gömlek	germ-lehk	shirt
göndermek	gern-dehr-mehk	send
göndermek	gern-dehr-mehk	to ship
görmek	ger-mehk	to see
görülmedik	ger-ryul-meh-deek	unusual/rare
görünüm	ger-ryun-yum	view
görüş	ger-ryush	opinion
görüşme	ger-ryush-meh	interview
gösterge	gers-tehr-geh	indicator
göstermek	gerr-stehr-mehk	to show
götürmek	ger-tyur-mehk	to take (away)
göz	gerz	eye
gözlük	gerz-lyuk	(eye) glasses
gram	grahm	gram
grip	greep	'flu
gurur	goo-roor	pride
güç	gyuch	power/strength

Güle güle.
gyu-leh gyu-leh
Goodbye. (said by person remaining)

gülme	gyul-meh	laugh
gülümsemek	gyu-lyum-seh-mehk	to smile

gümrük	gyum-ryuk	airport customs
gümüşten yapılmış	gyu-myush-tehn yah-pihl-mihsh	made of silver
gün	gyun	day

Günaydın.
gyun-ahy-dihn
Good morning.

günce	gyun-jeh	diary
güncel olaylar	gyun-jehl oh-lahy-lahr	current affairs
gündelik	gyun-deh-leek	daily
güneş engeli	gyu-nehsh ehn-geh-lee	sunblock
güneş gözlüğü	gyu-nehsh gerz-lyu-yyu	sunglasses
güneşin doğması	gyu-neh-sheen doh-mah-sih	sunrise
güneş yanığı	gyu-nehsh yah-nih-ih	sunburn
güneş	gyu-nehsh	sun
güneşin batması	gyu-neh-sheen baht-mah-sih	sunset
güneşli	gyu-nehsh-lee	sunny
güney	gyu-nehy	south
Güney Afrika	gyu-nehy ahf-ree-kah	South Africa
günlük	gyun-lyuk	daily
gürültü	gyu-ryul-tyu	noise
gürültülü	gyu-ryul-tyu-lyu	noisy/loud
güven	gyu-wehn	trust
güvenli seks	gyu-wehn-lee sex	safe sex
güvenmek	gyu-wehn-mehk	to trust
güzel	gyu-zehl	pretty/beautiful

H

haber	hah-behr	news
haber ajansı	hah-behr ah-zjahn-sih	news-agency
hacim	hah-jeem	volume
hafif	hah-feef	light(weight)
hafta	hahf-tah	week
hafta sonu	hahf-tah soh-noo	weekend
haklı	hahk-lih	to be right (following suffixes)

Haklısınız.
hahk-lih-sih-nihz
You're right.

hala	hah-lah	aunt (paternal)
halat	hah-laht	rope
halı	hah-lih	rug/carpet
hamak	hah-mahk	hammock
hamam	hah-mahm	Turkish bath
hamile	hah-mee-leh	pregnant

Hangi?
hahn-gee?
Which?

Hangisi?
hahn-gee-see?
Which one?

hanım	hah-nihm	woman
hap	hahp	tablet (medicine)
hapishane	hahp-ees-hah-neh	prison
harabe	hah-rah-beh	ruins
hareket etme	hah-reh-kehr eht-meh	departure
hareket etmek	hah-reh-keht eht-mehk	to depart

Harika!
hah-ree-kah
Great!

harita	hah-ree-tah	map
hasır	hah-sihr	mat
hasta	hah-stah	ill/sick
hastalık	hahs-tah-lihk	sickness/disease
hastane	hahs-tah-neh	hospital
haşiş	hah-sheesh	hash (drug)
hatıra	hah-tih-rah	souvenir
hatıra	hah-tih-rah	souvenir
dükkanı	dyuk-kah-nih	shop
hatırlamak	hah-teer-lah-mahk	to remember
hava	hah-wah	weather/air
havaalanı	hah-wah-ah-lah-nah	airport
havaalanı vergisi	hah-wah-ah-lah-nah wehr-gee-see	airport tax
havlu	hahv-loo	towel
hayal etmek	hah-yahl eht-mek	to hallucinate
hayat	hah-yaht	life
hayatta kalmak	hahy-aht-tah kahl-mahk	to survive
hayır	hah-yihr	no
hayvan	hahy-wahn	animal
hayvanat bahçesi	hahy-wah-naht bahh-cheh-see	zoo
hazımsızlık	hah-zihm-sihz-lihk	indigestion
hazır	hah-zihr	ready
hazırlanmak	hah-zihr-lahn-mahk	to prepare

(Hazirana) kadar.
(hah-zee-rah-nah) kah-dahr
Until (June).

hediye	heh-dee-yeh	present (gift)
hediye	heh-dee-yeh	gift
hekim	heh-keem	doctor
hemen	heh-men	almost
hemen	heh-men	
hemen	heh-mehn	immediately
hemşire	hehm-shee-reh	nurse

henüz değil	heh-nyuz deh-eel	not yet
hepsi	hehp-see	all
her gün	hehr gyun	every day
herzaman	hehr-zah-mahn	always
herbiri	hehr beer-ee	each
herhangi bir	hehr-hahn-gee beer	any
hesap	heh-sahp	bill
heykel	hehy-kehl	statue/ sculpture
hırsız	hihr-sihz	thief
hız	hihz	speed
hiç bir şey	heech beer shehy	nothing
hiç bir zaman	heech beer zah-mahn	never
hikâye	hee-kah-yeh	story
Hindistan	heen-dee-stahn	India
hisler	hees-lehr	feelings
hissetmek	hees-seht-mehk	to feel
hizmet	heez-meht	service (assistence)
hoş	hohsh	charming/ nice

Hoşça kalınız!
hohsh chah-kahl ih-nihz
Goodbye/Cheers!

hoş geldiniz	hohsh gehl-dee-neez	welcome
hüküm	hyu-kyum	prison sentence
hükümet	hyu-kyu-meht	government

I

ılık	ih-lihk	warm
ırk	ihrk	race (ancestry)
ırkçılık	ihrk-chih-lihk	racism

ısırık	ih-sih-rihk	bite (dog/insect)
ıslak	ihs-lahk	wet
ısmarlamak	ihs-mahr-lah-mahk	to order (food)
ıstırap çekmek	ih-stih-rahp chehk-mehk	to suffer
ışık(lar)	ih-shihk (-lahr)	light(s)
ızgara	ihz-gah-rah	to grill

i

İskoçya	ees-kohch-yah	Scotland

İyi akşam-lar
ee-yee ahk-shahm-lahr
Good evening.
İyi geceler.
ee-yee geh-jeh-lehr
Good night.
İyi günler.
ee-yee gyun-lehr
Good afternoon.
İyi yolculuklar!
ee-yee yohl-joo-look-lahr!
Bon voyage!

içerde	ee-chehr-deh	inside
içeride	ee-cheh-ree-deh	within
içki	eech-kee	drink (alcoholic)
içmek	eech-mehk	to drink/ to smoke
iğne	ee-neh	injection
iğne	ee-neh	needle
iki defa	ee-kee deh-fah	twice
iki hafta	ee-kee hahf-tah	fortnight
iki kişilik yatak	ee-kee kee-shee-leek yah-tahk	double bed
iki misli	ee-kee mees-lee	double
ikisi	ee-kee-see	both

il	eel	province
ilaç	ee-lahch	medicine
ile	ee-leh	with
ileride	ee-leh-ree-deh	ahead
ilginç	eel-geech	interesting
ilişki	ee-leesh-kee	relationship
ilk bahar	eelk bah-hahr	spring (season)
ilk ismi	eelk ees-mee	christian name
ilk yardım kutusu	eelk yahr-dihm koo-too-soo	first-aid kit

Note that words beginning with an undotted ı appear before this listing.

ilk	eelk	first
İmdat!	eem-daht	Help!
imza	eem-zah	signature
imzalamak	eem-zah-lah-mahk	to sign
-in dışında bırakmış	-een dih-shihn-dah bih-rahk-mihsh	excluded
inatçı	ee-naht-chih	stubborn
ince	een-jeh	thin
indirim	een-deer-eem	discount
indirim var	een-dee-reem wahr	on sale
inek	ee-nehk	cow
ingiltere	een-geel-teh-reh	England
inkâr etmek	een-kahr eht-mehk	to deny
inmek	een-mehk	disembark
insan	een-sahn	person
insan	een-sahn	human
hakları	hahk-lah-rih	rights
insanlar	een-sahn-lahr	people
ip	eep	string/rope
ipek	ee-pehk	silk
iptal etmek	eep-tahl eht-mehk	to cancel

ishal	ees-hahl	diarrhoea
istasyon	eestahs-yohn	station
istemek	ees-teh-mehk	to want/ to ask (for something)
iş	eesh	business/ work
işaret	ee-shah-reht	a signal
iş yapmak	eesh yahp-mahk	to deal
itiraf etmek	ee-tee-rahf eht-meck	to admit
itmek	eet-mehk	to push
iyi	ee-yee	good
İyi şanslar!	ee-yee shans-lahr	Good luck!
iyi	ee-yee	well
izin belgesi	ee-zeen behl-geh-see	permit
izin vermek	ee-zeen wehr-mehk	to allow
izin	ee-zeen	permission

jambon	jzahm-bohn	ham

kabahat	kah-bah-haht	fault/ offence
kabul etmek	kah-bull eht-mehk	to accept
kabul etmemek	kah-bool eht-meh-mehk	to refuse
kabzetilmek	kahb-zeh-teel-mehk	to be constipated
Kaç? kahch? How many?		
kadın pedler	kah-dihn pehd-lehr	sanitary napkins
kadın	kah-dihn	woman
kâğıt para	kah-iht pah-rah	banknotes

K

kâğıt	kah-iht	paper
kâğıttan bir yaprak	kah-iht-tahn beer yahp-rahk	sheet (of paper)
kahvaltı	kahh-wulıl-tih	breakfast
kahve	kahh-weh	coffee
kahverengi	kahh-weh-rehn-gee	brown
kalkış	kahl-kihsh	departure
kalacak yer	kah-lah-jahk yehr	accommodation
kalan	kah-lahn meek-tahr	rest (what's left)
kaldırmak	kahl-dihr-mahk	to pick up
kale	kah-leh	castle
kalem	kah-lehm	pen
kalıcı	kah-lih-jih	permanent
kalın	kah-lihn	thick
kalmak	kahl-mahk	to stay (somewhere)
kalp	kahlp	heart
kambiyo	kahm-bee-yoh	change (money)
kamera	kah-meh-rah	camera
kamp yapmak	kahmp yahp-mahk	to camp
kamp yeri	kahmp yeh-ree	campsite
kamyon	kahm-yohn	truck
kan	kahn	blood
Kanada	kah-nah-dah	Canada
kanama	kah-nah-mah	bleed
kan grubu	kahn groo-boo	blood group
kan tahlili	kahn tah-lee-lee	blood test
kanun	kah-noon	law
kanuni kılma	kah-noon-ee kihl-mah	legalisation
kapalı	kah-pah-lih	closed/shut
kapamak	kah-pah-mahk	to close
kapı	kah-pih	door/gate
kâr	kahr	profit
karanlık	kah-rahn-lihk	darkness
karantina	kahr-ahn-teen-ah	quarantine
karar vermek	kah-rahr wehr-mehk	to decide
kare	kah-reh	square (shape)
karı	kah-rih	wife
karın	kah-rihn	stomach
karşı	kahr-shih	against/ across/ opposite
karşılamak	kahr-shih-lah-mahk	to meet someone (planned)
karşısında	kahr-shih-sihn-dah	across
karton kutu	kahr-tohn koo-too	carton
kartpostal	kahrt-pohs-tahl	postcard
kas	kahs	muscle
kasa	kah-sah	cash register/ safe
kaset	kah-seht	cassette
kaşık	kah-shihk	spoon
kaşıntı	kah-shihn-tih	itch
kat	kaht	floor/ storey
katedral	kah-teh-drahl	cathedral
katı	kah-tih	solid
kavanoz	kah-vah-nohz	jar
kavga	kahv-gah	quarrel
kavga etmek	kahv-gah eht-mak	to fight
kavşak	kahv-shahk	crossroads
kaya	kah-yah	rock
kayadan bir duvar	kah-yah-dahn bee doo-wahr	rock face
kayaya tırmanma	kah-yah-yah tihr-mahn-mah	rock climbing

D I C T I O N A R Y

kaybeden kimse	kahy-beh-dehn keem-seh	loser
kaybetmek	kahy-beht-mehk	to lose
kayık	kah-yihk	boat
kayınpeder	kah-yihn-peh-dehr	father-in-law
kayınvalide	kah-yihn-wah-lee-deh	mother-in-law
kayıt	kah-yiht	recording (audio)
kaynamak	kah-yee-nah-mahk	boil
kaza	kah-zah	accident
kazak	kah-zahk	jumper/ sweater
kazanmak	kah-zahn-mahk	to earn/ to win
keçi	keh-chee	goat
kederli	keh-dehr-lee	sad
kedi	keh-dee	cat
kelime	keh-lee-meh	word
kenevir	keh-neh-veer	marijuana
kereste	keh-rehs-teh	timber
kesmek	kehs-mehk	to cut
keşfetmek	kehsh-feht-mehk	to discover
kılavuz	kih-lah-wooz	guide (person)
kır	kihr	country-side
kırık	kih-rihk	broken
kırmak	kihr-mahk	to break
kırmızı	kihr-mih-zih	red
kırtasiyeci	kihr-tah-see-yeh-jee	stationers
kısa	kih-sah	short (length)
kısa boylu	kih-sah bohy-loo	short (height)
kıskanç	kihs-kahnch	jealous
kış	kihsh	winter
kız	kihz	girl/ daughter
kız arkadaş	kihz ahr-kah-dahsh	girlfriend
kız kardeş	kihz kahr-dehsh	sister
kızartmış ekmek	kih-zahrt-mihsh ehk-mehk	toast
kibrit	kee-breet	matches
kilise	kee-lee-seh	church
kilit	kee-leet	lock (on door)
kilitlemek	kee-leet-leh-mehk	to lock
kilogram	kee-loh-grahm	kilogram
kilometre	kee-loh-meh-treh	kilometre
Kim? Who?	keem?	
kimi	kee-mee	some (animate)
kimlik	keem-leek	identification
kimse	keem-seh	person
kira parası	kee-rah pah-rah-sih	rent
kiralamak	kee-rah-lah-mahk	to hire/ to rent
kirletme	keer-leht-meh	pollution
kişi	kee-shee	person
kişilik	kee-shee-leek	personality
kitabevi	kee-tah-beh-vee	bookshop
kitap	kee-tahp	book
klasik sanat	klah-seek sah-naht	classical art
klasik tiyatro	klah-seek tee-yah-troh	classical theatre
klima	klee-mah	air-conditioning
koca(m)	koh-jah(m)	(my) husband

K

koklamak	kohk-lah-mahk	to smell
koku	koh-koo	smell (n)
kolay	koh-lahy	easy
koli	koh-lee	parcel
komedi	koh-meh-dee	comedy
komünist	koh-myu-neest	communist
konser	kohn-sehr	a concert
konservatif	kohn-sehr-wah-teef	contraceptives
konserve açacağı	kohn-sehr-weh ah-chah-jah-ih	can opener
konsolosluk	kohn-soh-lohs-look	consulate
kontaklens	kohn-tahk-lehns	contact lenses
kontrat	kohn-traht	contract
kontrol etmek	kohn-trohl eht-mehk	to check
kontrol noktası	kohn-trohl nohk-tah-sih	checkpoint
konu	koh-noo	question (topic)
konuşmak	koh-noosh-mahk	to talk
korkmak	kohrk-mahk	to fear
korku	kohr-koo	fear
korkunç	kohr-koonch	awful/terrible
korumak	koh-roo-mahk	to protect
korunmalı orman	koh-roon-mah-lih ohr-mahn	protected forest
korunmalı tür	koh-roon-mah-lih tyur	protected species
koşmak	kohsh-mahk	to run
koşu	koh-shoo	race (sport)
kova	koh-wah	bucket
koymak	kohy-mahk	to put
koyu	koh-yoo	dark (colour)
koyun	koh-yoon	sheep
koyun eti	koh-yoon eh-tee	mutton
köpek	ker-pehk	dog
köprü	ker-pryu	bridge (n)
kör	ker	blind
köşe	ker-sheh	corner
köy	kery	village
kral	krahl	king
kredi kartı	kreh-dee kar-tih	credit card
kucak	koo-jahk	cuddle (n)
kucaklama	koo-jahk-lah-mah	hug
kulak	koo-lahk	ear
kulaklar	koo-lahk-lahr	ears
kulaklı	koo-lahk-lih	hearing aid
kum	koom	sand
kurallar	koo-rahl-lahr	rules (of a game)
kurşunlu benzin	koor-shoon-loo behn-zeen	leaded (petrol/gas)
kurşunsuz	koor-shoon-sooz	unleaded
kurtarmak	koor-tahr-mahk	to save
kuru temizleme	koo-roo teh-meez-leh-meh	dry cleaning
kuru	koo-roo	dry (adj)
kurutmak	koo-root-mahk	to dry
kusmak	koos-mahk	to vomit
kusurlu	koo-soor-loo	faulty
kuş	koosh	bird
kutlamak	koot-lah-mahk	to celebrate
kutu	koo-too	box/tin can
kuvvet	koow-weht	strength
kuvvetli	koow-weht-lee	strong
kuzey	koo-zehy	north
küçük	kyu-chyuk	little/small
kül tablası	kyul tah-blah-sih	ashtray
kütüphane	kyu-tyu-pah-neh	library

DICTIONARY

kütüphane müdürü	kyu-tyup-hahn-ee myu-dyu-ryu	librarian

L

lamba	lahm-bah	lamp
lastik(ler)	lah-steek(lehr)	tyre(s)
laxsatif	lahk-sah-teef	laxatives
levha	lehv-hah	road sign
lezbiyen	lehz-bee-yehn	lesbian
lider	lee-dehr	leader
liman	lee-mahn	harbour/ seaport
lisan	lee-sahn	language
lokanta	loh-kahn-tah	restaurant
lokomotif	loh-koh-moh-teef	engine
lüks şey	lyuks shehy	luxury
lütfen	lyut-fehn	please

M

maaş	mah-ahsh	salary/ wage
maç	mahch	game/ match
madeni para	mah-deh-nee pah-rah	coins
maden-suyu	mah-dehn-soo-yoo	mineral water
mağara	mah-ah-rah	caves
mahal	mah-hahl	location
mahkeme	mah-keh-meh	law court/trial
makas	mah-kahs	scissors
makbuz	mahk-booz	receipt
makinist	mah-kee-neest	mechanic
makyaj	mah-kee-yajz	make-up
manav	mah-nahv	green-grocer
mantıklı	mahn-tıhk-lıh	sensible
manzara	mahn-zah-rah	scenery

manzara	mahn-zah-rah	view
marihuana	mah-ree-hoo-ah-nah	marijuana
masa	mah-sah	table
masaj	mah-sazj	massage
Mat!	maht!	Checkmate!
mavi	mah-vee	blue
mayo	mah-yoh	swim suit
medeni hal	meh-dehn-ee hahl	marital status
mektup (mail)	mehk-toop	letter
melodi	meh-loh-dee	tune
memleket	mehm-leh-keht	country (nation)
mendil	mehn-deel	tissues
menü	meh-nyu	menu
mercek	mehr-jehk	lens
merdiven	mehr-dee-wehn	stairway
Merhaba.	mehr-hah-bah	Hello.
mersi	mehr-see	thanks
mesaj	meh-sazj	message
meslek	mehs-lehk	profession
meslektaş	mehs-lehk-tahsh	colleague
meşgül	mehsh-gyul	busy
metre	meh-treh	metre
metro istasyonu	meh-troh ee-stahs-yoh-noo	subway station
meydan	mehy-dahn	main square
meydana getirmek	mehy-dah-nah geh-teer-mehk	to produce
meyve toplama	mehy-weh tohp-lah-mah	fruit picking
mezar	meh-zahr	grave
mide	mee-deh	stomach

244

mide ağrısı	mee-deh ah-rih-sih	stomach ache
migren	mee-grehn	migraine
mihmandar	meeh-mahn-dahr	guide (n)
milimetre	meel-ee-meh-treh	millimetre
milletlerarası otobüs	meel-leht-lehr-ah-rah-sih oh-toh-byus	long-distance bus
milli park	meel-lee pahrk	national park
milliyet	meel-lee-yeht	nationality
milyon	meel-yohn	million
mimarlık	mee-mahr-lihk	architecture
minibüs	mee-nee-byus	van
misafir	mees-ah-feer	guest
moda	moh-dah	fashion/style
modem	moh-dehm	modem
motor	moh-tohr	engine
(motor)bot	(moh-tohr)-boht	(motor) boat
motorsiklet	moh-tohr-seek-leht	motorcycle
motorsikletçi	moh-tohr-seek-leht-jee	motorcyclist
motorsiklete binmek	moh-tohr-seek-leh-teh been-mehk	to motorcycle
mum	moom	candle
musluk	moos-look	tap/faucet
mutfak	moot-fahk	kitchen
mutlu	moot-loo	happy

Mutlu yıllar!
moot-loo yihl-lahr!
Happy birthday!

Mutlu yıllar, nice senelere!
moot-loo yihl-lahr, nee-jeh seh-neh-leh-reh!
Many happy returns!

mücevherat	myu-jehw-heh-raht	jewellery
müdür	muu-duur	manager
mükemmel	myu-keh-mehl	excellent
mülteci	mool-teh-jee	refugee
müshil	myus-heel	laxatives
Müslüman	myus-lyu-mahn	Muslim
müthiş	myut-heesh	horrible
müze	myu-zeh	museum
müze müdürü	myyu-zeh myu-dyu-ryu	curator
müzik	myu-zeek	music
müzik gurubu	myu-zeek goo-roo-boo	band (music)
müzisyen	myu-zees-yehn	musician

N

Nasıl?
nah-sihl?
How?

nasihat	nah-see-haht	advice
ne ... ne ...	neh ... neh ...	neither ... nor ...
ne	neh	what
neden	neh-dehn	reason

Neden?
neh-dehn
Why?

nefis	neh-fees	delicious
nehir	neh-heer	river

Ne kadar?
neh kah-dahr?
How much?

nemlendirici krem	nehm-lehn-dee-ree-jee krehm	moisturising cream
nemli	nehm-lee	damp
nene	neh-neh	grandmother

Nerede?
neh-reh-deh?
Where?

Ne zaman?
neh zah-mahn?
When?

nezle nehz-leh cold
(ailment)

Niçin?
nee-cheen?
Why?

nişan- nee-shahn- engage-
lanma lahn-mah ment
(marriage)
nişanlı nee-shan-lih fiancée/
fiancé
nitelik nee-teh-leek quality
nitelikler nee-teh- qualif-
leek-lehr ications
Noel noh-ehl Christmas
Day
normal nohr-mahl standard
(usual)
nüfus nyu-foos birth
kâğıdı kah-ih-dih certificate
numara noo-mah-rah size (shoe)

O

Remember that ö is listed after o
as a separate entry.

o oh he/she
o(nu) oh(noo) the other
(one)
oda oh-dah room
oda pay- oh-dah to share
laşmak pahy-lahsh- a dorm
mahk
odun oh-doon firewood
ofsayt off-sahyt offside
oğlan oh-lahn boy
oğul (lu) oh-ool (loo) son
oda nu- oh-dah noo- room
marası mah-rah-sih number
oksijen ohk-see-zjehn oxygen
okul oh-kool school
okumak oh-koo-mahk to read

olası oh-lah-sih possible
olmak ohl-mahk to be
omuz(lar) oh-mooz(lahr) shoulder(s)
onlar ohn-lahr they
opera oh-peh-rah opera
operatör oh-peh- operator
rah-ter
orada oh-rah-dah there
oral oh-rahl oral
orgazm ohr-gah-zm orgasm
orijinal oh-ree- original
zjee-nahl
orman ohr-mahn forest
ormansız- ohr-mahn- defores-
laştırma sihz-lahsh- tation
tihr-mah
otogar oh-toh-gahr train station
orospu oh-rohs-poo prostitute
ortalıkta ohr-tah- abroad
lihk-tah
otel oh-tehl hotel
otoban oh-toh-bahn motorway
(tollway)
otobüs oh-toh-byus bus
otobüs oh-toh-byus bus stop
durağı doo-rah-ih
otobüs oh-toh-boos bus station
termi- tehr-mee-
nali nah-lee
otostop oh-toh-stohp to
yap- yahp-mahk hitchhike
mak
oturmak oh-toor-mahk to live
(somewhere)
oturmak oh-toor-mahk to sit
oynamak ohy-nah- to play
mahk (a game)
oyuncak oh-yoon-jahk toy (n)

Ö

öbür er-byur the other
öbür gün er-byur gyun day after
tomorrow

ödeme	er-deh-meh	payment
ödemek	er-deh-mehk	to pay
ödünç almak	er-dyunch ahl-mahk	to borrow
öfkeli	erf-keh-lee	angry
öğle	er-leh	noon
öğle tatili	er-lee tah-tee-lee	lunchtime
öğle yemeği	er-leh yeh-meh-yee	lunch
öğleden sonra	er-leh-dehn sohn-rah	afternoon
öğrenci yurdu	er-rehn-jee yoor-doo	youth hostel
öğrenci	er-rehn-jee	student
öğrenmek	er-rehn-mehk	learn
öğretmen	er-reht-mehn	instructor
öğretmen	er-reht-mehn	teacher
öksürük	erk-syu-ryuk	a cough
öldürmek	erl-dyur-mehk	to kill
ölmek	erl-mehk	to die
ölmüş	erl-myush	dead
ölüm	er-lyum	death
önce	ern-jah	before
öneri	er-neh-ree	proposal
önlemek	ern-leh-mehk	prevent
önünde	er-nyun-deh	in front of
öpmek	er-pmehk	to kiss
öpücük	er-pyu-jyuk	kiss
örnek	er-nehk	example
özel	er-zehl	private/ special
özel hastane	er-zehl hah-stah-neh	private hospital
özelleştirme	er-zehl-lehsh-teer-meh	privat-isation
özel ulak	er-zehl oo-lahk	express
özgeçmiş	erz-gehch-mish	resumé
özlemek	erz-leh-mehk	miss (feel absence)

P

pahalı	pah-hah-lih	expensive
paket (sigara)	pah-keht (see-gah-rah)	packet (cigarettes)
paket	pah-keht	package
palto	pahl-toh	overcoat
pamuk	pah-myuk	cotton
pantolon	pahn-tah-lohn	trousers
para cezası	pah-rah jeh-zah-şih	a fine
para	pah-rah	money
parça	pahr-chah	part/piece/ lump
pardon	pahr-dohn	pardon
park	pahrk	park (n)
park etmek	pahrk eht-mehk	to park
parlamento	pahr-lah-mehn-toh	parliament
parmak	par-mahk	finger
parmaklık	pahr-mahk-lihk	fence
parti	pahr-tee	party (fiesta!/ political)
pasaport	pah-sah-pohrt	passport
pasaport numarası	pah-sah-pohrt nyu-mah-rah-sih	passport number
patika	pah-tee-kah	track/path
patlak	paht-lahk	puncture
patron	pah-trohn	employer
paylaşmak	pahy-lahsh-mahk	to share (with)
pazar	pah-zahr	market
peki	peh-kee	OK
pembe	pehm-beh	pink
pencere	pehn-jeh-reh	window
peron	peh-rohn	platform (train/bus)
peşinden	peh-sheen-dehn	behind
petrol	peh-trohl	oil (crude)

peynir	pehy-neer	cheese
pil	peel	battery (dry)
pilav	pee-lahw	rice (cooked)
pire	pee-reh	flea
pirinç	pee-reench	rice (uncooked)
pis	pees	dirty/soiled
pişirmek	pee-sheer-mehk	to cook
pişmanlık duymak	peesh-mahn-lihk dooy-mahk	to regret
plaj	plazh	beach
plan	pee-lahn	itinerary
plastik	plah-steek	plastic
polis	poh-lees	police
polis memuru	poh-lees meh-moo-roo	police officer
politikacı	poh-lee-tee-kah-jih(lahr)	politician
popüler	poh-pyu-lehr	popular
posta kodu	pohs-tah koh-doo	postcode
posta kutusu	pohs-tah koo-too-soo	mailbox
posta ücreti	pohs-tah yuj-reh-tee	postage
posta	pohs-tah	mail
postalamak	pohs-tah-lah-mahk	to post
postane	pohs-tah-neh	post office
prehistorik sanat	preh-hee-stoh-reek sah-naht	prehistoric art
program	proh-grahm	program
puan saymak	poo-ahn sahy-mahk	to score
pul(lar)	pool(lahr)	stamp(s)
pusula	poo-soo-lah	compass

duvar (dış)	doo-wahr (dihsh)	wall (external)

radyatör	rahd-yah-ter	radiator
raf gibi düz çıkıntı	rahf gee-bee dyuz chih-kihn-tih	ledge
rahat	rah-haht	comfortable
randevu	rahn-deh-woo	date (appointment)
razı olmak	rah-zih ohl-mahk	agree
reçete	reh-cheh-teh	prescription
rehber	reh-behr	guide (person)
rehber kitabı	reh-behr kee-tah-bih	guidebook
rehberli tur	reh-behr-lee toor	guided trek
renk	rehnk	colour
resepsiyon	reh-sehp-see-yohn	check-in (desk)
resim	reh-seem	painting (the art)
resim(ler)	reh-seem-lehr	painting(s)
rezervasyon	reh-zehr-vahs-yohn	reservation
rezervasyon yapmak	reh-zehr-vahs-yohn yahp-mahk	to make a booking
ritim	ree-teem	rhythm
rock müzik gurubu	rohk myu-zeek goo-roo-boo	rock group
roman	roh-mahn	novel/fiction
röntgen	rernt-gehn	x-ray
rüşvet vermek	ryush-weht wehr-mehk	to bribe
rüşvet	ryush-weht	a bribe
rüya görmek	ryu-yah ger-mehk	to dream
rüzgâr	ryuz-gahr	wind

saat	sah-aht	hour/watch/clock

Saat kaçta?
sah-aht kahch-tah?
At what time?

sabalı	sah-bahh	morning
sabun	sah-boon	soap
saç	sahch	hair
saç fırçası	sahch fihr-chah-sih	hairbrush
sadık	sah-dihk	loyal
saf	sahf	pure
sağ	sah	right (side)
sağ ol	sah ohl	thank you (informal)

Sağa dönünüz
sah-ah der-nyu-nyuz
Turn right. (polite)

Sağa dönün.
der-nyun
Turn right. (informal)

sağcı	sah-jih	right-wing
sağır	suh-ihr	deaf
sağlık	sah-lihk	health
sahil	sah-heel	coast
sahip	sah-heep	owner
sahip olmak	sah-heep ohl-mahk	to have
sahne oyunu	sah-neh oh-yoon-oo	play (theatre)
sahne	sah-neh	stage
sakat	sah-kaht	disabled
sakin	sah-keen	calm/quiet
sanat	sah-naht	art
sanat galerisi	sah-naht gah-leh-ree-see	art gallery
sanatçı	sah-naht-chih	artist
sandal	sahn-dahl	boat
sandalet	sahn-dah-leht	sandal
sandalye	sahn-dahl-yeh	chair
saniye	sah-nee-yeh	second (time)
santimetre	sahn-tee-meh-treh	centimetre

saralı	sah-rah-lih	epileptic
saray	sah-rahy	palace
sargı	sahr-gih	bandage

sarhoş olmak
sahr-hohsh ohl-mahk
To be drunk.

sarp kayalık	sarp kah-yah-lihk	rock face
satın almak	sah-tihn ahl-mahk	to buy
satış	sah-tihsh	sales
departman	deh-pahrt-mahn	department
satmak	saht-mahk	to sell
satranç	sah-trahnch	chess
savaş	sah-vahsh	war
sayfa (kitap)	sahy-fah (kee-tahp)	page (of book)
saygı	sahy-gih	respect
sayıklayan	sah-yihk-lah-yahn	delirious
saymak	sahy-mahk	to count
sebep	seh-behp	reason
sebze	sehb-zeh	vegetables
seçimler	seh-cheem-lehr	elections
seçmek	sehch-mehk	to choose/ to vote
seks	sex	sex
seksi	sex-ee	sexy
selfservis	sehlf-sehr-vees	self-service
seminer	seh-meen-ehr	seminar (conference)
sempatik	sehm-pah-teek	sympathetic
sene	seh-neh	year
sepet	seh-peht	basket
seramik	seh-rah-meek	ceramic
serbest	sehr-behst	free (not bound)
sergi	sehr-gee	exhibition
sergilemek	sehr-gee-leh-mehk	exhibit
serin	seh-reen	cool
sert	sehrt	hard

ses	sehs	sound/voice
ses gücü	sehs gyu-jyu	level of sound
sevgi	sehw-gee	love (affectionate)
sevgili	sehw-gee-lee	lover
seyahat	seh-yah-haht	travel/journey
seyahat çeki	seh-yah-haht cheh-kee	travellers cheques
seyahat etmek	seh-yah-haht eht-mehk	to travel
seyahat kitapları	seh-yah-haht kee-tahp-lah-rih	travel books
seyahat mide bulantısı	seh-yah-haht mee-deh boo-lahn-tih-sih	travel sickness
şarkıcı	shahr-kih-jih	singer
sıcak	sih-jahk	hot
sıcaklık	sih-jahk-lihk	heat (n)
sıçan	sih-chahn	rat
sığır	sih-ihr	beef
sıkışmış	sihk-ihsh-mihsh	tight
sık sık	sihk sihk	often
sınıf sistemi	sih-nihf sees-teh-mee	class system
sınıf	zyum-reh	class
sınır	sih-nihr	border (frontier)
sıra	sih-rah	queue
sıradan	sih-rah-dahn	ordinary
sırt	sihrt	back (body)
sırt çantası	sihrt chan-tih-sih	backpack
sıvıyağ	sih-wih-yah	oil (cooking)
sigara	see-gah-rah	cigarette
sigara içmek	see-gah-rah eech-mehk	to smoke a cigarette
sigara kağıtları	see-gah-rah kah-iht-lah-rih	cigarette papers
sigorta	see-gohr-tah	insurance
sinema	see-neh-mah	cinema
sistit	sees-teet	cystitis
siyah	see-yah	black
siyah-beyaz film	see-yah beh-yahz fee-lm	B&W film
siyaset	see-yah-seht	politics
siz	seez	you (pol)
slayt	slahyt	slide (film)
soba	soh-bah	heater
soğuk	soh-ook	cold (temp)
soğuk su	soh-ook soo	cold water
sokak	soh-kahk	street/avenue
sokak müzisyeni	soh-kahk myu-zees-yehn-ee	busker
sol	sohl	left (not right)
solcu	sohl-joo	left-wing
soluk almak	soh-look ahl-mahk	to breathe
son	sohn	end/last
sonbahar	sohn-bah-hahr	autumn/fall
sonra	sohn-rah	after/later
sonsuza kadar	sohn-soo-zah kah-dahr	forever
son zamanlarda	sohn zah-mahn-lahr-dah	recently
sormak	sohr-mahk	to ask (a question)
soru sormak	soh-roo sohr-mahk	question (n)
sosyalist	sohs-yah-leest	socialist
soy	sohy	race (ancestry)
soyadı	sohy-ah-dah	surname

Ş

soymak	sohy-mahk	to rob
soyunma odası	soh-yoon-mah oh-dah-sih	changing room
sömürme	ser-muer-meh	exploitation
söylemek	sery-leh-mehk	to speak/ to tell
söz	serz	promise
sözlük	serz-lyuk	dictionary
sözlü rehber	serz-lyu reh-behr	guide (audio)
söylemek	sery-leh-mehk	to say
spor	spohr	sport
stüdyo	styud-yoh	studio
su	soo	water
susamış	soo-sah-mihsh	thirsty
su şişesi	soo shee-sheh-see	water bottle
sürpriz	syur-preez	a surprise
süt	syut	milk
süt ürün-leri	syut yu-ryun-leh-ree	dairy products

Ş

şahane	shah-hah-neh	wonderful
şaka	shah-kah	joke
şaka yapmak	shah-kah yahp-mahk	to joke
şampanya	shahm-pahn-yah	champagne
şampuan	shahm-poo-ahn	shampoo
şapka	shahp-kah	hat/cap
şarap	shah-rahp	wine
şarkı söyle-mek	shahr-kih sery-lehl-mehk	to sing
şarkı	shahr-kih	song
şarküteri	shar-kyut-teh-ree	delicatessen
şehir	sheh-heer	city

şehir duvar-ları	sheh-heer doo-wahr-lahr-ih	city walls
şehir merkezi	sheh-heer mehr-keh-zee	city centre
şehirler-arası	sheh-heer-lehr-ah-rah-sih	long distance
şehirler-arası otobüs	sheh-heer-lehr-ah-rah-sih	long-distance bus
şeker	sheh-kehr	sugar/ sweets
şemsiye	shem-see-yeh	umbrella
şenlik	shen-leek	festival
Şerefe! sheh-reh-feh!		
Good health!/Cheers!		
şırınga	shih-rihn-gah	syringe
şiddetli	shee-deht-lee	intense
şiir	shee-eer	poetry
şikayet	shee-kyah-yeht	complaint
şimdi	sheem-dee	now
şimdiden	sheem-dee-dehn	already
şimdiki	shim-dee-kee	present (time)
şirket	sheer-keht	company (business)
şişe	shee-sheh	bottle
şişe aça-cağı	shee-sheh ah-chah-jah-ih	bottle opener
şişman	sheesh-mahn	fat (adj)
şort	shohrt	shorts
şu(nu)	shoo(noo)	that one

T

taahhütlü mektup	tah-ah-hyut-lyu mehk-toop	registered mail

Ş

D I C T I O N A R Y

tabak	tah-bahk	plate
tacizlik	tah-jeez-leek	harrassment
tahmin etmek	tah-meen eht-mehk	to guess
takdir etmek	tohk-deer eht-meck	to admire
takip etmek	tah-keep eht-mahk	to follow (movement)
takma ad	tahk-mah ahd	nickname
taksi durağı	tahk-see doo-rah-ih	taxi stand
takvim	tahk-weem	calendar
talih	tah-lee	luck
talihli	tah-lee-lee	lucky
tamam	tah-mahm	OK
tam şimdi	tahm sheem-dee	right now
tamir etmek	tah-meer eht-mehk	to repair
tamirat	tah-mee-raht	repairs
tampon	tahm-pohn	tampons
tan (mayıs)- 'tan beri	tahn (mahy-ihs)' tahn beh-ree	dawn since (May)
tanımak	tah-nih-mahk	to recognise
tanımak	tah-nih-mahk	to know (someone)
Tanrı	tahn-rih	God
tansiyon	tahn-see-yohn	blood pressure
tapınak	tah-pih-nahk	temple
taraf	tah-rahf	side
tarak	tah-rahk	comb
tarihöncesi sanat	tah-ree-hern-jeh-see sah-naht	prehistoric art
tarife	tah-ree-feh	timetable
tarih	tah-reeh	date (in history)
tartışmak	tahr-tish-mahk	to argue
tartmak	tahrt-mahk	to weigh

tas	tahs	bowl
tasdik	tahs-deek	legalisation
taş	tahsh	stone
taşımak	tah-shih-mahk	to carry
taşıt pulu	tah-shiht poo-loo	car registration
tasalı	tah-sah-lih	worried
tasarım	tah-sahr-rihm	design
tat	taht	taste
tatil	tah-teel	holiday/ vacation
tatlı	taht-lih	sweet (n or adj)
tavşan	tahw-shan	rabbit
tavsiye etmek	tahw-see-yeh eht-mehk	to recommend
tavuk	tah-wook	chicken
taze	tah-zeh	fresh
Tebrikler!	teh-breek-lehr!	Congratulations!
tecavüz	teh-jah-wyuz	rape
teçhizat	tehch-hee-zaht	equipment
tehlikeli	teh-lee-keh-lee	dangerous
tehlikeye atan tür	teh-lee-keh-yeh ah-tahn tyur	endangered species
tehlike	tehy-lee-keh	risk
tek	tehk	unique
tek odalı	tehk oh-dah-lih	single room
tek yönlü (bilet)	tehk yern-lyu (bee-leht)	one-way (ticket)
tekerlek	tehk-ehr-lehk	wheel
tekerlekli sandalye	teh-kehr-lehk-lee sahn-dahl-yeh	wheelchair
tekme	tehk-mey	kick
tekrar	tek-rahr	again/ repeat
tekrarlamak	tehk-rahr-lah-mahk	to repeat

Tekrarlayın!	tehk-rahr-lah-yihn!	
Repeat!		
tel	tehl	wire
telefon	teh-leh-fohn	telephone
telefon etmek	teh-leh-fohn eht-mehk	to telephone
telefon kartı	teh-leh-fohn kahr-tih	phone-card
telefon kulübesi	teh-leh-fohn koo-lyu-beh-see	phone box
telefon rehberi	teh-leh-fohn reh-beh-ree	phone book
telefon santralı	teh-leh-fohn sahn-trah-lih	telephone exchange/ switchboard
televizyon	teh-leh-weez-yohn	television
telgraf	tehl-grahf	telegram
tembel	tehm-behl	lazy
temiz	teh-meez	clean (adj)
tepe	teh-peh	hill
tepsi	tehp-see	pan
tercih etmek	tehr-jeeh eht-mek	to prefer
tercüme etmek	tehr-jyu-meh eht-mehk	to make a translation
tereyağı	teh-reh-yah-ih	butter
terlemek	tehr-leh-mehk	to perspire
terzi	tehr-zee	tailor
Teşekkür ederim.	tesh-ehk-kyur eh-deh-reem.	
Thank you. (pol)		
teşekkür etmek	teh-shehk-kyur eht-mehk	to thank
teyze	tehy-zeh	aunt (maternal)
tıpa	tih-pah	plug (bath)
tıpkı	tihp-kih	same
tırmanmak	tihr-mahn-mahk	to climb

ticaret	tee-jah-reht	commerce
tipik	tee-peek	typical
tişört	tee-shert	T-shirt
tiyatro	tee-ah-troh	theatre
top	tohp	ball
Toz ol!	tohz ohl!	
Get lost!		
trafik	trah-feek	traffic
trafik lambası	trah-feek lahm-bah-sih	traffic lights
tramvay	trahm-wahy	tram
transit	trahn-seet	transit
transit yolcu salonu	trahn-seet yohl-joo sah-lohn-oo	transit lounge
traş etmek	trahsh eht-mehk	to shave
traş makinası	trahsh mah-kee-nah-sih	razor (electric)
tren	trehn	train (n)
tuhaf	too-hahf	strange
tur	toor	tour
turist	too-reest	tourist
turta	toor-tah	pie
turuncu	too-roon-joo	orange (colour)
tutucu	too-too-joo	conservative
tutuklu	too-took-loo	prisoner
tünaydın	tyun-ahy-dihn	Good evening.
tür	tyur	kind/type
tütün	tyu-tyun	tobacco
tuvalet(ler)	too-wah-leht (-lehr)	toilet(s)
tuvalet kağıdı	too-wah-leht kah-ih-dih	toilet paper
tuz	tooz	salt

U

uçak	oo-chahk	aeroplane
uçak ile	oo-chahk ee-leh	air mail
uçakla ile	oo-chahk-lah ee-leh	air mail

uçakla olmayan posta	oo-chahk-lah ohl-mah-yahn pohs-tah	surface mail
uçurum	och-oo-room	cliff
uçuş	oo-choosh	flight (aeroplane)
ucuz	oo-jooz	cheap
uluslararası	oo-loos-lahr-ah-rah-sih	international
umumi	oo-moo-mee	public
tuvalet	too-wah-leht	toilet
umurunda olmak	oo-moo-roon-dah ohl-mahk	to care (about)
un	oon	flour
unutmak	oo-noot-mahk	to forget
ustura	oos-too-rah	razor
utanç	oo-tahnch	embarassment
utangaç	oo-tahn-gahch	shy
utanmış	oo-tahn-mihsh	embarassed
uyku hapı	ooy-koo hah-pih	sleeping pills
uyku tulumu	ooy-koo too-loo-moo	sleeping bag

> *Can't find it?*
> *Try looking under 'Ü'*
> *in the next entry.*

uykulu	ooy-koo-loo	sleepy
uyumak	oo-yoo-mahk	to sleep
uyuşturucu	oo-yoosh-too-roo-joo	dope/ stoned
uyuşturucu etkisinde olan	oo-yoosh-too-roo-joo ht-kee-seen-deh oh-lahn	stoned (drugged)
uyuşturucular	oo-yoosh-too-roo-joo-lahr	drugs

uyuşturucu satıcısı	oo-yoosh-too-roo-joo sah-tih-jih-sih	drug dealer
uzak	oo-zahk	far/remote
uzay space	oo-zahy	outer
uzman	ooz-mahn	specialist
uzun ve zorlu bir yolculuk	oo-zoon weh zohr-loo beer yohl-joo-look	trek
uzun	oo-zoon	long
uzun yürüyüş için çizme (ler)	oo-zoon yyu-ryu-yyush ee-chin chiz-meh(lehr)	hiking boot(s)
uzun yürüyüş için yol(lar)	oo-zoon yyu-ryu-yyush ee-chin yohl(lahr)	hiking route(s)
uzun yürüyüş yapan	oo-zoon yyu-ryu-yyush yah-pahn	hiking
uzun yürüyüş yapmak	oo-zoon yyu-ryu-yyush yahp-mahk	to hike

Ü

üç kağıtçı	yuch kah-iht-chee	a cheat
üniversite	yu-nee-wehr-see-teh	university
üye	yu-yeh	member
üzerinde	yu-zehr-een-deh	over
Üzgünüm	yuz-gyu-nyum	I'm sorry.

V

vadi	wah-dee	valley
vakit	wah-keet	time
vantilatör	wahn-tee-lah-ter	fan (machine)

Y

var	wahr	to have
varmak	wahr-mahk	to arrive
varoş	wah-rohsh	suburb
vatandaş-lık	wah-tahn-dahsh-lihk	citizenship
ve	weh	and
vejetaryen	weh-zjeh-tahr-yehn	vegetarian
vergi	wehr-gee	tax
vermek	wehr-mehk	to give
vestiyer	wehs-tee-yehr	cloakroom
veya	weh-yah	or
veznedar	wehz-neh-dahr	cashier
videoteyp	wee-dee-oh-tehyp	video tape
virüs	wee-ryus	virus
vitamin	wee-tah-meen	vitamins
vize	wee-zeh	visa
vücut	wyu-joot	body

Y

yağ	yah	fat (for cooking)
yağlı	yah-lih	rich (food)

Yağmur yağıyor
yah-moor yah-ih-yohr
It's raining.

yağmur	yah-moor	rain (n)
yakın	yah-kihn	near
yakında	yah-kihn-dah	soon
yakışıklı	yah-kih-shihk-lih	handsome
yalan söyle-mek	yah-lahn ser-leh-mehk	to lie
yalancı	yah-lahn-jih	liar
yalnız	yahl-nihz	alone/only

yanık	yah-nihz	burn (n)
yanında	yah-nihn-dah	beside
yanlış	yahn-lihsh	mistake/wrong
yanmak	yahn-mahk	to burn
yapı işi	yah-pih eesh-ee	construction work
yapmak	yahp-mahk	to make/to do
yara	yah-rah	wound
yararlı	yah-rahr-lih	useful
yardım	yahr-dihm	help (n)
yargıç	yahr-gihch	judge
yarım	yah-rihm	half
yarın	yahr-ihn	tomorrow

Yasak değil(dir).
yah-sahk
It's allowed.

Yasaktır.
yah-sahk-tihr
It's not allowed.

yastık	yah-stihk	pillow
yastık yüzü	yah-stihk yyu-zyu	pillowcase
yaş	yahsh	age
yaşam	yah-shahm	life
yaşamak	yahsh-ah-mahk	to live (life)
yaşam stan-dardı	yah-shahm stahn-dahr-dih	standard of living

Yaşasın ...!
... yahsh-ah-sihn!
Long live ...!

yaşlı	yahsh-lih	old/aged (person)
yatak	yah-tahk	bed
yatakhane	yah-tahk-hah-neh	dormitory
yataklı vagon	yah-tahk-lih wah-gohn	sleeping car

Y

D
I
C
T
I
O
N
A
R
Y

yatak odası	yah-tahk oh-dah-sih	bedroom
yavaş yavaş	yah-wahsh yah-wahsh	slowly
yaya	yah-yah	pedestrian
yaya yolu	yah-yah yoh-loo	footpath
yaz	yahz	summer
yazar	yah-zahr	writer
yazmak	yahz-mahk	to write
yer	yehr	seat (bus/train)
yemek	yeh-mehk	eat/food
yengeç	yehn-gehch	crab
yeni	yeh-nee	new
Yeni Zelanda	yeh-nee zehy-lahn-dah	New Zealand
yeni	yeh-nee	recent
yeniden işleme sokulabilir	yeh-nee-dehn eesh-leh-meh soh-koo-lah-bee-leer	recyclable
yer	yehr	floor/place/space
yerel	yeh-rehl	local
yeşil	yeh-sheel	green
yeter	yeh-tehr	enough
yetişkin	ye-teesh-keen	adult
yıkamak	yih-kah-mahk	to wash (something)
yıkanmak	yih-kahn-mahk	to wash (oneself)
yıl	yihl	year
Yılbaşı	yihl-bah-shih	New Year's Day
Yılbaşı gecesi	yihl-bah-shih geh-jeh-see	New Year's Eve
yıldız(lar)	yihl-dihz(-lahr)	star(s)
yıllık	yihl-lihk	annual
yine	yee-neh	repeat
yok	yohk	none

yok etmek	yohk eht-mehk	to destroy
yoksul	yohk-sool	poor
yoksulluk	yohk-sool-look	poverty
yokuş yukarı	yohk-oosh yoo-kah-ih	uphill
yol	yohl	street/path/way
yolcu	yohl-joo	passenger
yolcu rehberi	yohl-joo reh-beh-ree	itinerary
yol gösteren köpek	yohl ger-ster-ehn ker-pehk	guidedog
yol haritası	yohl hah-ree-tah-sih	road map
yolculuk	yohl-joo-look	journey
yolculuk	yohl-joo-look	trip
yoldaşion	yohl-dahsh	companion
yorgun	yohr-goon	tired
yukarıya	yoo-kah-rih-yah	up
yumurta	yoo-moor-tah	egg
yuvarlak	yoo-wahr-lahk	round
yüksek (price)	yyuk-sehk	high
yükseklik	yyuk-sehk-leek	altitude
yün	yyun	wool
yürek	yyu-rehk	heart
yürümek	yyu-ryu-mehk	to walk
yüz	yyuz	face (n)
yüzde	yyuz-deh	percent
yüzme havuzu	yyuz-meh hah-woo-soo	swimming pool
yüzmek	yyuz-mehk	to swim/to bathe
yüzük	yyu-zyuk	ring (on finger)

Z

zama-nında	zah-mah-nihn-dah	on time
zarar	zah-rahr	injury/loss
zarf	zahrf	envelope
zayıf	zah-yihf	weak
zehir(li)	zeh-heer(-lee)	poison-(ous)
zemin kat	zeh-meen kaht	ground floor
zevk almak	zehwk ahl-mahk	have fun/enjoy
zevk için	zehwk ee-chin	for fun

zeytin(ler)	zehy-teen (-lehr)	olive(s)
zeytinyağ	zehy-teen-yah	olive oil
ziyaret etmek	zee-yah-reht eht-mehk	to visit
Zodyak	zohd-yahk	zodiac
zom	zohm	stoned (drugged)
zor	zohr	difficult
zührevi hastalık	zyuh-reh-wee hahs-tah-lihk	venereal disease
zümre	zyum-reh	class

MEETING PEOPLE

Across
2. sevgili — Dear ... [letter]
5. posteler — posters
7. kağit (para) — paper money
8. Kabul! — Agreed!

Down
1. kimlik — identification
3. tiyatro — theatre
4. boktan — crappy
6. (flört) etmek — to flirt

GOING OUT

Across
1. iskele — dock [noun]
5. burada — here
6. Yay — Sagittarius
7. aliş — purchase
8. çekici — charming

Down
2. kalabalik — crowded
3. liman (vergisi) — port tax
4. feribot — ferry boat
5. buyrun — Hello. [answering the phone]

FAMILY & INTERESTS

Across
2. gazete (kulübesi) — news kiosk
5. kiskanç — jealous
6. farketmez — It doesn't matter.
8. telekart — telephone debit card
9. çift (yataklı oda) — room with twin beds

Down
1. park — park [garden]
3. tekerlek — wheel
4. terazi — Libra [star sign]
7. tarife — timetable

CROSSWORD ANSWERS

IN THE COUNTRY

Across

1.	manda	water buffalo
5.	(dağ) tirmanma	(mountain) climbing
7.	gazete	newspaper
8.	dana rosto [2 words]	roast veal
10.	bezelye	peas

Down

2.	deniz	sea
3.	otobüs	bus
4.	kartpostal	postcard
6.	migren	migraine
9.	at	horse

HEALTH

Across

2.	mama (önlüğü)	bib [babies]
5.	biletleri	tickets
6.	defter	notebook
7.	akşam	evening
8.	İmdat	Help!

Down

1.	şeri	sherry
2.	mücevherat	jewellery
3.	meslektaş	colleague
4.	zarf	envelopes
5.	bagajim	bags

Abbreviations 10
Accommodation 63-70
  Paperwork 66
Address, Forms of 39
Addresses 53
Adjectives 24
  Comparison 24
Age 48
Agriculture 151
Ailments 157
Air 55
  Customs 55
Alternative Treatments 163
Amounts 183
Animals 150
Around Town 71-80
  Looking For 71
Articles (Grammar) 20
Astrology 96

Baby (Shopping for the) 112
Bank 71
Bargaining 107
Be Able 34
Be 28-29
Beach, At the 147
Bicycle 61
Boat 57
Body Language 37
Body, Parts of the 163
Bureaucracy 77
Bus 56
Business, On 170, 172

Calls, Making 76
Camping 141-152
  Crossword 152

Useful Words 141
Car 59
  Problems 60
Cardinal Numbers 183
Cards 102
Cases, Noun 21-23
Chemist 164
Cinema 94
Clothing 110
Colours 111
Common Interests 90
Comparison (Grammar) 24
  (Shopping) 116
Condiments 137
Consonants 16, 18
  Double 17
Contents 3
Conversation, Making 42, 45
Cooking Terms 140
Crosswords 50, 86, 104, 152, 166
Cultural Differences 47
Customs, Border 55

Dates 177
Days 176
Dentist 165
Desserts 132
Dictionaries
  English-Turkish 191
  Turkish-English 227
Differences, Cultural 47
Directions 51
Disabled Travellers 167
Dishes, Typical 129
Diving 148
Doctor 155
Drinks 137

INDEX

261

Eating Out 118
  Places to 119
Emergencies 185-190
  Health 185
  Police 186
Essentials (Phrases) 35

Family 87-90
  Crossword 104
  Travelling with 168
Feelings 49
Festivals 180-182
  Festive Expressions 181
  Toasts 182
  Weddings 181
Finding Your Way 51
First Encounters 40
Fish 135
Flora 151
Food 117-140
Fractions 184
Fruit 136

Games 102
Gay Travellers 168
Geographical Terms 149
Getting Around 51
Going Out 81-86
  Crossword 86
  Where to Go 81
Goodbyes 36
Grammar 19
  Adjectives 24
  Articles 20
  Negatives 33
  Nouns 20-23
  Possessive Pronouns 30
  Pronouns 24-25
  Questions 31

Verbs 25-30, 32-33
Greetings 36
Groceries, Essential 109

Have 29-30
Health 153-167
  Crossword 166
  Emergencies 153, 185
  Special Needs 162
  Useful Words 159, 161
  Women's 159
Hiking 141
  Path, On the 144
How to Use This Book 11

Idioms (Proverbs) 92, 145
In The Country 141
Infinitives 26
Insects 150
Interests 87-104
  Crossword 104
Introduction 9

Job, Looking For a 169-170

Kebaps (Roasted Meats) 130

Language Difficulties 43
Letters .... (see Staying in Touch)

Market, At the 134
Materials 110
Meals 119
  Special 117
Meat 134
Meet, Arranging to 83
Meeting People 35-50
  Crossword 50
Menu Decoder 120-128

Meze	133
Months	176
Music	90, 113
Nationalities	46
Need	34
Negatives	33
Nouns	20
Ablative	22
Accusative	21
Cases	21
Dative	22
Genitive	21
Locative	22
Nominative	21
Suffixes	23
Numbers	183
Cardinal	183
Fractions	184
Ordinal	184
Occupations	48
Opinions (on the Arts)	94
Ordinal Numbers	184
Paperwork	66
Path, On the (Hiking)	144
Paying (the Bill)	139
Pests	150
Photography	114
Pilgrimage	173
Places to Eat	119
Police , Dealing With	186
Polite Phrases	38
Possession	30-31
Post Office	73
Poultry	134
Prices	108
Pronouns	24

with Verbs	24
Pronunciation	15
Consonants	16, 17, 18
Transliteration System	17
Vowels	15, 16, 18
Proverbs (Idioms)	92, 145
Publications	112
Purchase, Making A	105
Questions	31
Religion	173
Romance	84
Affection, Showing	82
Salads	131
Seafood	129, 135
Seasons	177
Self-catering	134
Shopping	105-117
Bargaining	107
Looking For	105
Prices	108
Purchase, Making A	105
Sizes & Comparisons	116
Sights (In the Country)	150
Sightseeing	77
Signs	78
Sizes (Clothing)	116
Smoking	115
Soccer (Teams)	101
Social Issues	97
Soups	129
Souvenirs	110
Special Health Needs	162
Specific Needs	167-175
Spices	137
Sport	99-103
Cards	102

Games 102
Soccer 101
Useful Words 99, 101
Stars 96
Stationery 112
Staying in Touch 88
Streets, On The 75
Swearwords 83
Sweets 132

Taxi 58
Instructions 59
Telecommunications 74
Making a Call 76
Theatre 94
Tickets, Buying 53
Times 175
Telling the 175
Toasts 182
Toiletries 111
Tour, On 172
Tracing Roots & History 174
Traffic Snarls 54
Train 57

Transliteration System 17
Consonants 18
Vowels 18

Utensils (Eating) 119

Vegetables 132, 136
Stuffed 132
Vegetarian Meals 117
Verbs 25
Be 28-29
Future 28
Have 29-30
Imperative 28
Infinitives 26
Key Verbs 32, 33
Past 27
Present 26-27
Vowels 15, 18
Harmony 16

Weather 148-149
Weddings 181
Women's Health 159
Word Order 19

NOTES

NOTES

LONELY PLANET PHRASEBOOKS

Complete your travel experience with a Lonely Planet phrasebook. Developed for the independent traveller, the phrasebooks enable you to communicate confidently in any practical situation – and get to know the local people and their culture.

Skipping lengthy details on where to get your drycleaning ironed, information in the phrasebooks covers bargaining, customs and protocol, how to address people and introduce yourself, explanations of local ways of telling the time, dealing with bureaucracy and bargaining, plus plenty of ways to share your interests and learn from locals.

Arabic (Egyptian)
Arabic (Moroccan)
Australian
Introduction to Australian English, Aboriginal and Torres Strait languages
Baltic States
Covers Estonian, Latvian and Lithuanian
Bengali
Brazilian
Burmese
Cantonese
Central Asia
Central Europe
Covers Czech, French, German, Hungarian, Italian and Slovak
Eastern Europe
Covers Bulgarian, Czech, Hungarian, Polish, Romanian and Slovak.
Ethiopian (Amharic)
Fijian
French
German
Greek
Hindi/Urdu
Indonesian
Italian
Japanese
Korean
Lao
Malay
Mandarin
Mediterranean Europe
Covers Albanian, Croatian, Greek, Italian, Macedonian, Maltese, Serbian and Slovene

Mongolian
Nepali
Papua New Guinea (Pidgin)
Pilipino (Tagalog)
Quechua
Russian
Scandinavian Europe
Covers Danish, Finnish, Icelandic, Norwegian and Swedish
South-East Asia
Covers Burmese, Indonesian, Khmer, Lao, Malay, Tagalog (Pilipino), Thai and Vietnamese
Spanish (Castilian)
Also includes Basque, Catalan andGalician
Spanish (Latin American)
Sri Lanka
Swahili
Thai
Thai Hill Tribes
Tibetan
Turkish
Ukrainian
USA
Introduction to US English, Vernacular, Native American languages and Hawaiian
Vietnamese
Western Europe
Useful words and phrases in Basque, Catalan, Dutch, French, German, Greek, Irish, Italian, Portuguese, Scottish Gaelic, Spanish (Castilian) and Welsh

COMPLETE LIST OF LONELY PLANET BOOKS

AFRICA

Africa - the South • Africa on a shoestring • Arabic (Moroccan) phrasebook • Cairo • Cape Town • Central Africa • East Africa • Egypt • Egypt travel atlas • Ethiopian (Amharic) phrasebook • The Gambia & Sengal • Kenya • Kenya travel atlas • Malawi, Mozambique & Zambia • Morocco • North Africa • South Africa, Lesotho & Swaziland • South Africa, Lesotho & Swaziland travel atlas • Swahili phrasebook • Tunisia • Trekking in East Africa• West Africa • Zimbabwe, Botswana & Namibia • Zimbabwe, Botswana & Namibia travel atlas
Travel Literature: The Rainbird: A Central African Journey • Mali Blues • Songs to an African Sunset: A Zimbabwean Story

ANTARCTICA

Antarctica

AUSTRALIA & THE PACIFIC

Australia • Australian phrasebook • Bushwalking in Australia • Bushwalking in Papua New Guinea • Fiji • Fijian phrasebook • Islands of Australia's Great Barrier Reef • Melbourne • Micronesia • New Caledonia • New South Wales • New Zealand • Northern Territory • Outback Australia • Papua New Guinea • Papua New Guinea phrasebook • Queensland • Rarotonga & the Cook Islands • Samoa • Solomon Islands • South Australia • Sydney • Tahiti & French Polynesia • Tasmania • Tonga • Tramping in New Zealand • Vanuatu • Victoria • Western Australia
Travel Literature: Islands in the Clouds • Sean & David's Long Drive

CENTRAL AMERICA & THE CARIBBEAN

Bahamas, Turks & Caicos • Bermuda • Central America on a shoestring • Costa Rica • Cuba • Eastern Caribbean • Guatemala, Belize & Yucatán: La Ruta Maya • Jamaica • Panama
Travel Literature: Green Dreams: Travels in Central America

EUROPE

Amsterdam • Andalucia • Austria • Baltics States phrasebook • Berlin • Britain • Canary Islands • Central Europe on a shoestring • Central Europe phrasebook • Czech & Slovak Republics • Denmark • Dublin • Eastern Europe on a shoestring • Eastern Europe phrasebook • Estonia, Latvia & Lithuania • Finland • France • French phrasebook • Germany • German phrasebook • Greece • Greek phrasebook • Hungary • Iceland, Greenland & the Faroe Islands • Ireland • Italian phrasebook • Italy • Lisbon • London • Mediterranean Europe on a shoestring • Mediterranean Europe phrasebook • Paris • Poland • Portugal • Portugal travel atlas • Prague • Romania & Moldova • Russia, Ukraine & Belarus • Russian phrasebook • Scandinavian & Baltic Europe on a shoestring • Scandinavian Europe phrasebook • Slovenia • Spain • Spanish phrasebook • St Petersburg • Switzerland • Trekking in Spain • Ukrainian phrasebook • Vienna • Walking in Britain • Walking in Italy • Walking in Switzerland • Western Europe on a shoestring • Western Europe phrasebook
Travel Literature: The Olive Grove: Travels in Greece

INDIAN SUBCONTINENT

Bangladesh • Bengali phrasebook • Bhutan • Delhi • Goa • Hindi/Urdu phrasebook • India • India & Bangladesh travel atlas • Indian Himalaya • Karakoram Highway • Nepal • Nepali phrasebook • Pakistan • Rajasthan • South India • Sri Lanka • Sri Lanka phrasebook • Trekking in the Indian Himalaya • Trekking in the Karakoram & Hindukush • Trekking in the Nepal Himalaya
Travel Literature: In Rajasthan • Shopping for Buddhas

COMPLETE LIST OF LONELY PLANET BOOKS

ISLANDS OF THE INDIAN OCEAN
Madagascar & Comoros • Maldives • Mauritius, Réunion & Seychelles

NORTH AMERICA
Alaska • Backpacking in Alaska • Baja California • California & Nevada • Canada • Chicago • Deep South • Florida • Hawaii • Honolulu • Los Angeles • Mexico • Mexico City • Miami • New England • New Orleans • New York City • New York, New Jersey & Pennsylvania • Pacific Northwest USA • Rocky Mountain States • San Francisco • Seattle • South-West China • Southwest USA • USA phrasebook • Washington, DC & the Capital Region
Travel Literature: Drive thru America

NORTH-EAST ASIA
Beijing • Cantonese phrasebook • China • Hong Kong • Hong Kong, Macau & Guangzhou • Japan • Japanese phrasebook • Japanese audio pack • Korea • Korean phrasebook • Kyoto • Mandarin phrasebook • Mongolia • Mongolian phrasebook • North-East Asia on a shoestring • Seoul • South-west China • Taiwan • Tibet • Tibet phrasebook • Tokyo
Travel Literature: Lost Japan

MIDDLE EAST & CENTRAL ASIA
Arab Gulf States • Arabic (Egyptian) phrasebook • Cairo • Central Asia • Central Asia phrasebook • Iran • Israel & the Palestinian Territories • Israel & the Palestinian Territories travel atlas • Istanbul • Jerusalem • Jordan & Syria • Jordan, Syria & Lebanon travel atlas • Lebanon • Middle East • Turkey • Turkish phrasebook • Turkey travel atlas • Yemen
Travel Literature: The Gates of Damascus • Kingdom of the Film Stars: Journey into Jordan

SOUTH AMERICA
Argentina, Uruguay & Paraguay • Bolivia • Brazil • Brazilian phrasebook • Buenos Aires • Chile & Easter Island • Chile & Easter Island travel atlas • Colombia • Ecuador & the Galápagos Islands • Latin American Spanish phrasebook • Peru • Quechua phrasebook • Rio de Janeiro • South America on a shoestring • Trekking in the Patagonian Andes • Venezuela
Travel Literature: Full Circle: A South American Journey

SOUTH-EAST ASIA
Bali & Lombok • Bangkok • Burmese phrasebook• Cambodia • Ho Chi Minh City • Indonesia • Indonesian phrasebook • Indonesian audio pack • Jakarta • Java • Laos • Laos travel atlas • Lao phrasebook • Malay phrasebook • Malaysia, Singapore & Brunei • Myanmar (Burma) • Philippines • Pilipino phrasebook • Singapore• South-East Asia on a shoestring • South-East Asia phrasebook • Thailand • Thailand's Islands & Beaches • Thailand travel atlas • Thai phrasebook • Thai Hill Tribes phrasebook • Thai audio pack • Vietnam • Vietnamese phrasebook • Vietnam travel atlas

ALSO AVAILABLE: Brief Encounters • Not the Only Planet• Travel with Children •Traveller's Tales

For ordering information contact your nearest Lonely Planet office.

PLANET TALK

Lonely Planet's FREE quarterly newsletter

Every issue is packed with up-to-date travel news
and advice including:

- a letter from Lonely Planet co-founders Tony and
  Maureen Wheeler
- go behind the scenes on the road with a Lonely
  Planet author
- feature article on an important and topical travel
  issue
- a selection of recent letters from travellers
- details on forthcoming Lonely Planet promotions
- complete list of Lonely Planet products

To join our mailing list contact any Lonely Planet office.

LONELY PLANET PUBLICATIONS

AUSTRALIA
PO Box 617, Hawthorn 3122, Victoria
tel: (03) 9819 1877 fax: (03) 9819 6459
e-mail: talk2us@lonelyplanet.com.au

USA
150 Linden Street,
Oakland, CA 94607
tel: (510) 893 8555
TOLL FREE: 800 275-8555
fax: (510) 893 8572
e-mail: info@lonelyplanet.com

UK
10a Spring Place,
London NW5 3BH
tel: (0171) 428 2800 fax: (0171) 428 4828
e-mail: go@lonelyplanet.co.uk

FRANCE:
1 rue du Dahomey, 75011 Paris, France
tel: 01 55 25 33 00 fax: 01 55 25 33 01
e-mail: bip@lonelyplanet.fr

**World Wide Web: http://www.lonelyplanet.com
or AOL keyword: lp**